940.
53494
LEV

DOLTON PUBLIC LIBRARY DISTRICT

3 1146 00271 4347

B71

500

D0073054

DOLTON PUBLIC LIBRARY DISTRICT
708 849-2385

THE LAST DEPOSIT

THE LAST DEPOSIT

Swiss
Banks
and
Holocaust
Victims'
Accounts

ITAMAR LEVIN

Translated by Natasha Dornberg

Foreword by Edgar Bronfman and Israel Singer
Foreword by Avraham Burg

Westport, Connecticut
London

Library of Congress Cataloging-in-Publication Data

Levin, Itamar.
  [Pikadon aharon. English]
  The last deposit : Swiss banks and Holocaust victims' accounts
/ Itamar Levin ; translated by Natasha Dornberg ; forewords by
Edgar Bronfman, Israel Singer, and Avraham Burg.
     p.   cm.
  Includes bibliographical references and index.
  ISBN 0–275–96520–1 (alk. paper)
  1. Banks and banking—Corrupt
practices—Switzerland—History—20th century. 2. Jewish
property—Switzerland. 3. Jews—Europe—Claims. 4. Holocaust,
Jewish (1939–1945)—Economic aspects. I. Title.
HG3204. L4813   1999
940.53'494—dc21   98–53398

British Library Cataloguing in Publication Data is available.

Copyright © 1999 by Itamar Levin and Natasha Dornberg

All rights reserved. No portion of this book may be
reproduced, by any process or technique, without the
express written consent of the publisher.

Library of Congress Catalog Card Number: 98–53398
ISBN: 0–275–96520–1

First published in 1999

Praeger Publishers, 88 Post Road West, Westport, CT 06881
An imprint of Greenwood Publishing Group, Inc.
www.praeger.com

Printed in the United States of America

∞™

The paper used in this book complies with the
Permanent Paper Standard issued by the National
Information Standards Organization (Z39.48–1984).

10 9 8 7 6 5 4 3 2 1

"Your wife will be like a fruitful vine within your house; your children will be like olive shoots around your table."

—*Psalms 128:3*

For Irit, Ariel, and Aviad

With love and gratitude

CONTENTS

Photo essay follows page 121.

FOREWORD: STRUGGLE FOR THE RESTORATION OF HUMAN DIGNITY

AFTER ENDURING THE nine circles of hell and being left alive, many Holocaust survivors and the heirs of those murdered were forced to face the insensitivity and malevolence of the Swiss bankers. The Swiss bureaucrats demanded death certificates for the owners of Swiss bank accounts and refused to consider the fact that death camps like Auschwitz did not provide such documents.

The scandal of the Holocaust victims' dormant bank accounts led to a unique historical development that tested anew the connection of Swiss financial ties to the Nazis. The information revealed pertaining to Switzerland's role in financing and laundering Nazi Germany's money, and Swiss control of gold stolen both from banks and individuals—including Jews—in occupied Europe, uncovered the darker side of the legend of Swiss neutrality.

The global press fulfilled a central role in creating international pressure on the Swiss government and banks, and in this area, Itamar Levin's pioneering and intensive work is very important. The international press understood that this issue was not simply about monetary claims, but about a struggle to do historic justice—to reveal the truth about the behavior of countries and peoples in Europe and outside that collaborated with the Nazis and stood aside during the horror of the destruction of the Jewish people.

When we founded the World Jewish Restitution Organization (WJRO) in 1993, along with a wide umbrella of Jewish organizations, with the cooperation of the government of Israel, we believed that we were adjudicating the law of history in rewriting the last chapter of the Holocaust. The fact that a series of countries, under international pressure and with the courage of a new generation, are dealing with the darker chapters of the past, proves the moral importance of the struggle.

The Nazis stripped the Jews of everything—their rights, their property, their very status as human beings. The struggle to restore Jewish property, though inadequate compensation for all that the Jews lost, is designed to restore the human dignity and basic human rights taken away from the six million lost in the Holocaust.

Edgar Bronfman
President
World Jewish Congress

Israel Singer
Secretary-General
World Jewish Congress

FOREWORD:
NO GREATER HUMAN JUSTICE

NO LESS THAN fifty years passed before the Jewish people could deal not only with the horrifying murder, terrifying in its proportions, of six million Jewish men and women, aged and children, but also with the looting of tremendous proportions of Jewish property.

Many of the surviving generation, survivors of the ghettos and camps, preferred to leave the nightmare behind them and start a new life, free of the horrible memory. Two generations elapsed, and thanks to Itamar Levin and others in the Jewish and international press, the subject of looted possessions came to the surface and was placed on humanity's agenda.

And thus was revealed the affair of the disappearance of Jewish property during the Holocaust. In this way it became clear that not only the Nazis, already well catalogued in documents, looted the victims. All of Europe was partner to robbing the victims and appropriating the property of those sent to death camps. Starting with the man in the street, who took over the homes of the murdered and stole their property on the day they left, and on to administrations that collaborated with the Nazis and nationalized abandoned property, and including the bank management that hid and made inaccessible any possible information about the victims' accounts in their safes and cellars.

I remember Itamar Levin's first report in *Globes*, an article that revealed a little of what had been hidden, and in its wake, bit by bit, the entire story laid out in this book began to unfold. At that time, I approached the late Prime Minister Yitzhak Rabin, who not only saw it as our generation's duty to those murdered, but gave me his blessing in the name of the government of Israel to set about this task.

The dimension of the robbery is so vast, so expansive, that I believe Itamar Levin's is just the beginning of revelations yet to come. No week goes by in which another detail in the story is not discovered—more hidden information, more stolen property, more testimony of larceny. Although I do not believe it will be possible to uncover everything hidden for decades, we must strive to return most of the property to its rightful heirs, the Jewish people. This will not atone for the deeds already done, and certainly not the loss of life, but there could be no greater mission of human justice.

Avraham Burg
Speaker of Knesset
Former Jewish Agency Chair

PREFACE

ON JULY 23, 1997, the world witnessed the collapse of Swiss banking's famous wall of secrecy. On that day, Georg Krayer, President of the Swiss Bankers Association, along with Jewish Agency Chair Avraham Burg and Secretary-General of the World Jewish Congress, Israel Singer, made a stunning presentation to the world. The three provided the media with a list of 1,872 names of the owners of bank accounts in Switzerland that were opened before 1945 and with whom there had been no contact for at least ten years. The Swiss Supervisor of Banks Kurt Hauri announced at that time that the names of all the account holders who may have been murdered in the Holocaust would be published in this manner in the future.

It was exactly three years earlier, in July 1994, that I first heard about the problem of Holocaust victims' deposits in Swiss banks. That month Israel's financial daily *Globes* had dispatched me to Switzerland to prepare an article about ultraorthodox Jews vacationing in the Alps. Shortly after I arrived in the resort town of Davos, I ran into Professor Yehuda Blum in the hallway of the Etania Hotel. Blum, a former Israeli ambassador to the United Nations, a Holocaust survivor, and a well-known international law expert, asked the purpose of my visit. When he heard my answer, he said, "The real story of the Jews in Switzerland is the bank accounts left by Holocaust victims. Go check into it."

Since then, I have been privileged to follow the affair from close quarters and to contribute my modest part in bringing it to the public and media agendas in Israel and abroad. I saw how the banks were forced to switch from the position of dismissing the problem as solved and declaring there were no more dormant accounts to admitting decades of bad behavior, agreeing to an independent, international investigation, and publicizing the owners' names for thousands of remaining dormant accounts. I witnessed Swiss government remarks, which began by claiming that this was a problem between private banks and their private clients. Finally, the Swiss government was forced to debate the matter for months on end and take an active role in efforts to resolve the crisis. I have read hundreds of pages that exposed Switzerland's real face during World War II. It was not just an island of democracy and prosperity in the heart of Hitler's Europe, which all of us had been taught to believe, but also a vital financial support for the Third Reich.

The purpose of this book is to reveal as many details as possible about the affair of the Holocaust deposits. It will deal with Swiss wartime policies, only insofar as they touch on the fate of the money Holocaust victims held in Switzerland. In recent years Bern has proposed a series of explanations for its wartime behavior, some of which, in retrospect, may even be considered acceptable. But surely there is no excuse for the condescending, arrogant, insulting attitude the Swiss banks exhibited to the Holocaust survivors or the victims' heirs when they attempted to get their money from the banks after the war. From this perspective, the accounts and moneys may aptly be seen as a symbol of liberal, democratic Europe's treatment of the living skeletons that came out of Auschwitz, Treblinka, the Warsaw Ghetto, and hundreds of other places that decimated the continent's Jewish population.

The book has two distinct sources: archival and contemporary materials. This stems from the fact that the book deals with documented past events, most of whose participants have already passed away, and current events, the documentation of which is still classified, but whose heroes are still with us. In any case, an attempt was made to verify the credibility of the sources as much as possible, either by comparing testimony through analysis or because I witnessed some of the described events. My work as a journalist, however, prevents me from revealing a few of my sources. The chapter notes cover as much information as possible without revealing their names.

On two key issues I made use of excellent prior publications. The first is the report by Swiss historians Peter Hug and Marc Perrenoud on the deposits problem, as handled by Switzerland until the mid-1970s, a work based on thousands of Swiss documents and deserving of becoming a cornerstone of future research. The second is the Eizenstat report on gold trade between Switzerland and Germany and the negotiations for the return of the gold after World War II. This American report is based on about 15 million documents and is the most up-to-date summary of the subject. Nonetheless, concerning both reports, I did not hesitate to add details, analysis, and even criticism in places where I felt there was a need.

A long list of people helped me in the past four years in the ongoing research necessary for this book. Among them were Avraham Burg, Israel Singer, Greg Rickman, Yoram Majorek, Batia Lashem, Gilad Livnah, Thomas Borer, Zvi Barak, Rolf Bloch, Avi Becker, Akiva Lewinsky, Elan Steinberg, Pierre Monod, Hanan Ben-Yehuda, Avraham Hirschson, Silvia Matile-Steiner, Eldad Adar, Naftali Lavi, Moshe Zanbar, Shraga Ilam, Ron

Zweig, Dian Porat, Arnon Magen, and Christopher Olgiati. All deserve thanks.

For the ability to dedicate so much time to covering the affair of the deposits, I am grateful to my place of employment and my family. The Israeli financial daily *Globes* provided me with financial and professional support, while my family provided me with encouragement, without which I could never have allowed myself to focus to such an extent on the Jewish property in Europe, specifically the bank accounts in Switzerland.

In the *Globes* group I owe a special thanks to Editor Hagai Golan, former editor in chief Adam Baruch, the late Assistant Editor Nahum Baratz, and former editor of the weekly supplement, Dudi Green. The group's late general manager, Haim Bar-On, will be remembered fondly for his characteristic generosity and the availability of the group's resources for my work on the Jewish property issue and the completion of research for this book. Natasha Dornberg was much more than a talented, industrious translator. Throughout the work on this book, she has provided the perfect dose of advice, assistance, and humor.

Three generations of my family also saw me through the many years, which involved frequent trips abroad and long hours of work. My parents, Elazar and Esther Levin, who taught me to love the Jewish people and chase justice, and my wife Irit and our sons Ariel and Aviad give all my work a reason.

The exposure of the Swiss deposits affair awoke many European countries to investigate the fate of property of Holocaust victims; some of them have even acted to right the wrongs, primarily Norway. Others began investigating this chapter in their history, of whom Austria stands out.

If a lesson can be learned, it is the principal one that the Jewish people will not give up what is rightfully theirs. There are those who claim that dealing with property in the same breath as the Holocaust is an insult to the memory of the victims and cheapens the Holocaust. I do not believe this is true. The fact that the Holocaust was the worst crime in history does not mean that stolen property should remain in the hands of those to whom it does not belong. The dead cannot be resurrected, but everything that can be done, must be done. If this means a struggle for bank accounts, buildings, land, synagogues, and torahs, then that is what is necessary.

Anyone who makes peace with the fact that the thieves will continue to benefit from what they looted after (and sometimes before) the murder of Europe's Jews, grants legitimacy to the continuation of the Holocaust in its material aspects. Anyone who ignores the cry for justice is allowing the world—which did not lift a finger to save the Holocaust victims—to continue to inherit from those murdered. The Jewish people owe it to themselves and the dead to make every effort to ensure that the assets of those who perished will help memorialize and educate future generations about Holocaust history and Jewish history. This is the heart of the struggle described on these pages.

GENERAL NOTES

1. The Swiss franc and U.S. dollar exchange rate changed drastically from 1995 to 1997 when the Swiss economic crisis caused a 20 percent devaluation of the local currency. In mid-1998, the exchange rate was about 1.5 francs to the dollar, and in 1999 about 1.6 francs to the dollar.

2. Calculation of current values of the Swiss franc in comparison to earlier time periods was done according to the official Swiss Consumer Price Index, and is current through the end of 1996. The following is a test of how to calculate current values against previous years:

- to calculate the current value of the Swiss franc in contrast to 1933 values, multiply by 7;
- in contrast to 1939 values, multiply by 6.7;
- in contrast to 1940 values, multiply by 5.2;
- in contrast to 1945 values, multiply by 4.5;
- in contrast to 1950 values, multiply by 4.2;
- in contrast to 1962 values, multiply by 3.5;
- in contrast to 1964 values, multiply by 3.3;
- in contrast to 1974 values, multiply by 2.

3. The price of an ounce of gold in 1945 was $35. The price of an ounce of gold in 1998 was less than $300, and in mid-1999, $250–260.

4. To calculate the current value of the U.S. dollar in mid-1997:

- in contrast to 1945 values, multiply by 8.9;
- in contrast to 1946 values, multiply by 8.2;
- in contrast to 1947 values, multiply by 7.2;
- in contrast to 1952 values, multiply by 6.

5. In the text the abbreviation UBS stands for Union Bank of Switzerland. Following its merger with Swiss Bank Corp. in 1998, the new, merged entity is also known as UBS, but the abbreviation now stands for United Bank of Switzerland. The third largest bank in Switzerland in the years described in the book was Credit Suisse, which is now the second largest.

1

"THE ENCOMPASSING FOG"
Europe's Jews Transferred Millions to Switzerland

BY THE END of 1996, after months of incessant attacks on himself and his colleagues had left their mark on a top-ranking Swiss banker, he lost his Swiss banker's characteristic cool and stated publicly what he had apparently thought for quite some time: "The Jews murdered in Auschwitz were barefoot; they didn't have bank accounts in Switzerland," he pronounced.

The leaders of the Jewish organizations described the comments as anti-Semitic, but were they historically accurate? If the answer is yes, the entire affair of Holocaust victims' Swiss bank accounts is endowed with much more modest proportions than those to which the Jewish organizations, former U.S. Senator Alfonse D'Amato, Israeli Knesset members, the Israeli government, and even the U.S. government, lay claim.

If, indeed, Europe's Jews were wretchedly poor, from where did these alleged billions of dollars come, as those attacking the banks claimed? And if the wealthy did manage to extract themselves from the Nazi's grasp, they could have withdrawn their money after the war, and there would have been no problem about "dormant accounts," as the bankers call the problem. If the truth is on the bankers' side, then the entire affair can be closed, and certainly at the international level it has reached since mid-1995.

What was the economic status of Europe's Jews prior to the Holocaust? There is still no organized, comprehensive, academic answer to that question, although economist Helen Junz is conducting the first independent research on that question at this writing. She is preparing for the Volcker Commission—a joint committee of Jewish organizations and the Swiss Bankers Association (SBA)—detailed research into the economic standing of Europe's Jews before World War II. Junz is also investigating whether the Jews could have transferred money abroad, and if so, what sums were transferred, and where.

By the end of 1997, Junz had completed a preliminary sampling of the prewar economic status of Jews in Germany, Holland, and Poland. She estimated that Germany's Jews could have transferred abroad assets currently valued at $5.5 billion. Holland's Jews actually transferred at least

$2 billion in current values. Poland's Jews had property valued at an overall sum of $22 billion; Junz has not yet determined how much of it was transferred out of the country.[1]

Let us assume, for our purpose, that Germany's Jews transferred abroad half the sum at their disposal, about $3 billion, and that Poland's Jews transferred abroad just 10 percent of their property, $2 billion. It has already been determined that Holland's Jews transferred $2 billion abroad. Let us also assume that just one-fourth of that money went to Switzerland. Then, from these three countries alone, $1.7 billion in current values made their way to Switzerland. At this writing, the banks have admitted only a few tens of millions.

The Nazis understood the economic capabilities of their victims better than anyone else. When writer Gitta Sereny asked Franz Stangel, commander of the Treblinka concentration camp, why the Jews were liquidated, his answer was clear and unambiguous: the Nazis wanted the Jews' assets, and added that it was their property that enabled Germany to purchase vital iron from Sweden.[2] The gigantic robbery of Jewish property, the entire dimension of which will probably never be known, proves unequivocally that Europe's Jews were not barefoot.

Anyone who claims that fund transfers were a marginal phenomenon simply cannot handle the thousands of tales of money transfers, sometimes of significant sums, by Jews, from all over Europe to Switzerland. In the 1960s, about 7,000 Jews claimed that they knew about family members who had transferred money; some could even testify about their own accounts in Switzerland.

Since 1995, 5,000 people have made similar claims to the Swiss Bankers Association. The association's ombudsman, Hanspeter Haeni, fully admits that "I don't think any of them are lying, but a long time has passed, many things have happened, and they cannot prove it." In New York, in 1996–1997 about 31,000 survivors and heirs joined three class action suits against the banks, with prima facie claims that their relatives had bank accounts in Switzerland.

On the other hand, in the list of 1,800 dormant account holders the Swiss banks published in July 1997, only about 20 percent of the names appeared Jewish, something we will expand on later in this chapter. In October 1997, the banks announced that they had 64,000 dormant accounts that belonged to Swiss citizens, and admitted the possibility that many of them were trustees for the real beneficiaries, many of whom were probably Jews. World Jewish Congress secretary-general, Israel Singer, saw as early as the 1980s written testimony that no less than 17,000 Polish Jews transferred money to Switzerland.[3]

Is it possible that all these people are trying to hitch a free ride on the public outcry, and get their hands on money they are not entitled to? First, as we have stated, the Swiss Bankers Association admits that it believes all the petitioners. Second, and more important, testimony about the existence of bank accounts in Switzerland appeared two generations before the affair burst onto the public scene.

The Israeli Foreign Ministry files in the state archives contain dozens of citizens' petitions from the beginning of the 1960s, asking for assistance in finding their money or the money of their relatives that had disappeared without a trace in Swiss banks. The petitioners were regular citizens or their lawyers, the remnants of families from various countries, different professions, and varying economic classes. In addition, documents from the 1940s indicate a significant percentage of Jewish depositors in the New York branch of Swiss Bank, one of the three leading banks in Switzerland.

It is now clear that the depositors maintained strict secrecy about their activities. The primary reason for this was the laws forbidding trading in foreign currency in most European countries. But there is another, much simpler reason for the uncertainty surrounding the accounts. Generally, the husband or father handled all financial matters, particularly those connected with his business. How many women or children knew exactly, where all the family's money was located?

For the purposes of secrecy and caution, many depositors apparently used third parties—local friends, lawyers, or businesses. This is very significant, as the banks looked all along for Holocaust victims' accounts by searching for Jewish names. The fact is that many Jews bear names that are not necessarily Jewish. Others acted through companies they owned that did business in Switzerland, and clearly a company name doesn't give away its owners' religion. As the Swiss looked entirely for individual Jewish depositors, there was no way to locate moneys deposited in corporate accounts.

Those who personally deposited money in Switzerland put cash and securities in their accounts, generally preferring checking accounts with immediate accessibility rather than the limits imposed on savings accounts. Checking accounts, however, did not accumulate interest over the years, but were slowly eroded by regular bank fees. The fees were collected despite the fact that the accounts were inactive, and despite the fact that the usual custom is to charge fees relative to the number of transactions. Securities from Eastern European countries, where most of the Continent's Jews lived, lost almost all their value over the years. In contrast, there are only a few accounts of European Jews opening safe-deposit boxes before the Holocaust, boxes that may have contained valuables whose value usually remained in tact, such as gold and jewelry.

Here are a few examples from the Israeli Foreign Ministry files. In August 1961 the ministry asked about the fate of the accounts of the Uzias and Louisa Hoennigsberg, because they wanted to try to dissolve some of the "general fog" surrounding the question of accounts in Switzerland. The heirs' counsel reported that in 1936, the couple transferred 12–16,000 British pounds to Switzerland. In 1961 values, this was 470,000 francs, not including interest. If we assume that the interest rate was about 3 percent annually, the value of the account in 1961 is close to 1 million francs. The banks claimed that year that they found just 6 million francs belonging to Holocaust victims.

A later investigation showed that a deposit of 1,000 British pounds in UBS can be proven.[4] In 1962 values, without interest, this was 34,000 francs, and with 3 percent annual interest it is close to 70,000 francs. This is still a large sum, hinting that Jewish depositors were not paupers, and did not endanger their lives just to deposit chump change.

Haim Rottenberg reported that his brother and sister-in-law, who lived in Germany, deposited money in Swiss banks before the war. Engineer Aaron Zeslavski asked about assets deposited by his uncle, Dr. David Tomarkin of Riga. Haim Berger Lazar told of his uncle, Isaac Berger, a Romanian textile merchant, who did business in Switzerland and deposited money there. Ozis Baumbach of Lvov (Ukraine) and his family were also clients of a Swiss bank, according to testimony from his niece, Yona Keller.

Jacob Altman raised the possibility that his sister and brother-in-law, "who were senior bank officials in a Jewish bank in Kovno, Lithuania, and handled money transfers, invested their own money in securities in Switzerland, secretly, as there was a law at that time against taking money out of Lithuania." Shlomo Romm asked for the ministry's assistance concerning "my brother Lazar Romm, born in Riga in 1897. A wood merchant by trade, but essentially a stock market player, he kept his money and securities in banks in Switzerland and England. My brother and his entire family were murdered during World War II by the Nazis."

Lawyers petitioned, in typical style, about the accounts their clients sought. One particularly interesting letter came from attorney Ruth Diegi in the name of Irena Jablonovski, concerning Isador Serena who died in Warsaw in 1941. It contains certain assumptions that are true in most of the cases.

The late Serena told my client before his death, that he had deposited significant sums of money in Swiss bank's before the Second World War. My client doesn't know in which banks they were deposited, and if they were deposited in the deceased's legal name or in a pseudonym. My client assumes that the money was deposited in the big banks in the major cities in Switzerland, and believes there is a possibility the deceased chose a fake name, due to the ban existing before the war on the removal of money from Poland.

Other lawyers wrote about a wealthy Hungarian leather merchant who kept "a lot of money" in Switzerland, and another Hungarian Jew who deposited "significant sums and valuables."[5]

Finally, Mina Meirovitz's letter. This is a short, hand-written letter in Yiddish, on simple stationery, sent in July 1961 to then Minister of Finance Levi Eshkol, later Israel's prime minister: "I hereby request his Honor to be of assistance to me, in finding money my two sisters from Lithuania transferred to Switzerland. My sisters and their children were lost in the Holocaust, and I don't want the money to go to waste. In hopes of a response, Meirovitz Mina."[6] Can anyone claim that Mina Meirovitz is greedy, trying to get rich off the Swiss bankers?

The best proof about the accounts is in the Swiss banks' own documents. The wall of banking secrecy has cracked a little in recent years, due to a series of reports, and there are now at least six lists of account holders in Swiss financial institutions. In all the lists, the number of names of Jewish descent is prominent, much higher than the proportion of Jews in the general population, and it is very likely that this is only a partial list of Jewish accounts. Of the six lists, three are of dormant accounts in all the banks, two list the clients of the American branch of Swiss Bank Corp. in the early 1940s, and one contains the names of clients of the Geneva branch of the investment firm, Société Général de Surveillance.

The Geneva list was discovered in the National Archives in Washington, D.C., by U.S. Senator Alfonse D'Amato's staff, who will later play a central role in our story. It includes the names of 182 people who deposited $29 million with the company in various currencies, or $350 million in current values. At least thirty of the depositors were Jews from Romania, Bulgaria, Greece, Hungary, and France.

Among the depositors were Avrham Adolf Isvornau, $13,000; Simon Herschkovitz, 150,000 francs; Isaac Feldstein, 738,257 francs and $19,574; Robert Levy, 5,707 francs; Jerassim Margulis, 20,000 francs; Sigmund Mendelson, $2,000; Maurice Moise Rothman, 11,220 francs and $4,200; Emil Friedlander, 119,980 francs; Mrs. Laufer, 183,109 francs; Leib Herascovici, 80,525 francs; Moshe Adler, 22,108 francs; Nissim Hasan, 23,774 francs; Baruch Halpern, 269,000 francs; Angi Landau, 899,930.40 francs. All the amounts are in nominal terms; current values are twelve times higher. Prominent again are the sizable amounts, contradicting the small sums the banks reported throughout the years.[7]

Two of the lists of dormant accounts reveal the names of customers whose moneys the Swiss government transferred to the Hungarian and Polish governments as part of secret agreements to compensate Swiss citizens whose property was nationalized by those countries (see the account in Chapter 3). Hungary received moneys from thirty-three accounts. The complete list was not published, but it was reported that almost all the names on the list were Jewish.[8]

The list of fifty-five account holders whose money was transferred to Poland was published in full and has no less than thirty-one Jewish names,

ROUMANIE

Soldes créditeurs

M. Adler, Bucarest	FrS	22,018.85
Mondy Agent, Bucarest	"	22,219.70
Agraproduct, Bucarest a/bloque (vente 432 T. pois par W. Kundig & Co. Zurich	"	330,110.00
Agraproduct, Bucarest c/financier	"	493,095.67
Leo Alpern, Bucarest	"	14,123.00
Arion Samuil, Bucarest	"	20,703.90
Mihail Atias, Bucarest	"	5,000.00
Mme. Cocutza M. Brôh, Bucarest	"	43,989.10
Leon Bălian, Bucarest	$	1,591.75
Leon Bălian, Bucarest	FrS	400.55 (debit)
Leon Bălian, Constantza (actions Selecta SAR, Bucarest)	Nom.Lei	1,400,000.00
Bălian & Co. S.A. Bucarest	Frs	4,557.40
Bălian & Co. S.A. Bucarest	Fbg	31,282.08
Emil Neumann Borcovici, Braila	FrS	15,772.05
Kriker Bouhartzian, Bucarest	"	9,993.30
Alexandru P. Bratulescu, Bucarest	"	9,992.80
Serban Salviny Orgeon, Bucarest	"	3,000.00
Jancu Chitzos, Bucarest	"	5,953.05
Jancu Chitzos, Bucarest	$	3,013.66
Ing. Androi V. Chrissoghelos No.567	FrS	54,850.50
Ing. Androi V. Chrissoghelos No.936	"	579,263.50
Compenie Cifio S.A. Bucarest	"	36,780.53
H. Cohl, Bucarest	"	9,974.60
D. Constantinescu, Bucarest	"	7,500.00
D. Constantinescu, Bucarest c/Depot Francs OR		3,800.00
Ernst Ozallek, Bucarest	Frs	205,112.25
Ernst Ozallek, Bucarest	$	1,270.38
Coret. A. Dimitropol, Bucarest	FrS	8,100.00
Eug. Dornhelm, Timisoara	"	35,000.00
"Ergodo" Radu G. Dumitrescu, Bucarest	"	3,272.65
S.A.R. de Transporturi Egor, Bucarest	"	258,381.05
S.A.R. de Transporturi Egor, Bucarest c/bloque	"	10,500.00
S.A.R. de Transporturi Egor, Bucarest (en billets de banque)	Frs	250,000.00
Adolph J. Ellenbogon, Bucarest	FrS	5,925.80
Externa, S.A., Bucarest	"	1,600.00
Constantin Foltoianu, Bucarest	"	523,919.14
Mme Adela Feldman, Bucarest	"	25,000.00
Isaac Feldstein, Bucarest c/927	"	736,792.60
Isaac Feldstein, Bucarest c/bloque	$	19,444.38
Isaac Feldstein, Bucarest	"	130.00
Isaac Feldstein, Bucarest c/suspens	FrS	1,465.00
Isaac Feldstein, Bucarest	Francs OR	32,500.00

Jahrol

Société Général de Surveillance's list of Romanian clients, June 18, 1945. (U.S. National Archives; Senator D'Amato's office) including Laizar Birnbaum, Leib Zelig Bloch, Bruno Blumenfeld, Levin Blumental, Mercelli Buber, Ernest Epstein, Michael Friedberg, Moshe Glicksman, Stanislav Goldstein, Walter Levi, Mendel Luschek, David Kaspar-Selinger, and Isaac Weizman.[9]

The third list is the one published by the Swiss Bankers Association in July 23, 1997. It contains more than 1,800 names of the owners of 1,750 accounts in various banks. Examining the list only according to the sound of the names indicates that about 20 percent of the depositors were Jewish.[10] How can such a low percentage be explained if the banks actually located all the remaining accounts they still had? The only reasonable explanation, assuming there were many more Jewish-owned accounts, is that the banks can no longer find the documents as they were destroyed years before, as we will prove later in this chapter.

The clients of Swiss Bank Corp.'s American branch were revealed by foreign currency control documents in the U.S. Treasury, which investigated all the Swiss banks in the United States in the early 1940s. This was done as part of freezing Swiss assets because Switzerland conducted trade with Nazi Germany. The first report, from October 1940, included hundreds of names. Accounts containing $14.5 million ($160 million in current values) were located, of which about $1 million (now $11 million) belonged to accounts registered to Jewish-sounding names. They therefore accounted for 7 percent of the branch's clients. It is also important to remember that Jews may have deposited money through trustees, whose names were not Jewish.

The Jewish deposits came from all over Europe, including Poland, Czechoslovakia, Yugoslavia, France, Turkey, Romania, and Hungary. This is sure proof that geographic distance was not an insurmountable obstacle to opening a bank account in Switzerland. Some of the depositors are described as "without citizenship," hinting at refugees, some are explicitly listed as refugees, and some whose citizenship was revoked due to their Jewish descent. In some of the accounts, there are only a few dollars left, which indicates withdrawals, along with fees imposed by the bank.

There are a few prominent names on the list, like Baron Maurice de Rothschild, $98,492.70, the equivalent of $1 million in current values, and three members of the famous Guggenheim family who had close to $60,000 ($600,000 in current values). Other names are Betty Brandes, $14,353.69; Moise Asckenasy, $61,020.60; Stanislav Feigenbaum, $12,499.10; Michel Kahn, $4,698.60; Adolf Marcus, $5,000; Joseph Muri, $24,609.63; Berthold Weinberg, $9,072.67; Vera Stein, $10,103.15; Isidor Pollak, $8,962.25; Arthur Kahn, $6,994.05; Friedrich Gottlieb, $15,266.60; Ida Marx, $9,345.56; Zalman Paves, $15,279.55; Simon Borer, $7,288.40; Bella Wermas-Rosenberg, $19,605.[11]

The number of Jewish names is even more prominent in the second list, which revealed the numbered accounts in Swiss Bank Corp.'s New York

No. of Bank...........................
Swiss Bank Corporation

Demand Deposits (Due to Individuals)

Name and Address of Account		Nationality	Amount	Blocked	Free
Filsu-Haubensak, Hermann	Basel, Switzerland	Unknown	14,999.50	14,999.50	
Fischer-Schaetti, Eugen	Zuerich, Switzerland	Swiss	50.05	50.05	
Fleischer, Eliz.		Unknown	1,000.00	1,000.00	
Fleischhacker, Bruno	St. Gallen, Switzerland	German	3,323.40	3,323.40	
Fleischhacker, Oskar Accred. a/c	Muenchen, Germany	Unknown	1,477.25	1,477.25	
Flury, Max	New York City	do.	1,500.00	1,500.00	
Fondatton, Angelo	Glaris, Switzerland	Swiss Co.	35,735.35	35,735.35	
Fondation de Famille "Silveretta"	Geneve, Switzerland	Swiss Co.	5,292.55	5,292.55	
Fondation, Elisabeth	Geneve, Switzerland	do	63.49	63.49	
Fondation, Maria	do	do	700.78	700.78	
Fotsch, Edwin	New York City	Unknown	6.25	6.25	
Frank Helmuth	Genoa, Italy	Stateless	1,153.70	1,153.70	
Frank, Johann		Unknown	1,874.48	1,874.48	
Frank-Picard, Marcelle	Montevideo, Uruguay	do	10,053.70	10,053.70	
Freud, Friedrich	New York City	do	113.02	113.02	
De Freire de Andrade, Mme. Nadege	Alto Estoril, Portugal	Portugal	3,358.91	3,358.91	
Frey, Bernhard	Neugut, Switzerland	Unknown	65.10	65.10	
Frey, Frederico	Florenz, Italy	Swiss	2,451.20	2,451.20	
Frick, Max J.		Unknown	7.50	7.50	
Frischknecht, Ferdinand	St. Gallen, Switzerland	do	112.50	112.50	
Fritz, Max	Zuerich, Switzerland	do	24,545.50	24,545.50	
Frueh, Jean	Grindelwald, Switzerland	do	804.45	804.45	
Furrer, Dr. Hugo	Ascona, Switzerland	do	2,865.50	2,865.50	
Gabay, Adil	Istanbul, Turkey	Turkey	22,563.35		22,563.3
Gansser, Rodolfo	Lugano, Switzerland	Swiss	999.50	999.50	
Ganz, Arthur	New York City	Unknown	853.22	853.22	
Ganz, J. & Frischknecht, H.	Bagdad, Iraq	Swiss partners	998.30	998.30	
Ganz, Dr. Ernst Jt. a/c	Kuesnacht, Switzerland	Swiss	3,930.36	3,930.36	
Garfunkel, Frau Rosa	Zuerich, Switzerland	do	2,618.10	2,618.10	
Gassman, Charles	Biel, Switzerland	do	1,020.95	1,020.95	
Geiringer, Josef, Dr.	Sao Paulo, Brazil	German	1,834.80	1,834.80	
Gerber, Alfred	Thun, Switzerland	Unknown	1,225.00	1,225.00	
Gerber, Otto	Berne, Switzerland	Swiss	163.65	163.65	
Gerbers, Ernst	Sohne, Switzerland	Unknown	32.71	32.71	
Ges. Der Ludw. Von Roll Schen Eisenwerke, A. G.	Gerlafingen, Switzerland	Swiss	470,710.09	470,710.09	
Gerngross, Ludwig		Unknown	211.29	211.29	
Gibel, Eduard Jt. a/c	Dietikon, Switzerland	Swiss	4,994.50	4,994.50	
Giovanoli, E. N.	Basle, Switzerland	do	4,499.75	4,499.75	
Girod, Henri	Court	do	5,186.46	5,186.46	
Glaisanor, S. A.	Fribourg, Switzerland	Swiss Co.	163.49	163.49	
Gleim, Franz	Guyaquil, Ecuador	do	39.82	39.82	
Gloor, E.	London, England	Swiss	11,390.70	11,390.70	
Gloor, Max	Aarau, Switzerland	do	48,995.22	48,995.22	
Gloor-Wehrli, Walter Jt. a/c	Leutwil, Switzerland	do	4,499.50	4,499.50	
Gnepf-Germann, Walter	Zurich, Switzerland	do	758.83	758.83	
Goetschel, Les Fils De Marc	La Chaux de Fonds, Switzerland	do	2,997.50	2,997.50	
Golay, Louis Auguste	Le Sentier, Switzerland	do	431.34	431.34	
Golay, Mme. Mathilde	Le Sentier, Switzerland	do	451.07	451.07	
Golay, Mme. Mathilde Blocked a/c Opn. Coll.	Le Sentier, Switzerland	do	40.91	40.91	
Golay-Buchel & Cie, S.A.	do	do	701.24	701.24	
Goldray, S. A.	Geneve, Switzerland	Swiss Co.	48.30	48.30	
Goldstein, Dr. Erich	Santiago de Chile	Palestine	239.84		239.84
Goldstein, Dr. Isaak	Zuerich, Switzerland	Swiss	6,324.87	6,324.87	
Gonzenbach, Adolf Compte/Jt.	Caracas, Venezuela	do	8,349.44	8,349.44	
Goth & Co., A. G.	Basel, Switzerland	do	2,683.77	2,683.77	
Gottlieb, Leo Jt. a/c	Cologny, Switzerland	do Res. U.S.A.	1,139.13	1,139.13	
Graef, Frln. Margrith	Zofingen, Switzerland	Unknown	1,011.75	1,011.75	
Graf, Max	Brugg, Switzerland	Swiss	1,775.09	1,775.09	
Gresly, Direktor Herbert	Liesberg, Switzerland	do	14,999.50	14,999.50	
Griessmann, E.J.	London, England	Unknown	2.43	2.43	
Grillo, Lucas	Chiasso, Switzerland	do	13,798.50	13,798.50	
Grimm, B. & Co.	Bangkok, Thailand	Thailand Corp. (Swiss)	26.50	26.50	

Swiss Bank Corporation's New York branch list of clients, October 16, 1940. (U.S. National Archives; Senator D'Amato's office)

.ription
Accounts

E.X. 8074   Karl Petschek and/or Wilhelm Petschek
                    Citizen of Czechoslovakia, now Haitian Passport No. 319
                    Entered U.S. November 25, 1940
                    Address: 2 Kensington Road, Scarsdale, New York

E.Y. 8075   Julio Koenig
                    Palmoticesa 18/I, Zagreb, Yugoslavia
                    Firm's name: "Union" tvornica kandita i Cokolade, Zagreb, Yugo.
                    Cover Address: Laborit A.G., Chur, Switzerland

C.Z. 1001   Isaac Cohen and/or Mrs. R. Cohen
                    Istanbul, Turkey
                    Cover Address: A. L. Marty, Paradeplatz 6, Zurich, Switzerland

C.Y. 1002   Radu Xenopol and/or Mrs. Thyra Xenopol
                    Rue Romana 55, Bucharest, Rumania
                    Cover Address: c/o Arbitrium Handels A.G., Alpenstrasse 9,
                                        Zug, Switzerland
                    Code used: 1 ton for $1000.00 - 2 tons for $2,000.00, etc.

C.X. 1003   Nicolas Lichiardopol
                    Orsova, (Jud Severin), Rumania
                    Cover Address: Dobrivoye Maximovic a Tekija na Dunaver, Yugoslavia
                                        (Moravska Banovina)
                    Code signature: Thousand Three

C.W. 1004   Dr. Walter Strate and/or Mrs. Lydia Strate
                    Bucharest, Rumania
                    Cover Address: Dr. Walter Strate, c/o Arbitrium Handels A.G.
                                        Alpenstrasse 9, Zug, Switzerland
                    Code Signature: Thousand Four

F.Z. 1026   Alesandro Fernandez
                    Irun, Spain
                    Cover Address: c/o Vda. de A. Fernandez e Hijo
                                        31-39 Marche aux Souliers, Antwerp, Belgium

F.Y. 1027   Federico O. Bemberg
                    Buenos Aires, Argentina
                    Cover Address: C. Gortchacow (no street and city given)

F.X. 1041   Ch. Felix Keller
                    Horn, Lucerne, Switzerland
                    Code Signature: F. K. Mille quarante et un
                    Swiss citizen

F.E. 1046   Zalmen Paves
                    Bucharest, Rumania
                    Power of Attorney dated Oct. 17, 1941, held by
                    Nathan L. Paves, 17251 Moenort Street, Detroit, Michigan

Swiss Bank Corporation's New York branch list of numbered accounts, February 12, 1945.
(U.S. National Archives; Senator D'Amato's office)

branch. The U.S. authorities located 126 names in all, of which fifty-one appear to be Jewish. This is 40 percent of the accounts, and Treasury officials noted that many of the depositors were refugees from Nazi-occupied countries. Generally, only Jews had reason to hide their property from Nazi eyes.

A number of names from the list exemplify its nature. Zalman Paves, who also had a regular account, opened account number FE-1046. Berthold Weinberg, Friedrich Gottlieb, Arthur Kahn, and Isidor Pollack had numbered accounts as well as regular accounts. Julie and Milka Fischer of Zagreb, Yugoslavia, registered a cover address in Swiss Bank's Zurich headquarters. Moris Finzi's account, DZ-8051, was opened by Jehuda Altman of Hadera, Palestine, and its cover address was Erna Englaender in Hollywood, California.

Elizabeth Deutsch of Yugoslavia opened an account in February 1940, by transferring $50,000 ($500,000 in current values) from her brother George Schultz's numbered account. According to the list, the documents for Schultz's account, were to be sent to Gotthard Wielich of Asona, Switzerland. Other Jewish names included Emil Borger, Endre Schrieber, Egon Ehrenstein, Jakob Adanja, Vera and Alexander Klein, Georg Loe-Beer, Emil and Alter Mayer, Louis and Lina Graber, Otto and Betty Burgaur, Jacob and Emil Laib, Elsi Boyer, Hugo Keller, August Low-Bar, René Ullman, and Simon Marx.[12]

How much money did Europe's Jews deposit in Swiss banks? The answer will never be known, since the relevant documents no longer exist. During negotiations between Israel and Switzerland in the 1950s and 1960s that preceded legislation to transfer dormant accounts to the Swiss government, the Swiss banks and government threw out a variety of different numbers, some of which were not even in the same ballpark. The banks, which should have known better than anyone how much money was involved, naturally tried to minimize their estimates whenever possible. As early as December 1947, the Union of Swiss Jewish Communities demanded that the Swiss Ministry of Finance take steps to reach a moral solution to the problem of deposits without heirs. The Swiss Bankers Association responded to the Ministry of Finance and said that all this involved just 500,000 francs (4.5 million francs in current values).[13]

The Swiss government, which had no figures of its own, was forced to rely on the banks' figures and estimates by its own officials. There is no document that testifies to any attempt by Bern to conduct an independent investigation as part of the government's supervision of its banks. This was just the beginning of a long-term government policy that resulted in the fact that no one supervised or controlled the banks' actions in this affair for decades.

For instance, an Israeli consul in Bern, D. Rubek, reported to Israel's

Foreign Ministry in October 1956 on his talks with Swiss president Markus Feldman. Their conversation followed a proposal by the Union of Swiss Jewish Communities to establish a government trust fund to hold property without heirs.

After the government passed the Communities' proposal on to the bankers . . . the Bankers' Association notified that a further investigation by the banks indicated that the total property [without heirs] in the banks' hands amounted to no more than 1 million francs! The bankers therefore say that for such a small sum it isn't worth endangering the principle of banking secrecy, so important for the Swiss economy. The president himself commented that it was hard to believe the truth of this information; I told him that I had heard from reliable sources of finding sums much greater than 1 million francs.[14]

In June 1960, Israel's ambassador to Bern, Joseph Linton, reported that in a discussion with Warren Blumberg of the U.S. embassy, he was told about a conversation held in Switzerland between Blumberg and another American, Seymour Rubin. Rubin was the head of the U.S. delegation to the Paris Convention in 1945, after which he aided Jewish organizations in handling the deposits problem.

Blumberg reported to Linton what Rubin had reported to him:

He met with the secretary general of the Swiss Bankers' Federation [should be Association] to discuss the problem of property without heirs. They didn't reach an agreement, but Rubin proposed sending him a memorandum that would answer the problems the bankers raised. Rubin was told offhandedly, that the banks currently estimate the accounts as 35,000 francs and no more! I am doubtful any use will come of Rubin's conversation with the bankers or his proposal to send a memorandum. It is possible I might agree if we were talking about 900,000 francs, but regarding just 35,000 francs, what can we expect of these people? Negotiation with them on this basis could only postpone any government action concerning the proposed law [to transfer the moneys to the government].[15]

Thirteen months passed, and in July 1961, the banks had another estimate altogether. The Israeli embassy in Bern reported to the Foreign Ministry in Jerusalem about a meeting held by then president of the World Jewish Congress, Nachum Goldmann, with the president of the Swiss Bankers Association (whose name is not mentioned in the document). Goldmann warned his counterpart that the "Jewish organizations and institutions that he represents will not put up with any attempted sabotage by the banks of the proposed law recently submitted to them concerning the property without heirs." The Swiss commented, that at most 2 million francs was at stake.[16] Even this estimate, the highest given by the banks, was very different from the amount the banks actually transferred just two years later—6 million francs.

There are many reasons for the uncertainty about the value of the deposits, and they are very important to understanding the development of the affair. As has already been noted, the depositors themselves maintained secrecy, because opening Swiss accounts constituted a violation of the law in most European countries, and because, in many families, financial matters were handled solely by husbands and fathers. This was especially true in those instances where a father used his international business to transfer money or revenue from his business to Switzerland. In other cases, many Jews apparently acted through intermediaries in order to ensure greater secrecy. The depositors and the intermediaries most trusted the Swiss banks' well-known policy of secrecy, which created one of the most absurd situations in the entire affair. Secrecy, originally designed to protect all depositors, including Jews, has been used against their heirs for generations.

In the 1950s, the banks claimed over and over that the small sums involved did not justify tampering with their secrecy guidelines. They even stated, explicitly, and legitimately from their point of view, that giving up their secrecy would harm their businesses, as many chose Swiss banks under the assumption that their names would never be revealed.

In April 1983, attorney Franz Kalherles, then chair of the Swiss Bar Association, testified to an Israeli court that "The Nazis sent letters and special messengers to Swiss banks, in order to discover the lists of German Jews who deposited their money there. They made every possible effort, including bribing and threatening officials, to uncover the lists. It was then decided to enact a law determining that conveying financial and economic secrets constitutes a punishable offense."[17] The Swiss law was enacted in 1934 and remains in effect today. Anyone who reveals banking secrets will be arrested.

The biggest problem in the investigation is the lack of documentation. The banks, the Swiss Bankers Association, and the Swiss government have all provided conflicting information since 1994, in answer to this simple question: what happens to the documents associated with dormant accounts in which there have been no transactions for ten years or more?

Under normal circumstances, no one would expect the banks to keep all the documents related to its accounts for many decades, and certainly not before the age of microfilm and computers. Had they done so, Zurich would have become one big archive. When the banks started getting into trouble with their different versions about the deposits, they encountered a trap concerning the documents. If documents still exist, the banks will be required to present them for careful examination, the results of which are likely to be embarrassing. If the documents were destroyed, there will be a massive public outcry.

What is now clear beyond a shadow of a doubt, is that the banks are authorized, under certain circumstances, to close dormant accounts and destroy the documents. The Swiss Foreign Ministry's official answer to my question in February 1997, was that

According to Article 962 of the Swiss Code of Obligations, banks as well as other enterprises are obliged to keep business records—such as records of openings of accounts and records necessary to identify the account holders—for at least ten years. The term of ten years starts with the closing of an account. In general, an account may only be closed upon the order of the account holder, since there is no Swiss legislation which would allow the closing of dormant accounts, as known in other states. Hence basic records may not be destroyed as long as an account still exists. Nevertheless, the law of a few Swiss cantons authorized banks to close dormant accounts subject to public notification. Yet in September 1995 the Swiss Bankers Association issued guidelines forbidding Swiss banks from closing dormant accounts. The Swiss Federal Banking Commission supervises the banks' compliance with the guidelines.

The key sentence here is "the law of a few Swiss cantons authorized banks to close dormant accounts." The large Swiss banks are, in fact, holding companies, owning the banks in each of the twenty-three Swiss cantons. For all intents and purposes, each bank is a separate company directly and wholly owned by a parent bank, usually headquartered in Zurich. In addition, there are hundreds of smaller banks in Switzerland that only have branches in one or a few cantons.

Supervising banks is carried out on two levels: (1) according to cantonal laws concerning the local subsidiary banks, and (2) according to federal law concerning the national parent banks. The deposits belong solely to the subsidiary banks. Therefore, nothing stands in the way of the following scenario: Let us suppose that in Canton A it is forbidden to close dormant accounts, and in Canton B it is allowed. The parent bank decides that it wants to close all the dormant accounts in all its branches. It therefore asks its bank in Canton A to sell its dormant accounts to its sister company in Canton B, which then closes the accounts. Ten years after closure, the bank destroys all the documents, and no traces of the accounts remain.

This process, which appears illogical, stems from two loopholes. The first loophole is that in Switzerland, as opposed to many countries, there is no governmental custodian that is legally entitled to deal with property without heirs. Therefore, the banks are responsible for handling accounts without heirs.[18]

The second loophole, the option to destroy documents, is a logical and accepted practice worldwide. In Switzerland, however, the banks are not required to even maintain minimal records of any kind that document the existence of an account and the circumstances of its closure. Such records are not complicated to set up, and could easily take up just one line: account number, client name, date of closure, circumstances of closure, and an authorized signature. It is also essential to the banks' internal regulation, in order to prevent fraud, but it does not exist in most of the banks. In September 1995, the banks were required by the Bankers Association, beginning in January 1996, to avoid the destruction of documents relating to dormant accounts. But the bank had already had decades to destroy documents, and now, even the new prohibition gave them three months to dismantle their records.

What happens to property without heirs? The official and authorized answer to this question was provided by attorney Silvia Matile-Steiner, the Bankers Association's legal secretary, in October 1994:

Even under normal circumstances, it can happen that we don't hear from a customer for several years. The bank tries to establish contact with him, and when the bank believes there is no chance of contacting the client, for instance if letters to the customer return again and again, the bank must keep the account open another ten years. Sometimes the banks keep the accounts for 15–20 years. Then the bank closes the account, and keeps the money for another ten years in the bank's own account. Afterwards, the money becomes the bank's.[19]

Here it is, plain and simple: the account is closed, the documents are destroyed, and the money is appropriated by the bank.

Did the banks take advantage of these loopholes? This question is pivotal: If the procedure existed but was not implemented, then the money still exists and should be returned to the heirs or to the Jewish people. If the procedure was implemented, then this is a serious disaster to the reputation, integrity, and credibility of the banks.

In October 1994, six months before the storm broke, most of the major banks refused to answer my questions regarding the fate of dormant accounts. Their usually blunt answers were along the lines of, "the problem was solved by the 1962 law," or they directed me to a document in a similar vein from the Bankers Association. Only Swiss Bank Corp. agreed to provide more detailed information, which came from Dr. Martin Wirz, senior legal counsel to bank management: "If someone deposits securities or bonds in a bank, there is no limitation on the time of deposit, and the heirs can come even after 100 years and receive them," Wirz said. "The time limit applies to cash deposits, which must be kept for ten years after notifying the client of plans to close the account. However, we have never sent such a notification to a client with whom we lost contact, and the heirs will receive all the money plus interest accrued."[20] The reality, however, was different, and was revealed by the answers provided over decades by the various banks to clients—not journalists—who approached them for information.

For the first investigation of the subject for the Israeli business daily

Globes in September and October 1994, I approached some of the major banks, asking to locate a possible account belonging to a deceased family member. Their answers to my questions, when they did not know I was a journalist, exposed their real behavior toward petitioners. The answers were not identical, displaying the weakness of the Swiss government's supervision, which allowed the banks to behave as they pleased in a matter as sensitive as maintaining account documents.

The Julius Baer Bank and UBS presented two opposing approaches to account documents. The former claimed that it saved the relevant documents without any time limit. A bank official in Geneva said that after ten years the bank could destroy documents pertaining to specific transactions and instructions given for the account, but not the documents related to opening the accounts, "also for the benefit and protection of the bank."

It later became clear that the Julius Baer Bank does keep account-opening documents, but with regard to accounts opened before 1940, it has primarily only the owners' signature samples. By their nature, signature samples do not generally allow secure identification of the depositor. The first organized procedures at the bank on this matter were implemented only at the beginning of the 1970s, and accountants who examined Julius Baer's documentation believe that "the chances of locating documents from before 1946 are circumstantial."

In contrast, an official of UBS, then the largest bank in Switzerland, said, "We don't have to keep documentation of account opening. The law states that we only have to keep documents for ten years."[21] Accountants who examined UBS's documentation in 1997 determined that only the Basel and Bern branches of the bank had information on accounts opened between 1934 and 1946 and that it no longer exists. These two branches represented just 15 percent of all UBS's bank's deposits as of 1945. In the Bern branch, 25,000 cards with the details of accounts closed before 1977 were found that included the names of clients and the dates of closure. The accountants found, however, that the information on the opening dates of the accounts was unreliable, and that apparently most of the accounts were opened after the end of World War II. The conclusion was unequivocal: there was no way to create a database concerning the accounts closed by UBS.[22]

On the other hand, in 1996, the World Jewish Congress uncovered a document regarding an attempt by Radu Lecca, a Romanian officer who was among those chiefly responsible for the Final Solution in that country, to withdraw money from Volksbank (now part of Credit Suisse) in Zurich. The money consisted of bribes Lecca took from Jews to save their lives and in 1963 he attempted to withdraw the money. We will see the significance of this discovery later, but for the moment, the answer Lecca received is important: There is no possibility of finding moneys deposited before 1944, as "all the relevant business documents were destroyed a long time ago."[23]

Arthur Andersen's examination of Credit Suisse in August 1997 uncovered details of 1.5 million "banking relationships" that had been closed, including the names of the clients, dates of opening, and dates of closure. About 250,000 of those relationships (the nature of which was not clarified by the accountants) were closed between 1933 and 1949. It was also reported that similar details regarding the bank's Zurich branch were uncovered, although not regarding its other branches. Two other findings are important: accounts disappeared as the result of banking fees, and the bank sometimes sold the assets deposited in the accounts in order to cover their fees.[24]

The decisive evidence that the banks customarily destroyed documents came to light in December 1997, when historians Peter Hug and Marc Perrenoud published the report requested by the Swiss government about its agreements with Poland and Hungary, under which Holocaust victims' assets were transferred to Warsaw and Budapest. We will discuss this report in greater detail in Chapter 3, and deal here with only one instance the two uncovered, the Traschel account affair.

Otto Traschel was a Swiss citizen who emigrated to eastern Germany in the 1920s. In 1925, Traschel opened a savings account in the Savings Bank of Obersimmental: after that, contact with him was lost. In April 1935, the bank announced in Bern's official canton newspaper that Traschel's dormant savings account contained 3,430.65 francs (about 23,000 francs in current values), and that if there was no contact with the owner within ten years, the account would be closed and the money "will be absorbed into the bank's reserve fund." This did, in fact, happen in 1945, but to the bank's great embarrassment, Traschel's son appeared in 1953 and presented the savings book. But even the involvement of the Swiss Foreign Ministry did not enable the son to receive the money. Hug and Perrenoud also note that in the official newspaper of the Bern canton in 1935, when the intention to appropriate the Traschel account was declared, no fewer than seventy-seven other notices about similar accounts also appeared.[25]

Decades later, the situation had not changed. In September 1996, at the height of the storm surrounding the dormant accounts, Credit Suisse informed a Jewish woman from Buenos Aires, who claimed to be the heir to an account opened at the bank in the 1930s by her grandfather, a Holocaust victim, "We regret to inform you that we cannot perform the examination. The duty to preserve business documents is effective in Switzerland for ten years. Therefore, we cannot track bank transactions conducted before 1986."[26]

This viewpoint is reinforced in the findings of Volcker Commision accountants who conducted a sampling in the summer of 1997 of the documentation in a number of Swiss banks. In the Banque Cantonale Vaudoise, it was found that documents more than ten years old are regularly destroyed in order to make space in the bank's archives.

Similar policies were found at Spar und Leikhasse and Bauman & Cie.

In the St. Gallische Kantonalbank, there is no uniform policy. Each branch acts as it chooses, but none of them keeps documents more than ten years if the account is closed. This is also true at the Banque Cantonale de Genève. Picket & Cie. admitted explicitly that if an account is dormant for five years, it closes the account and transfers the money to a "general account," which is essentially the bank's own property.

In 1997, Swiss Bank prepared a list of 60,000 accounts that were closed before 1945, including the names of clients, opening dates, closure dates, and closure reasons, and promised to make the list available to the Volcker Commission accountants. Meanwhile, the Volcker Commission reported that they could not determine the documentation status at Swiss Bank, which was then the third largest bank in Switzerland and is now part of the merged United Bank (UBS). They noted, however, that since the war, Swiss Bank had swallowed up forty other banks, and it appeared that it appropriated for itself the dormant accounts in those banks.[27]

The proof of closure of dormant accounts by the banks is so abundant and conclusive, that the U.S. government determined that this is what happened. In October 1997, then Under Secretary of State Stuart Eizenstat, special envoy for the restitution of property in Europe, said that "The exact number of accounts under Jewish ownership in Swiss banks will never be known, as some were liquidated by the banks over the years."[28] After two-and-a-half years of the Jewish struggle, Washington accepted the Jewish organizations' position on the most central question of what happened to the dormant accounts.

Nonetheless, the examination by the Volcker Commission accountants finally showed that not all the documents were destroyed. In January 1999, Commission chair Paul Volcker stated that he expected the commission to locate 3,000 to 15,000 accounts that had belonged to Holocaust victims. This estimate is based on the fact that when Yad V'Shem (the central Israeli institution for Holocaust research) transmitted 500,000 Holocaust victims' names to the commission, it was found that about 3,000 of them had accounts in Swiss banks. Since Yad V'Shem has the names of about 3 million victims, Volcker concludes that about 15,000 names of victims who held accounts will be discovered.[29]

Considering the only-partial preservation of documents and that Yad V'Shem has only about half the victims' names, it is clear that the number of accounts in Swiss banks owned by Holocaust victims amounted to tens of thousands—as the Jewish organizations had claimed throughout the years.

The very likely possibility of the lack of enough documents about dormant accounts has great practical importance. First, it means that it will be very difficult, maybe even impossible, to find the accounts and restore the property to the heirs. Second, it can now be concluded that an investigation of the entire affair is not likely to lead to real results, unless it becomes clear that the remaining documents are sufficient as a representative sampling of all the documents.

The investigation conducted by the Volcker Commission concerning the banks' handling of victims' accounts, is based primarily on the work of four international accounting firms—KPMG, Price-Waterhouse, Arthur Andersen, and Coopers & Lybrand. Accountants know how to work when they have documents in front of them, but their work is useless when they have to make do with fragmented testimony and assumptions. A senior international accountant, who heard about the documentation problem, told me, "if that is the case, my colleagues will work for a long time and receive a lot of money, but won't find anything."

The other alternative, examining the banks' balance sheets, is also not practical. The proposal is to examine how much the banks' assets increased during 1933–1945 and calculate the portion of that amount from closing dormant accounts. The banks, however, did not keep the working papers on which the balance sheets are based, since they are not required to. All that is left are the reports themselves, from which it is impossible to conclude the volume of dormant property that the banks appropriated for themselves.

It can be concluded that various investigations would have great difficulty in restoring property to its rightful owners, the depositors' heirs. They would also have difficulty determining the sums involved, in order to reach a settlement with the Jewish organizations concerning the accounts without heirs. Therefore, as long as such a serious documentation problem existed, the only possible solution was a global settlement with the organizations and the claimants together, as was reached in August 1998.

The amount of the settlement was determined in negotiations that took into account existing documentation, the possible proportion of Jewish clients out of all the banks' clients prior to the Holocaust, and the likelihood that those clients were murdered and none of them withdrew their money. To this was added a sum that the banks paid to salvage their reputations, particularly with class action suits amounting to tens of billions of dollars and the threat of sanctions in the United States pending against them.

The settlement was negotiated by the major Jewish organizations, headed by the World Jewish Congress and the Jewish Agency. These two organizations led the way beginning in 1994 for the return of the deposits. The status of the Jewish organizations in the matter, primarily their right to conduct negotiations with Switzerland and the banks, and their right to manage the money they received, is one of the central issues in the settlements made after World War II concerning the fate of German property and the property of Nazi victims. We will discuss this complex issue in Chapter 2.

2

"SWITZERLAND WILL EXAMINE FAVORABLY"
Victims' Money Was Designated for Refugee Rehabilitation

IN 1945, MANY German nationals had assets outside their homeland, in both Allied and neutral countries. Germany itself had deposited a great deal of property—including assets looted from occupied countries and victims of the Nazi regime—in Switzerland, Sweden, Spain, Turkey, Portugal, and even in the United States. After the war, the victorious Allies held huge claims against the defeated Germany and its allies Italy, Hungary, Bulgaria, and Romania. The combination of these problems led the Allies into a debate that lasted several years concerning the fate of German assets, primarily if they were to be used to rehabilitate Germany, rehabilitate Europe, and pay reparations to the victors.

The longest and most difficult discussions were conducted between the Allies—the United States, Britain, and France—and Switzerland, an island of prosperity and peace in war-torn Europe. When the Allies discussed the fate of German property, they also discussed the future of property without heirs, primarily the assets in the bank accounts of Holocaust victims. Switzerland did not want to part with them, which, although only deposited in the country, contributed greatly to its economic prosperity. Moreover, if the assets were not claimed by their owners, the banks could appropriate them for themselves, and the Swiss government was not at all opposed to accepting tax revenues on this income.

The fate of German property held in neutral countries, primarily Switzerland, was first discussed at the rank of heads of state at the Potsdam Conference in July–August 1945. The United States was represented by President Harry Truman, Britain by Prime Minister Winston Churchill and later his replacement Clement Attlee, and the Soviet Union by Joseph Stalin. At Potsdam, it was decided that the Allies would appropriate all German property held outside of Germany, as the property inside the country fell into their hands when they occupied German territory. The conference's participants left the discussion of what exactly would be done with the money for a later date.[1]

This phase began on November 9, 1945, when the representatives of the eighteen Allies met in Paris, without the Soviet Union, which had waived its portion of the German property. The United States proposed using 6 percent of the German property in neutral countries to rehabilitate war refugees. At that time, in camps across the continent, there were hundreds of thousands of refugees, including 60,000–70,000 Jews. Someone had to finance their maintenance and rehabilitation, and the United States believed that it was appropriate for Germany to do just that, through state and citizen assets. The U.S. proposal was to direct 2 percent of the German assets to assisting Holocaust survivors. Britain opposed this, fearing the money would be used for the emigration of Jews to Palestine, which they had severely limited since 1939.

After about a month of negotiations, the Allies agreed to budget $50 million ($445 million in current values) toward refugee rehabilitation. Half the sum was slated to come from "non-monetary" gold captured in Germany, in other words, gold looted from victims of the Nazi regime, primarily Holocaust victims. This included jewelry and gold dental work. The other half, determined by the Paris Agreement signed on December 21, 1945, "shall be met from a portion of the proceeds of German assets in neutral countries which are available for reparation." And then came the article (Article 8) that is important for our purposes: "Governments of neutral countries shall be requested to make available for this purpose [refugee rehabilitation] (in addition to the sum of 25 million dollars) assets in such countries of victims of Nazi action who have since died and left no heirs."[2]

In simple terms, the neutral countries were asked to investigate the scope of assets they held that could be assumed to belong to Nazi victims who had left no heirs. The Allies had determined that these assets be made available to rehabilitate war refugees. For the Swiss, this meant that it had to carefully scan the banks, insurance companies, investment firms, and law offices to locate Nazi victims' assets and make them available to rehabilitate survivors.

With a little goodwill, Bern could have found a way to respond to the request, whose logic, morality, and basic justice were irrefutable. Bern could have determined, for instance, that an account for whom no heirs had appeared, let us say by May 1946, a year after the end of the war, would be considered property without heirs and thus be available for rehabilitation. Arrangements to ensure compensation for the banks, if heirs suddenly appeared after the agreed date, could also have been made. In practice, however, Switzerland instituted a policy of intentionally dragging its feet.

The Americans and the British had trouble with the Swiss that continued for months after the implementation of the Paris Agreement, primarily concerning German property in Switzerland, as the Swiss denied the Allies' right to claim the property. In February 1946, the Allies invited a Swiss delegation to Washington to discuss the German property. The talks began in March and lasted through a crisis-ridden three-month period, and Washington officials began to discuss imposing sanctions on Switzerland. On the periphery of the talks, the issue of property without heirs was also raised.

The Washington Accord, signed on May 25, 1946, was primarily a settlement with Switzerland in consideration of the looted gold that Bern had purchased from Germany and the thawing of Swiss assets in the United States. Among other things, Switzerland promised the Allies immediate receipt—at the expense of liquidating German property in Switzerland—of 50 million francs ($12 million in 1946 or $98 million in current values) for the purpose of rehabilitating refugees. It is important to emphasize that the money was slated to come from German property, and not from property without heirs. We will see later how Switzerland dragged its feet on this matter as well.[3]

And what about the property without heirs? This matter was discussed in two secret "accompanying letters" not published at the time the agreement was signed. In the first letter, representatives of the United States, Britain, and France asked Swiss minister Walter Stucki "to submit to the kind consideration of your Government, in the interests of victims whose assets were looted by the Germans and whose property may come to light in Switzerland, the proposal to institute a simple, inexpensive administrative procedure [for recovery] taking account of the penury and frailty of these victims." Stucki responded, "Despite the fact that I believe that the Swiss legislative body has not been proven inefficient [in locating victims property], I will not sidestep raising your request to my government."

In his second letter, Stucki stated, "On the point of signing the Agreement relating to German assets in Switzerland dated this day, I confirm that my government will look favorably on the question of introducing the measures necessary to place at the disposal of the three Allied governments [the United States, Britain, and France] (for the purpose of aid and assistance [for refugees]) the amount of assets in Switzerland belonging to victims of the acts of violence recently perpetrated by the former German government, who died without heirs."[4]

This letter is the principal legal basis for the repeated demands made on Switzerland to locate the assets of Holocaust victims without heirs, and make them available for the rehabilitation of refugees. Naturally, this does not allow Switzerland to evade in any way the return of property to existing heirs. Switzerland, however, avoided taking any action until 1962, and when it finally did, it transferred most of the money to the local Jewish community, and not to organizations helping survivors.

Those entitled to the property without heirs, according to a binding international agreement, are the Jewish Agency and the American Joint Distribution Committee, known as the Joint. Their status was established in June 1946, when the Americans tired of the British anti-Jewish policy in Palestine. The United States decided to again raise the issue of financing the rehabilitation of refugees, which had remained open in the Paris Agreement at the end of 1945. In an obvious hint at its intentions, the U.S. Department of State decided that Eli Ginzburg, a young economist and director of the United Jewish Appeal in the United States in the years 1941–1942, and who later became an economics professor at Columbia University, would head the delegation.[5]

The talks were held in Paris in June 1946, immediately following the signing of the Washington Accord. The participants were the United States, Britain, France, Czechoslovakia, and Yugoslavia, the five countries that made up the committee in charge of implementing the December 1945, Paris Agreement on the rehabilitation of refugees.

In the preliminary talks Ginzburg held with representatives of the various countries, he discovered that Britain's primary concern was that moneys designated for refugee rehabilitation would be directed toward Jewish settlement in Palestine. It is a reasonable assumption that the British feared the possibility that the moneys would finance the Jewish underground and purchase weapons for the Hagana, the core of the armed forces of Jewish settlement in Palestine—subject to the Jewish Agency. In the end, it was agreed that the Jewish Agency and the Joint would not be mentioned in the agreement itself, but in an accompanying letter that was sent to the director of the International Refugee Organization.

Thus, the June 14 agreement dealt with the distribution of the $25 million established in the Paris Agreement. The money was to come from three sources: realization of the nonmonetary gold uncovered in Germany, realization of German assets in neutral countries, and the property without heirs left in those countries (Switzerland, Sweden, Spain, Portugal, and Turkey). Of the nonmonetary gold, 90 percent was slated for Jewish refugees, and of the property without heirs, 95 percent was also slated for them. In total, $22.5 million was designated for Jewish refugees via the Jewish Agency and the Joint, while $2.5 million was designated for non-Jewish refugees via the International Refugee Organization. In current values, this amounts to $185 million specifically to aid Holocaust survivors.[6]

The agreement indicates that when Switzerland was asked to return property without heirs, its legal owner became the Jewish Agency. The agency then transferred its rights to the Israeli government in the 1950s, and it, in turn, authorized the World Jewish Restitution Organization (WJRO), consisting primarily of the Jewish Agency and the World Jewish Congress, to act on the property matter in the 1990s. There are, therefore, solid legal grounds for the Jewish organizations' demand to receive and manage the moneys.

It is important to note that the June 14, 1946, agreement annulled the difference between German property and property without heirs. In the original Paris Agreement of December 1945, two parallel routes were established: the transfer of $25 million in German property held in neutral countries to refugee rehabilitation, along with a request that the neutral countries locate property without heirs and make it available for the same purpose. In the second Paris Agreement of June 14, 1946, both sums are combined. In total, $25 million is slated for refugee rehabilitation, which will come from German property and property without heirs. This was a significant gain for Switzerland, which was not even a party to the 1946 talks between the Allies.

But this was not enough for Switzerland, despite being required to transfer far less to the Allies than had originally been planned. For years, Switzerland evaded fulfillment of its part in the international agreements. It should be noted again that this did not pertain to transferring Swiss property, but to German property, and, most significantly, Jewish property.

In September 1946, only three months after the signing of the Washington Accord, Switzerland began its delaying tactics. Its first play was to claim that it wanted to know what was being done in the United States concerning the return of property without heirs to Holocaust victims, on both the federal and individual state levels. The second maneuver was a dispute between Switzerland and the United States on how to calculate the exchange rate of the reichsmark (the currency issued by the Reichsbank, the central bank of Nazi Germany) on German deposits in Switzerland. These tactics delayed Swiss fulfillment of its obligations concerning the liquidation of German assets slated to be transferred to the Allies for rehabilitation of Germany and Europe, and refugee resettlement. The United States and Britain rejected the connection that Bern created between the exchange rate and refugee aid, but did not succeed in changing the Swiss position.

In March 1947, Edward Warburg, chair of the American Jewish Congress, approached Acting Secretary of State Dean Acheson with the request that the Swiss be reminded of their commitments. Warburg asked that Switzerland pay as soon as possible no less than 20 million ($34 million in current values) of the 50 million franc advance it had promised. He noted the distress of the Jewish Agency and the Joint in handling refugee resettlement, and that they could not continue to borrow money to finance their activities, which endangered the entire operation. Acheson promised to do everything possible, in coordination with Britain and France.

Acheson kept his word. At the beginning of May 1947, the State Department drafted a request to Switzerland asking for immediate payment of $5 million, and forwarded it to the British and French embassies in Washington. Before the Allies had time to send the request to Bern, the Swiss suddenly suggested that they immediately pay the entire 50 million francs. Now the tables were turned. The United States rejected the proposal, arguing that Switzerland had to fulfill all its commitments according to the Washington Accord, the first and foremost of which was the payment of $58 million (250 million francs) against the gold it purchased from Germany.

In a telegram to the American embassy in Paris, a State Department official explained the American position: "The Department wants to avoid any charges that it has bargained on the Accord for all IARA [Interallied Reparation Agency] countries in order to advance one special case," in other words, refugee aid. But in the meantime, American public opinion, both Jewish and general, began to pressure the administration, demanding the adoption of a more favorable policy toward the refugees.

The pressure led to a change in U.S. policy. After consulting with Britain and France, in February 1948, almost two years after the signing of the accord, the United States asked Switzerland to transfer the first 20 million francs for refugee aid. The United States ignored everything that had happened in the intervening months since the Swiss proposal to pay the entire 50 million francs, and returned to its May 1947, position of an advance on the overall payment. For some reason, it took the Swiss another four months to respond, and the money was only transferred to the Allies in July 1948.[7]

Another issue about which the Swiss were stubborn related directly to the property of Holocaust victims. The Washington Accord required the Swiss to freeze the assets belonging to Germans within its borders. As a result, the assets of Nazi victims were also frozen. The U.S. representatives to the Washington talks discovered, maybe a little late, that on this point they had gotten something they had not wanted at all: All assets were frozen. Since Congress was demanding that Nazi victims get their property back, even if they were formally included in the definition, "Germans in Germany," whose property was frozen, there is no question that there was a great deal of logic, not to mention justice, in this approach. It was inconceivable to further hinder the victims, most of whose property was stolen from them before and during the war, by not returning the property they had transferred to safety beyond the Alps.

One of the U.S. representatives to the Washington talks, Randolph Paul, reached a gentlemen's agreement with his Swiss colleagues that Nazi victims' property would not be frozen, but due to time constraints, their agreement was not put into writing. Nonetheless, U.S. officials dealing with the matter received the impression that the Swiss intended to release assets belonging to the victims.

At the end of 1948, it became clear that this was not the case. In November 1948, the International Refugee Organization reported to U.S. Secretary of State George Marshall that the Swiss Clearing Office, was continuing to freeze victims' assets, and asked for U.S. assistance in solving the problem. The State Department responded that it hoped the matter would be discussed shortly, with the aim of reaching a less harsh Swiss approach concerning the release of victims' assets.

Prior to talks between the Allies and Switzerland in May 1949, the United States asked to remove the assets of Nazi victims from the sphere of the Washington Accord. In the March preparatory meetings, however, the British and the French refused to support the United States' proposal. The British claimed that such an action on behalf of the victims would be discriminatory and neglect the primary goals of the agreement: the receipt of all German assets outside Germany. The United States, therefore, did not raise the subject in May.

It is a reasonable assumption that the Swiss did not know about the differences of opinion among the Allies concerning victims' property, but they certainly felt in mid-1949 that their position in the negotiations was better than it had been previously. One reason for this was the worsening Cold War, which obliged the United States to maintain correct relations with Switzerland against the Soviet threat. Another reason was explicitly stated in a Swiss Foreign Ministry document in mid-1949, which summarized the talks from May and June:

The negotiations which lie behind us took place in an atmosphere which may be distinguished favorably in every respect from that in which the Washington agreement negotiations took place three years ago. Whilst on that occasion [the Washington talks], we came under strong pressure, were treated with obvious mistrust, almost as if we had secretly been Hitler's friends, this time we found a definite spirit of friendliness and readiness to understand particularly on the part of our American treaty partners. Not a single member of the big US delegation in 1946 was in attendance. We were dealing with an entirely new set of people altogether, and they were not under so much Jewish influence or imbued with Morgenthau's spirit [Henry Morgenthau, the Jewish secretary of the treasury 1934–45].[8]

In other words, Switzerland felt no pressure to transfer the promised funds for refugee rehabilitation, since Morgenthau was no longer in a position of power.

Later in 1949, pressure began to build on the Truman administration that it demand payment of the remaining 30 million francs. Jacob Javits—a member of the House of Representatives and later one of Israel's greatest friends in the Senate—entered the picture. In May 1949, Javits approached Secretary of State Acheson and asked that the United States demand the remaining payment from Switzerland immediately, which was sent in January 1950, with no response. An additional demand sent in March 1950 was answered negatively in May. Bern argued that there was no legal ground requiring Switzerland to make any additional gesture to the refugee organization. This was a weird answer, to put it mildly, as Switzerland had promised in the Washington Accord to transfer 50 million francs, and had so far transferred only 40 percent of the total.

Bern also had a technical justification for its refusal: The money was to come from the liquidation of German assets in Switzerland, a process delayed by various problems between Switzerland and other countries. Put simply, Switzerland had returned to the linkage between refugee aid and the liquidation of German assets. Since the exchange rate problem was essentially solved, however, Bern now indicated another problem: the the release of assets frozen by the United States during the war as German property, which Switzerland claimed as its own.[9] Switzerland succeeded in retaining that link for three years, and avoided transferring the money, despite the fact that it was vital to aid Holocaust refugees.

Where the United States had failed, the Jewish organizations did not stand a chance. A clear example of the futile contacts between the Jewish organizations and Switzerland is the meeting held in Bern in July 1949, between representatives of the World Jewish Congress, the Jewish Agency, the Joint, the American Jewish Committee, and Swiss minister of justice, Eduard von Steiger.

The meeting was described in a report written by Jewish Agency representative Shlomo Adler-Rudell. According to Adler-Rudell, von Steiger emphasized that the Swiss government was aware of the seriousness of the problem, and asked for information from the Jewish representatives. Max Isenbergh, of the American Jewish Committee, emphasized the "principle according to which Jewish assets without heirs or claimants should be used for the welfare, rehabilitation and resettlement of Jews," and explained that the aid was urgently needed. Von Steiger offered the floor to Mr. Alexander, the official in charge of the matter, to report on the steps under consideration.

a) First, it must be determined if, and of what extent, there are assets without heirs and claimants. For this purpose, every bank and private citizen will be required to register with an official Swiss office the assets of foreign citizens with whom there has been no contact since May 9, 1945, within three months of the introduction of the law.

b) Afterwards, there will be a need to insure the assets against future changes by freezing them.

c) Some steps will have to be taken to locate the legal heirs, who are unaware of the existence of the assets.

d) It will be necessary to solve the problem of the death certificate [of Holocaust victims].

e) It will be necessary to examine the question of who is entitled to the assets, Switzerland or their [the owners'] country of origin.

f) All these problems must be solved in legislation. He [Alexander] promised that if the moneys were transferred to the Swiss government, they would be used for refugee rehabilitation.

Later in the meeting, attorney F. R. Biennenfeld of the World Jewish Congress discussed at length the question of who is entitled to the property without heirs—Switzerland or the victims' countries of origin. Naturally, the Jewish organizations tried to convince Switzerland that they were entitled to the assets, as that would make it easier for them to use the assets for refugee rehabilitation. If it were determined that the countries of origin were entitled to the property, it meant separate negotiations with each country, most of which were under Communist rule and might have appropriated the moneys for themselves. Biennenfeld tried to make a convincing argument that it was "against the public interest" to transfer the assets without heirs to the governments of the countries of origin, as "the previous governments in those countries created the problem of property without heirs by murdering the owners." For his part, von Steiger promised that banking confidentiality would not be an obstacle to an agreed-upon solution. Adler-Rudell continued:

When the meeting had gone on about an hour and a half, von Steiger summarized the situation as follows: his office would examine the laws and steps taken in other countries, particularly those mentioned by Mr. Isenbergh. They would be grateful to receive a summary [in writing] of the reasons listed by Biennenfeld why the countries of origin could not demand the assets. Thirdly, he expected [the Jewish organizations to provide] a general declaration of the details of management of the fund to be established. The overall impression of all the participants in the meeting was that the Swiss government, or at least the Ministry of Justice, was interested in solving the problem in a just manner.[10]

In retrospect, the report of the meeting in July 1949 is one of the most interesting documents in the entire affair. First, it clearly indicates some of the key problems that would continue to accompany the situation for years: who is entitled to the property without heirs, what do in lieu of a death certificate, and would banking confidentiality be revoked in order to return the property. Second, it indicates the naiveté of the Jewish side, which was convinced that the list of problems dropped at its doorstep indicated the Swiss desire to solve the problem. It would be several years before those who negotiated with Bern would understand that these problems were often no more than an excuse for inaction.

Third, in this early meeting some groundwork was laid that was only implemented thirteen years later in the 1962 law that ordered the owners of dormant assets to report them to the government: the requirement to report assets for which contact with the owners had been lost, the depositing of those assets in a public office of some sort, and the attempt to locate heirs before the money was transferred for refugee aid. Fourth, as early as 1949, some of the principles in effect today were put forward: the establishment of a fund common to the Jewish organizations and the Swiss government that the Swiss government would control and which would assist needy Jewish refugees—the exact plan for the "humanitarian fund" the Swiss and the Jewish organizations established at the beginning of 1997 (see Chapter 12).

In practice, Switzerland continued to refuse to transfer to the Jewish organizations the remainder of the advance it had promised in the Washington Accord, and it certainly took no steps concerning the property without heirs. The red tape concerned the much wider problem of implementation of one of the primary parts of the Washington Accord: liquidation of German assets in Switzerland. During 1950–1952, lengthy discussions were held between the Allies and Switzerland on this matter. Meanwhile, Bern negotiated with Bonn concerning the fate of German assets within Swiss borders.

At the end of the process, two agreements were achieved in August 1952. On August 26, an agreement was signed between Switzerland and Germany, the Bonn Agreement, in which Bonn would pay Bern 121.5 million francs (480 million francs in current values) against the sum Switzerland was to pay to the Allies out of German assets. The payment was to be financed by exercising German assets that had not been demanded, including the assets of Holocaust victims. Until the German government received the revenues from selling its citizens' assets, it would borrow the sum from a consortium of Swiss banks.

Two days later, on August 28, an agreement was signed between Switzerland and the Allies, the Bern Agreement, that dealt with Swiss debts. Instead of transferring to the Allies half of the German assets within its borders, the Swiss promised to pay the same 121.5 million francs, then worth $28.3 million. From this sum, Switzerland deducted the 20 million francs paid in 1948 as an advance to the International Refugee Organization (which then had transferred 90 percent of the money to the Jewish Agency and the Joint).

At the same time, Switzerland announced in a confidential letter accompanying the Bern Agreement that it had no Holocaust victims' assets whose heirs were unknown and were entitled to them. Switzerland promised nonetheless that if such assets were discovered, it would favorably consider using them to aid Nazi victims, a similar phrase to that used in the Washington Accord.[11]

The Bern Agreement was a great achievement for Switzerland. First, Switzerland announced in 1947 that the value of the frozen German assets within its borders amounted to 398 million francs, then worth $98 million ($706 million in current values). This sum was designated to be divided equally between Switzerland and the Allies. But, instead of transferring $50 million to the Allies, Switzerland transferred $23.6 million (the amount determined in the Bern Agreement, minus the advance paid to the International Refugee Organization).

Second, Switzerland did not pay anything from its own coffers, but received immediate reimbursement from Germany. This was fine, since as has been said a number of times, Switzerland was supposed to stop holding property that was not theirs. It continued to hold a great deal of German property, however, and its banks even profited on the loans they gave West Germany to finance the agreement.

The agreements between Switzerland and the Allies and Switzerland and Germany finally enabled the transfer of the rest of the Swiss debt to the International Refugee Organization, but only after they dragged things out. In September 1953, one year after the Bern and Bonn Agreements, Switzerland transferred $3 million ($18 million in current values) to the International Refugee Organization. In 1955–1956, the Allies transferred another $3.5 million in the name of Portugal, completing the $25 million quota determined ten years earlier in the Paris Agreement. The Swiss contribution was only $7.7 million, despite the fact that there were German assets and property without heirs of a much greater scope within its borders. Sweden, which had a much lower volume of this sort of asset, contributed nearly twice as much, $13.5 million.[12]

The Bonn and Bern Agreements put the activities of the Swiss Clearing Office in Zurich, which had been established by the Swiss government in 1934, into high gear. The clearing office was managed by the Swiss central bank, the Swiss Bankers Association, the Association for Trade and Industry, and the Swiss Center for Trade Promotion. The office's initial job had been to facilitate transfers and payments according to Swiss clearing agreements with foreign countries.

During World War II, the office was in charge of implementing the freezing of assets of citizens of sixteen foreign countries, and also handled requests to release them under special circumstances. Among other things, they handled the freezing of German assets in Switzerland. The office's files therefore contain information on the assets of Jews who escaped from Germany to Switzerland. Copies of about ninety of the office's reports are kept in the Public Record Office in London,[13] and only two of those files deal with Jews.

The most interesting of the cases is report number 81, concerning Dr. Ursula Buschbeck, 51, who held various assets in Switzerland that are not listed in the report. Even after the war, Buschbeck could not get into Switzerland, and only after masquerading as a German did she succeed. Jewish refugees were particularly unwanted, unlike German refugees, who were warmly welcomed. Her case also emphasizes the rigid bureaucracy encountered by petitioners, despite the fact that Buschbeck presented, as the report explicitly states, "documents and authorizations" that confirm her version of what happened to her.

Ms. Buschbeck studied in Zurich until she received her PhD. She later spent time in Switzerland a number of times. At the beginning of the war, she returned to Germany, where she was subject to Nazi persecution due to race [a hint that she is Jewish]. After her German passport was revoked, she was arrested and released after a year and a half imprisonment. She was expelled from her home and place of residence, and lost all means of supporting herself. Under Nazi pressure, she was forced to give up her German citizenship permanently. In order to avoid further persecution and additional imprisonment, Buschbeck did everything in her power to reach Switzerland. Her efforts were in vain. Only at the end of the war, did she manage to receive from the German authorities what is known as a "foreigners passport" which notes she is "without citizenship."

She presented this document to the Swiss authorities in order to receive an entry visa to that country, but her request was denied because she was without citizenship. Later, she repeated the request posing as a German citizen, and this attempt was successful. The French military government gave her the necessary permissions to travel to Switzerland, and provided her with "travel papers in lieu of passport," as she had successfully proven she suffered persecution and that she still felt her personal safety was at risk even after the end of the war.

She reached Switzerland in the middle of November [1947] in order to spend three months here for her personal rehabilitation. . . . The travel papers [from the French military government] included the following comment, noted by the occupying powers: "the owner of this pass is explicitly forbidden from making any transaction or withdrawal from a bank account or other asset abroad, in which a German citizen is an interested party and could claim rights."

Nonetheless, we can ask ourselves, if these travel papers, granted by the occupying forces in 1947, could influence or annul the passport granted in 1945 by the German authorities which stated Ms. Buschbeck was without citizenship, or renew German citizenship if she is interested. Under these circumstances, the above comment cannot be construed to mean that Ms. Buschbeck cannot make use of the means belonging to her in Switzerland, but that she is not authorized to conduct commercial transactions for the benefit of German citizens. The text itself deals with this possibility.

After this legal argument, outstanding primarily for not raising any moral arguments, the Swiss Clearing Office recommended releasing Buschbeck's assets.

In 1946, the Swiss government authorized its Clearing Office to break into the safe-deposit boxes of German citizens, or those considered German prisoners. The official purpose was to prevent the defeated Nazis from trying to appropriate the property, but it is unclear what the connection is between this action and the seizure of the property of Nazi victims. KPMG accountants who examined the matter in 1997 for the Volcker Commission determined that the value of the property removed from the safes was 1.9 billion francs in nominal values, approximately 10 billion francs in current values.

When the break-ins were reported in a meeting of the Volcker Commission in September 1997, World Jewish Congress secretary-general Israel Singer bombarded the accountants with questions: "Whose property was it? What happened to it?" He also questioned the representative of the Swiss government, Thomas Borer: "Where is the report certainly given your government on the fate of the property?" None of these questions were answered. The accountants and Borer, who were rather embarrassed, promised to provide the answers at one of the committee's upcoming meetings.[14] As of this time, explanations for the break-ins have not been provided. This is just one instance in which it became clear how cynically Switzerland handled the property of Nazi victims. The most prominent incidents were the agreements between Switzerland and Hungary and Poland, which will be described in Chapter 3.

3

"CRUELLY IRONIC"
Switzerland Exploits Property without Heirs for Its Own Purposes

THE HEARING ON Holocaust victims' deposits in the U.S. Senate Banking Committee on October 16, 1996, did not arouse the same level of interest as the first hearing initiated by committee chair Senator Alfonse D'Amato, six months earlier. That hearing appeared to be another move in D'Amato's incessant attacks on the Swiss banks concerning Holocaust victims' accounts, and on Switzerland itself for its close economic ties with Nazi Germany. Since this was the second hearing, expectations were low for revelations.

But D'Amato surprised the participants. He pulled from history's dusty shelves two agreements that Switzerland signed with Poland and Hungary, under which Switzerland transferred to those countries close to 100 dormant accounts belonging to Polish and Hungarian citizens. D'Amato claimed that this was Jewish property used to compensate Swiss citizens whose property in Poland and Hungary was nationalized when they were taken over by the Communist Party.[1]

Like many other issues that D'Amato made into headlines, the agreements with Poland and Hungary were known to researchers of the period. D'Amato, however, gave these historical matters current significance. Before the hearing, a handful of historians knew about them. The public at large knew nothing about them, and the agreements largely did not affect or interest them. D'Amato pulled them out with perfect timing, and revealed how Switzerland exploited Jewish property without heirs for its own benefit.

Swiss reaction to the revelations in the Senate Banking Committee was stuttered, possibly because Bern needed time to figure out exactly what it was all about. The Polish government announced that the agreement with Warsaw was illegal and promised to try and locate the heirs of the account holders whose funds were transferred to Poland, so that their money could be returned to them. Hungary explained that it received the money after Switzerland decided that each country was the beneficiary of the assets of its murdered citizens' who left no heirs.[2]

The Swiss response came two weeks later on October 29. The Foreign

Ministry charged historians Peter Hug and Marc Perrenoud with preparing a report on the agreements with Poland and Hungary. The two worked at a dizzying pace and submitted their report on December 19, 1996. (The English-language version used for the purposes of this book was published one month later.) The speed at which they worked did not adversely affect the quality of the job, and the Hug-Perrenoud report has become a very important source not only on the agreements with Poland and Hungary, but on everything concerning Swiss handling of property without heirs.

In the background of the two agreements was the importance, from the Swiss perspective, of trade with Eastern Europe. After World War II, Bern tried to prove to the Allies—who were hostile due to its actions during the war—how important Switzerland was to them, and therefore decided to develop its own ties with Eastern Europe.[3]

At the end of the 1940s, however, the blossoming trade stood in the shadow of the problem of nationalization of property in Eastern Europe. Poland had nationalized Swiss property at a value of 100 million 1949 francs of the total Swiss investment estimated at 300–360 million francs (to reach 1999 values, multiply by 4.3).

Hungarian nationalization affected Swiss assets valued at 60 million francs, about one-fifth of Swiss citizens' assets in that country. One-third of Swiss assets in Bulgaria were nationalized, at a value of 20 million francs. Czechoslovakian nationalization affected Swiss assets valued at 120 million francs of a total 162 million francs in assets. The worst damage to Swiss investors was in Romania; whose government nationalized Swiss assets valued at 75 million francs, about three-quarters of all Swiss assets there.

Switzerland paid its citizens compensation for a large portion of the nationalized assets, and later requested negotiations with the nationalizing countries in an attempt to retrieve at least some of the money it had paid out. Poland promised to pay Switzerland 53.5 million francs in 1949 values, about half the value of the nationalized property. In 1950, Hungary promised to pay Switzerland 30 million francs, once again, about half the value of the nationalized property.[4]

Was there a direct connection between the agreements and the fate of the deposits left in Switzerland by murdered citizens of those communist countries? Hug and Perrenoud prove that there was no direct connection, refuting D'Amato's claim. But, there is no doubt that there was a definite link between the two issues. It should be emphasized that most of the accounts transferred to Poland and Hungary belonged to Jews.

Swiss-Polish trade in the second half of the 1940s was multifaceted and problematic. Switzerland imported from Poland about one-fourth of the coal essential to industry, which could no longer be imported from a devastated Germany. In exchange, Poland wanted to purchase machinery, aluminum, chemicals, and more from Switzerland. There were problems however, that made trade between the two countries difficult: Polish assets in Switzerland were frozen in July 1945, when the Communists rose to power, but it badly needed loans from Swiss banks. And, of course, there was the question of compensation for the nationalized property.

These issues required years of complex and exhausting talks, in which the question of the bank deposits—the majority of Polish assets in Switzerland—was included from the start. The Polish side raised the matter in January 1946, when the trade talks began. Bern's official representative, Max Troendle, replied that the banks and insurance companies were obligated to try and locate their clients. If the Swiss government had insisted on implementing this stance in its contacts with the banks, it is possible that the entire deposits affair would have looked very different.[5]

What did the banks think of this? Swiss Bankers Association (SBA) chair Rudolph Speich, in the second round of talks with the Poles in February 1946, expressed a view that was apparently very similar to that of the government, but he did have a few important reservations:

The desire of the Swiss banks to trace all the account holders and [I should like to] emphasize that the banks have no interest in keeping those deposits without any contact with the owners of such securities. However, banking law does not authorize the disclosure of any details whatsoever to third parties who cannot prove that they have a right over these assets.

It is thus the duty of the Polish state to start the legal procedure required to obtain a declaration of absence [of the account owner], then to ensure that no heirs exist and finally, to contact the depositary or bank who, when in possession of the necessary documents, will be only too happy to hand over the assets in question. Of course, Swiss banking establishments will endeavor to renew contact with their Polish clients as soon as communications are restored and so long as they are not in receipt of instructions from their clients to retain all correspondence at the bank's premises.[6]

This document indicates that the SBA believed at the time that the country of origin of the owner of a dormant account was not entitled to inherit the account. Application of this principle could have simplified things for the Jewish organizations.

Also, in 1946, the banks were demanding "appropriate documentation" of the existence of the accounts and the fate of their owners, a nearly impossible demand directed at the third party (the Polish government), accompanied by a refusal to provide that party with information. Speich's remarks specifically refer to correspondence to missing clients kept at the relevant bank branch, and state that the banks take no steps to locate those missing clients, as we described in Chapter 1.

Poland rejected the SBA's position on the spot, and requested a list of dormant account owners. As expected, the Bankers Association refused the request, using as justification, banking confidentiality. Later, in October 1946, the Poles first linked the problem of the deposits to the question of compensation for nationalization: Warsaw stated that it still could not ensure payment of compensation, but suggested using Polish property without heirs in Switzerland as compensation for the nationalization. Switzerland did not respond, and the talks continued fruitlessly throughout 1947–1948.[7]

In December 1948, the Swiss cabinet decided that the time had come to solve the disputed matter with Poland, and appointed a delegation of government and business representatives, including the Bankers Association, to conduct talks with Warsaw. The talks began at the start of 1949, and Poland explicitly asked to receive "insurance policies, bank deposits, and current accounts in existence in Switzerland in the name of Polish nationals who had died or gone missing during the war without leaving heirs." The Swiss delegation responded that the Poles were deluding themselves concerning the scope of the assets. An investigation at insurance companies found 110,000 francs (462,000 francs in current values), and an investigation at the banks located current accounts, savings schemes, and securities worth 200,000 francs (840,000 francs in current values).

After this first round of talks, the SBA tried again to check with its members to find out just how much money was involved. The investigation was conducted in June 1950, and the banks reported assets worth 598,000 francs (2.51 million in current values): 541,000 francs in securities in Swiss francs, and 46,000 francs in securities in foreign currency, as well as 11,000 francs in dormant assets abroad.[8] It is very interesting that the banks did not find, at least they claimed, a single penny in current accounts. Did Polish citizens not open such accounts? Or had the banks already managed to close them? Or had commissions and fees chewed away at the accounts until they disappeared? These questions remain unanswered.

Negotiations with the Poles continued throughout the first half of 1949, until on June 25, an agreement was signed in Warsaw to solve the problems between the two countries. Among other things, Poland promised to pay Swiss citizens compensation for nationalization totaling 53.5 million francs. The property without heirs was not handled in the agreement itself, but in an accompanying letter, which related to Polish nationals with whom there had been no contact since May 9, 1945.

The letter resolved that five years after the nationalization compensation agreement was instituted, all the banks and insurance companies in Switzerland would close the deposits, accounts, and policies. The money would be transferred to the Swiss central bank in the name of the Polish government, which promised to compensate the legal heirs should they appear later. The Swiss government reported during the talks that based on esti-

Dolton Public Library District

271-4347

mates, this pertained to 2 million francs (10 million francs in current values).[9]

The reason that the property without heirs was handled in an accompanying letter was the Swiss desire to keep its agreement with Poland a secret. As described in Chapter 2, Switzerland had promised to favorably examine making the property without heirs available for refugee rehabilitation, and transferring it to Poland clearly contradicted this obligation. The Swiss government hid the details of the agreement with Poland even from the Federal Assembly (Parliament), which had to ratify the agreement. Only the principles of the pact were submitted to the Parliament, and the sole thing said about the deposits was that "a mechanism has been created that does not damage civil law."[10]

The Jewish organizations learned the details of the agreement almost immediately and were quick to protest. In October 1949, Max Isenbergh, a representative of the American Jewish Committee, met with Felix Schnyder and Denise Robert of the Swiss Foreign Ministry. Isenbergh stated that he had received the impression from his meeting with Minister of Justice Eduard von Steiger in July 1949, that positive steps would be taken to solve the problem of property without heirs, and that he was shocked by the agreement made with Poland.

Schnyder claimed that the deposits themselves were not going to be transferred, but that Poland was to be offered credit against them. We now know that he was not telling the truth. Isenbergh was not impressed with this answer and said the central problem still remained: The deposits would not serve humanitarian purposes, as the Swiss government had promised. Schnyder replied that Poland would probably use the money for humanitarian aims, a claim completely unsupported by the agreement between Switzerland and Poland.

In his report on the meeting, Isenbergh cited his remarks to von Steiger that

the former owners of this property had sent it to Switzerland for the precise purpose of putting it beyond the reach of their government, and in doing so they had trusted in the reliability of Switzerland as a banking nation. It is clear that the former owners would not want to have their property returned to the successor government . . . whose control they wished to escape. It is difficult to consider Switzerland's making such a return as less than a failure to live up to the admirable banking standards for which she is known.

By handing over the property to the Polish Government, Switzerland had in effect used it for its own benefit. They had give it as a quid pro quo to assure Polish acceptance of the Polish-Swiss Accord as a whole [at the center of which was compensation for the nationalization]. From our point of view, it appeared cruelly ironic that these assets of victims of persecution should now be used as a kind of consideration in bargaining with the country from which they were sent for safe

Dalton Public Library District

haven. We thought that Switzerland would be regarded by world public opinion as falling short of her usual standards of public morality in this incident.

Schnyder reiterated that he understood the Jewish organizations' point of view, but stated that other than moral satisfaction, nothing would be gained by publication of the matter.[11]

Contacts continued at higher levels. At the beginning of November 1949, Foreign Minister Max Petitpierre met with the presidents of the Swiss Jewish community, attorney Georges Brunschvig and Paul Guggenheim. Brunschvig and Guggenheim asked the Swiss government to promise that if the money was in fact transferred to Poland, it would serve humanitarian aims. Petitpierre answered that the ministry was considering such an option, and asked them for a written memorandum explaining the community's position on the issue. Naturally, this was lip service. The agreement was already signed, and Switzerland would not have reopened the issue after years of negotiations, just to respond to demands from the Jewish community.[12]

In the end, no details of the agreement were brought to the attention of Federal Assembly members. Only members of the committees that handled it in the two houses of Parliament knew all the details. Their discussions, however, held behind closed doors, revolved around the summarized statement from the cabinet, and not the complete document. The agreement was ratified by a large majority on December 22, 1949.[13]

The United States, Britain, and France also did not succeed in changing the Swiss position. The three countries appealed to Bern on December 20, 1949, two days before the Parliament vote, and asked for an explanation about the Swiss-Polish agreement. They wanted to know why Switzerland had blatantly violated the essence of the Washington Accord concerning the objective of the property without heirs. That agreement did not require Switzerland to make this property available for victim rehabilitation, but promises in the spirit of "will examine favorably," as the agreement was worded, carry great weight in international diplomacy.

Switzerland did not even bother to reply directly to the three powers. Instead, on February 1, 1950, the Foreign Ministry issued a press release explaining the legal source of the agreement. The ministry relied on an 1891 law concerning the property of Swiss nationals abroad, and claimed that inferences could be taken from it about the property of foreign nationals in Switzerland. The press release also emphasized the Polish government's commitment to compensate heirs, if they should appear, and claimed that the Washington Accord did not cover relations between Switzerland and Poland.[14]

In March 1950, after three months without a reply to their inquiry, the embassies of the United States, Britain, and France reminded Bern's Foreign

Ministry that they were still waiting for an answer. Another five weeks passed before the Foreign Ministry replied on April 26. It claimed that the Washington Accord and Paris Agreement did not prevent Switzerland from implementing the agreement with Poland, and that the current agreement ensured the rights of any heir likely to appear in the future. Locating Nazi victims' assets remaining in Switzerland and the decision on their future use had been revealed as a very difficult task. "Before making any decision on the matter, the federal authorities believe there is a need to know the scope of involved assets," the ministry added.[15]

In essence, the Swiss said that they were unilaterally retreating from the Washington Accord concerning victims' assets, as it was hard for them to locate them, and it was possible that it was not worth all the trouble when the volume of the assets was considered. In light of this approach, it is no wonder that another twelve years of struggle went by before Switzerland passed legislation to locate the deposits, an altogether appropriate step in fulfilling its obligations.

Switzerland invoked lengthy red tape in implementing the agreement with Poland as well. Bern was supposed to transfer to Poland the deposits without heirs, at a nominal value of 598,000 francs, five years after the June 1949, agreement with Warsaw took effect. Actually, Switzerland received at least some of its money and did not hasten to pay its share.

In July 1955, six months after the date for implementation of the agreement, the SBA and the Association of Insurance Companies sent memos to all their members with a reminder about the agreement with Poland, and recommended how to reduce the volume of property to be returned. Among other things, they suggested using Poland's 1939 borders—much smaller than those of 1955—as the definition of a "Polish national residing in Poland" whose property should be returned to Poland. The banks and insurance companies were further instructed not to transfer moneys of those whose disappearance during the war was in any doubt.[16] These instructions directly touch on the Jewish deposits affair, as they hint at one of the possible means the banks used to reduce the volume of accounts transferred to the government according to the 1962 law. This law required all those holding property without heirs to report it to the Swiss government if they believed the original owners had been murdered by the Nazis. (The law is described in detail in Chapter 5.)

On September 15, 1955, nearly six years after the agreement was ratified by Parliament, the SBA reported to the Foreign Ministry on the results of the location of Polish assets among its members: 22,300 francs (87,000 francs in current values). This was only 3 percent of total Polish assets the banks located in June 1950, after ratification of the agreement. The banks even waved the results proudly, as the association wrote to the ministry that "This meant that [the] storm over the exchange of letters [concerning the property without heirs] was without any real foundation and was a repetition of the Americans' suspicion that we had been handling Nazi riches."[17]

We now know that the American suspicions were well founded, and that Swiss banks did hold money for senior Nazis. But what happened to the moneys located in 1950? There is only one logical answer: The banks' machinations, following the association's instructions, were successful, and the scope of the assets was reduced to minute amounts. Would it be too much to assume that similar maneuvers were implemented in the deposits of Holocaust victims, which at the time, were not the subject of any agreement, or public controls?

Despite the fact that the sun involved was now reduced to mere pennies, Switzerland continued to buy time. Talks with Poland conducted in Warsaw in November 1955 and January 1956, ended unproductively, just as the Swiss government hoped. As the volume of trade between the two countries dropped, and Switzerland needed less Polish coal than in the past—having moved partially to electricity and gasoline and resuming the purchase of coal from West Germany—it had less interest in solving the problems with Poland.

In February 1958, three years after the date for transfer of the moneys, the Swiss embassy in Warsaw informed the local Foreign Ministry that "it has become clear the investigation is lengthier and more complex than we had at first expected. It has only recently been possible to complete the examination, and the relevant Polish assets in Poland are 17,549.50 francs [65,000 francs in current values]. Concerning the insurance companies, the sum is 849 francs [1,820 francs in current values]."

Above and beyond the further odd reduction in the value of the assets, the Swiss embassy's notice did not contain an ounce of truth, to put it mildly. One investigation was completed in June 1950, and another in September 1955. In any case, the banks transferred the moneys to Warsaw in two installments in July and August 1960, and by then had managed to further reduce the sum to 15,498 francs (57,300 francs in current values). The insurance companies transferred the entire 849 francs that they had reported.[18]

It should be noted that Poland also did not meet its obligations in full under the 1949 agreement, although it did more so than Switzerland. While Switzerland did not transfer a penny to Poland on the appointed date, by the end of 1963, at the end of the period determined for the payment of nationalization compensation, Poland paid half the promised sum (53.5 million francs). Destitute Poland paid tens of millions of francs, while wealthy Switzerland evaded repayment (not payment, but repayment) of a few thousand francs.

As a result, there was a need for further talks by the mid-1960s on a subject supposedly closed in 1949. In the end, Poland agreed to sever the link between nationalization compensation and the problem of the deposits, possibly due to the report Switzerland made concerning the scope of property without heirs. In June 1964, the two countries signed an "accompanying agreement" to the one signed in 1949, and Poland completed the payment of compensation. Now, only the problem of the deposits remained unresolved.[19]

In 1962, during the first round of talks that ended in an agreement two years later, Warsaw again raised the issue about receiving the deposits without heirs. Its appeals went unanswered, and in February 1964 the Polish foreign minister asked to receive, at the least, a list of the accounts involved. The Swiss embassy in Warsaw feared that the point of the demand was to allow the Communist government to pressure the owners or their heirs to give up the deposits in vital foreign currency, a fear which could not be ruled out.

In response, the Swiss announced that the money had been transferred to Poland's account with the Swiss central bank in 1960, but the Poles had trouble locating the transfer in their bank statement. The Poles also wanted to explain the enormous gap between the 1949 estimates (2 million francs) and the sum actually transferred (16,000 francs). The Swiss promised to check and provide an answer, but failed to do so.[20]

In the meantime, in December 1962, the Swiss Parliament ratified the law for the handling of property without heirs of Nazi victims, but a problem arose: How to compromise between the instructions of that law and the agreement with Poland, if further assets of Polish citizens were later discovered? The 1962 law determined that the money would be collected by a dedicated Claims Registry and transfered to a special charity fund. The agreement with Poland, however, granted Warsaw total ownership of deposits of its citizens who were killed.

In 1964–1965, the Swiss ministries of foreign affairs, finance, and justice held in-depth discussions on the question of how to settle this contradiction. In December 1964, the ministry of Justice determined that payments to Poland (and Hungary) would conflict with the 1962 law. Nevertheless, the cabinet decided in August 1965 to transfer directly to Poland property discovered under the 1962 law, bypassing the charity fund that held all the property, without even reporting this to Parliament.[21]

The Swiss cabinet thus violated a law that it had initiated and submitted to Parliament. It is thus possible that in the background of this decision was the same maneuver we will later see with Hungary: recognition of Poland as the heir of the property of its citizens who died leaving no heirs. Using this logic, an heir exists, and therefore no moneys need to be transferred to the charity fund. Clearly, this argument empties the law of all content, as it can be used to transfer all the moneys to the depositors' countries of origin.

End of story? Certainly not. It is true that in October 1965, Switzerland had already informed Poland of its government's decision (made two months earlier, but the Swiss continued to bide their time), which enabled Warsaw to finally receive the moneys. It took another ten years, however, for the money to actually be transferred. The Claims Registry, established under the 1962 law, methodically hid information from the Polish government, among other things, as part of its policy of not trying at all to locate heirs in Eastern European countries.

In 1970, the Swiss National Bank remembered to inform the Claims Registry that it had to transfer the Polish assets to Poland's account in the central bank, but the registry continued to find new excuses in order to avoid doing so. The registry even pretended to be concerned about Polish interests when it claimed that it was better for Warsaw if the money remained in the hands of the registry itself, which invested the money at 5 percent annual interest, while Poland received no interest at all from the Swiss National Bank. Furthermore, the registry claimed, it was necessary to act slowly in order to ensure that no other country would know of the special arrangement with Poland.

In the meantime, it became clear to the Claims Registry that the scope of Polish assets without heirs was thirty times greater than had been reported in 1955—16,000 francs. In 1970 values, the volume of assets amounted to 500,000 francs (1.1 million francs in current values), a figure relatively close to the 1950 report by the banks (598,000 francs), although it was 65 percent lower in current values. Of the reported assets, the registry managed to return only 10 percent to the owners, so 450,000 francs in assets remained without claimants.

Instead of immediately reporting this to the Polish government, the Claims Registry conducted a number of clandestine tests to locate owners, in cooperation with Jewish and other concerns.[22] No other incidence is known in which the Claims Registry exhibited such diligence in seeking owners; it usually works in the opposite way. Only its motivation not to implement the agreement with Poland led the registry to do what it should have been expected to do all along: search for owners and heirs.

The matter progressed only when the Swiss government prepared to open new economic talks with Poland. As was the case all along, when Switzerland had an economic interest of its own, it knew perfectly well how to honor agreements, and when Switzerland had little interest, it also had little willingness to honor its commitments. Meanwhile, Poland completed the payment of nationalization compensation according to the 1964 "accompanying agreement," and in October 1971, talks between the two countries resumed.

In February 1972, the Swiss cabinet again determined that it was possible to transfer the money directly to Poland's account in the Swiss National Bank, thus remaking a decision it had made seven years earlier. The actual transfer was made on August 6, 1975, and the Polish government received 463,594.55 francs (880,000 francs in current values), the sum of the property without heirs discovered under the 1962 law. Although Switzerland transferred the money, it refused to submit to Poland the names of the account owners whose assets were transferred to Warsaw. In Hug and Perrenoud's opinion, even if Poland had received a list, it probably would not have succeeded in locating the legal claimants. It is not clear, however, on what basis Hug and Perrenoud made that determination.[23]

As mentioned earlier, Switzerland entered into talks with Hungary in March 1950 that were based on two starting points: Bern hoped to expand mutual trade, and Budapest hoped to receive the property without heirs. Washington took note of the talks, and in May 1950, the United States officially expressed concern about the transfer of property without heirs to Hungary, which it estimated at 15 million francs (64 million francs in current values). Switzerland ignored the appeal.[24]

In July 1950, Switzerland and Hungary signed an expansive economic agreement, and among other things, the letters accompanying the agreement determined that

The Hungarian delegation suggested that assets situated in Switzerland belonging to Hungarian nationals who were last resident in Hungary and had died without leaving heirs, to which no one had made claim since January 20, 1945, date of the armistice in Hungary, should be considered to have become the Hungarian state's. These assets claimed as property of the Hungarian state should be transferred to the Hungarian government.

For its part the Hungarian government would be ready to indemnify those persons who proved before expiry of the period of limitation that they were in a position to raise justified claims to such property. The [Hungarian] government would recognize the competence of Swiss courts in any legal dispute between rival claimants and Swiss defendants.

It is accordingly open to Hungarian beneficiaries to demand the release of property situated in Switzerland in accordance with Hungarian law on inheritance. This would be equally true where under Hungarian law, in the absence of other heirs, the Hungarian state or one of its institutions, for example the so-called Jewish Fund [the meaning is unclear], was the beneficiary.

All cases in which the Hungarian side show that a Hungarian national who had his last domicile in civil in Hungary had died without heirs, the competent Swiss authorities will be as helpful as possible to the Hungarian authorities, in inquiring whether he [the legator] had left assets in Swiss banks or insurance companies.

Hug and Perrenoud justifiably comment that the wording of the agreement does not create any link between compensation for nationalized Swiss property and the problem of the deposits.[25] As we will see later, however, the link existed in practice and in declaration, when it was clear to Switzerland that the receipt of compensation for nationalized property involved a solution to the deposits problem in a manner satisfactory to Hungary. The press release concerning the agreement did not even hint at the matter of the deposits, and Bern kept its agreement secret on the matter, which directly contradicted its promise to transfer the moneys for refugee rehabilitation.

The agreement was defined as "confidential," although the head of the Swiss delegation, Max Troendle, clarified that "the intention is that it may not be published, and not that it is secret." In light of this, all parts of the agreement were brought to the attention of the commerce committees of both houses of Parliament. Troendle claimed in one of the debates that "we limited ourselves to the provision of declarations in keeping with Swiss law" and the agreement's accompanying letters are not part of it.[26] This was neither the first nor the last time that the Swiss cabinet gave only partial and even misleading reports to Parliament on the sensitive issue of property without heirs.

Relations between Hungary and Switzerland worsened after the Soviet invasion of Budapest in 1956, and talks ceased. Only after 1963, when political relations improved and mutual trade increased again, did the deposits issue return to the agenda. In talks held in February 1964, a link was created, at least indirectly, between the problems bothering Bern and Budapest. Bern raised the issue of compensation for the nationalization of 362 Swiss assets in Hungary, and Budapest included the problem of the deposits in its list of subjects needing resolution.[27] Both countries focused mainly on the question of how to reconcile the 1962 law with the promise given Hungary, and Bern promised to investigate and respond.

If someone failed to notice the link the Hungarians created between deposits and nationalization, the Hungarian consul in Bern, Layosh Rack, clarified his country's intention to pay compensation against deposits and set the two off against each other. There is no doubt the Hungarians were sure that they would receive tens of millions of francs, as they had nationalized 60 million francs worth of Swiss assets.

There were differences of opinion inside the Swiss government concerning the Hungarian demand to receive moneys while promising to act to locate the heirs. While Swiss officials were still arguing, however, in October 1964, Hungary expressed disappointment that it had not yet received an answer to its last appeal on the matter, ten months earlier. In response, the Swiss embassy in Budapest hinted that it was possible an answer would be provided in November, with the resumption of the trade talks.

The government assigned the Ministry of Justice to examine whether the 1962 law did, in fact, damage the rights of foreign countries, while authorizing the Foreign Ministry to recognize the Hungarian "counterdemands" concerning the property without heirs. The link between deposits and nationalization was now confirmed at Bern's highest levels.

It became immediately clear to the Swiss government, however, that it had a serious problem in implementing the promises it had given Warsaw and Budapest, as they contradicted the 1962 law concerning property without heirs. Bern clung to the didactic solution proposed by the Ministry of Justice that has already been mentioned in the Polish context: to recognize Hungary's right to inherit from its citizens who died without heirs. After such recognition, the property in Switzerland no longer fell into the framework of the 1962 law, as the property had heirs, and that law applied only to property without heirs.

In August 1965, therefore, the government decided to transfer 325,000 francs (1 million francs in current values) from the fund of property without heirs to an account called Foreign Ministry—nationalization compensation—Hungary. The money had not yet been transferred to Hungarian authority, as the government decided to submit, "at the right time," a bill to "settle Hungary's counterdemands."

At this point, the link between the two issues reached its peak. Holocaust victims' assets were transferred to an account explicitly called "nationalization compensation." Even if technically those funds did not serve as compensation for Swiss citizens, as Hug and Perrenoud state, there is no doubt that they were used as a bargaining tool between Hungary and Switzerland, clearly bypassing the law that determined what was to be done with them.

Hungary was not enthusiastic about the Swiss action, and called the answer it received "entirely negative" and "hurtful." Budapest claimed that the Swiss obligation to supply it with all the necessary information stemmed from the principle of good faith, otherwise Switzerland could keep the property forever under the claim that Hungary had not proven ownership. Hungary again promised that it would transfer the property without heirs to a fund to assist in the rehabilitation of war survivors. This promise, however, was only lip service designed to allow Switzerland to "sell" the idea to local public opinion. As we have seen, Hungary's real stance was that it would use the moneys to cover some of the nationalization compensation to be paid to Swiss citizens.[28]

The deadlock in the talks continued for more than a year, primarily due to the difficulty in estimating the value of the Swiss assets that had been nationalized. Finally, in November 1965, a nationalization compensation agreement was reached. Hungary would pay full compensation for the nationalization of 52 assets, and nearly complete compensation for the nationalization of 37 assets, thus providing compensation for 89 of the 172 assets nationalized. The Hungarian payment amounted to 1.8 million francs in 1971 values (4.8 million francs in current values), and was in addition to the payment of 30 million francs Hungary had promised in 1950. It was only paid in 1971, due to differences of opinion on the valuations of the nationalized assets and the exchange rate at which payment would be made.

With the signing of the nationalization compensation agreement, the Swiss government began to deal with the deposits issue, which shows the link was maintained all along. Switzerland informed Hungary of the sum already credited to Budapest—325,000 francs. How did Bern reach this figure? As in the Polish case, the sum also decreased with time. The Claims Registry announced in December 1964 that it had located Hungarian assets without heirs valued at 460,550 francs (1.5 million francs in current terms).

Claims Registry lists reveal that a total of fifty-three Hungarian accounts were located, one at a value of 100,000 francs, one at 119,000 francs, and six valued at more than 20,000 francs each. In that case, how did the sum shrink by one-third? The Swiss Foreign Office later claimed that heirs had been found for accounts at a value of 135,000 francs. Hug and Perrenoud cast doubt on the accuracy of this claim, in light of the Claims Registry's known methods (see Chapter 5), but propose no other explanation.

In the end, Hungary basically waived its demand to receive information concerning the property without heirs. It therefore transferred to Switzerland a long list of Hungarian claimants and asked Switzerland to examine it. Bern's Ministry of Justice examined only the names of the account holders that Hungary claimed had fallen victim to Nazi persecution, and ignored all other claimants. Only two claimants were located: Eugen Halasz, who had 842 francs in a current account in Credit Suisse, and Rudolph Wintenberg, who owned 77,973.75 francs in gold coins, current accounts, and securities at UBS. In current values, Halasz had 2,740 francs and Wintenberg had 254,000 francs.

In 1966, talks between the two countries ceased due to a deadlock on the question of calculating nationalization compensation. When a breakthrough was achieved, it was possible to achieve a comprehensive agreement. On resumption of the talks, the head of the Hungarian delegation, Layosh Reti, said that there was no need to publish the details of an agreement concerning the property without heirs. It was possible Budapest feared the ramifications of the minute sum found, although it is more likely that as Hungary had no intention of transferring the moneys to refugee rehabilitation—but planned to use it for its own needs—it preferred that no one know of the moneys it would receive. Naturally, Bern did not oppose maintaining confidentiality, if only as it was clear to Switzerland that it was again in danger of hostile public opinion and diplomatic attacks for its use of the property without heirs.

In order to maintain secrecy, the Swiss government hid the details of the agreement not only from the public, but also from Parliament. The agreement was signed in August 1971, ratified by the cabinet in March 1972 (another odd delay), and submitted to Parliament two months later. It was officially reported that Switzerland would receive 1.4 million francs in nationalization compensation, while the real number was 1.8 million. The 400,000 franc difference was almost identical to the sum of property without heirs transferred to Hungary, 325,000 francs. The moneys were transferred in February 1975, and compensation was paid to entitled Swiss citizens in December 1976.[29]

Hungary and Poland were the only two countries to receive from Switzerland their citizens' property without heirs. Hug and Perrenoud examined the rest of the countries that could have reached similar agreements with Switzerland, namely, Bulgaria, Yugoslavia, Romania, and Czechoslovakia, but did not find any proof of the existence of additional agreements. Bulgaria and Yugoslavia did not even raise the issue.[30]

Romanian Jews did deposit money in Switzerland, and as part of its trade talks with Bucharest, Bern prepared for the possibility that it would be asked to return those deposits to the Romanian government. In the trade agreement signed in August 1951, Swiss comment on the problem is included and is extremely carefully worded:

The Swiss delegation had knowledge of the practical difficulties that would be encountered in identifying assets belonging to Romanian nationals who have died in specific circumstances. That is why Switzerland has declared that, in all cases where the Romanian authorities prove that a national of their country, whose last place of permanent residence was in the territory of Romania, is deceased without heirs, the relevant Swiss authorities will do everything possible to assist the Romanian authorities in ascertaining whether the deceased has left assets in Swiss banks or insurance companies.

As regards inheritable property of deceased Romanian citizens with no heirs, where the Romanian authorities presume that such property is located in Switzerland, the Swiss delegation has, at the request of the Romanian delegation, declared that where the same conditions and circumstance prevail, the Swiss government will not treat any Romanian claims to such property less favorably than it would any similar claims from other government.

The Swiss declaration was not put to the test, as Romania, for reasons of its own, did not raise the issue again.[31]

Finally, Czechoslovakia. This country was particularly aware of the problem of property without heirs, as it was one of the five countries in charge of the Paris Agreement, which also dealt with the fate of the property in neutral countries. By May 1946, Prague had appealed to Bern's Foreign Ministry, asking for assistance in locating accounts of Czech citizens murdered by the Nazis. The Swiss Foreign Ministry was in no rush to answer, and the request was transferred to the Ministry of Justice only in October; they answered the Czechs in November.

The Swiss response noted the legal and administrative difficulties in responding to the Czech request, and added that "In any event, there is no question of transferring any unclaimed assets in Switzerland to the Czechoslovak national administration, because by virtue of the Washington Accord, such assets must, where possible, be placed at the disposal of the three Allied governments, for purposes of aid and relief." This was entirely true, but, as we have seen, Switzerland renounced the Washington Accord when it needed to (the agreements with Poland and Hungary), and then claimed that no obligatory agreement was reached in Washington on the question. This response tied Prague's hands, and the Czechs showed no further interest in the matter until the 1960s.

Prague only woke up in November 1963, apparently due to the Swiss legislation in 1962 for the location of property without heirs. At the end of 1963, by the first day of talks on nationalization compensation for Swiss citizens, the Czechs raised a number of issues for discussion, including the property of Holocaust victims in Swiss banks. The Swiss representatives responded with a review of the steps their country was taking. The subject remained on the agenda in the bilateral talks for the next three years.

At the end of the talks in June 1967, a number of letters were signed in Prague, one of which related to the property without heirs. It was drafted in only general terms, in which Switzerland essentially promised to transfer to the Czechs information on deposits that were found, in keeping with the 1962 law. In fact, the Swiss Foreign Ministry avoided transmitting any information to Prague, despite a number of requests.[32]

The Swiss government discussed the Hug-Perrenoud report on February 26, 1997. On that day, the government approved the establishment of a fund to aid Nazi victims (see Chapter 12), and very few noticed its decision due to the Hug-Perrenoud report. The government announced its willingness to immediately transfer to "interested governments and organizations" the names of all the account owners located under the 1962 law. In practice, only the names of account owners from Poland and Hungary were published, while the rest of the names were not even included in the two lists of dormant accounts Switzerland published in July and October 1997.

The government also declared its willingness to compensate any heir from former Communist countries, despite emphasizing that the moneys from these accounts were transferred to the charity fund established under the 1962 law. This willingness has not yet been put to the test. At the end of the press release, Hug and Perrenoud's "fast, important and useful" work was halfheartedly praised, and noted that certain points needed further refinement. The ball was then passed to the historians' committee for the investigation of Swiss policy during World War II, headed by Professor Jean François Bergier. It is indicative that the government notice did not even mention a word of thanks to Hug and Perrenoud.[33]

Swiss handling of Holocaust victims' property in Eastern Europe indicates much more than the limited conclusions about the use of Polish and Hungarian victims' assets as bargaining tools for the benefit of Bern's economic and political ends. As we have seen, Switzerland clearly violated the spirit of the law for the return of property without heirs, and possibly even the law itself. It ignored its commitments under the Washington Accord to make this property available for refugee rehabilitation, unless it felt comfortable waiving the agreement in order to reject demands from other countries for those assets.

Bern ignored external pressure, including that from the United States and acted only according to its own self-interest, and gave no thought at all to the question of morality or justice. Switzerland slowly implemented the signed agreements with Poland and Hungary and only when it was necessary. In order to avoid hostile public opinion, the cabinet did not hesitate to hide uncomfortable facts from the world and from the Parliament it asked to ratify these agreements.

In light of this behavior, it is no wonder that in the 1950s Israel and the Jewish organizations did not succeed in making Switzerland return Jewish deposits. These Swiss actions also explain why it acted so feebly to return the property in the 1960s and 1970s. It had no material self-interest of its own in the matter that would stimulate it to more positive action.

4

"CRYING AND SCREAMING"
A Dozen Years of Frustration with the Swiss Banks and Government

SWISS BANKS PROPEL the local economy, and in this way they are no different from their counterparts all over the developed world. They also bring foreign deposits of billions of dollars into the country every year, employ thousands of people, and support many thousands of associated businesses. The banks are the strongest sector of the Swiss economy. This is important to remember in order to understand why the Swiss government, even if it wanted to, could not force the banks to act seriously to restore the deposits of Holocaust victims.

The Swiss banks owe their greatest prosperity to World War II. A Swiss government report of 1947 determined that "In the middle of a war-torn and tumultuous Europe, Switzerland became a haven where everyone could find asylum for themselves or their property. The influx of capital in 1941 was such that our central bank was forced to introduce restrictions on transfers of capital from countries linked to the dollar, initially with regard to foreigners and, shortly afterwards, the Swiss themselves."[1]

Swiss bankers could not rest on their laurels in the years following the war. While the world saw Switzerland as a safe financial refuge due to its well-known secrecy policy, there were arguments inside the country regarding this very issue. There were those who proposed easing the policy slightly, in order to prevent Swiss citizens from depositing moneys hidden from income-tax authorities. Others claimed that foreign citizens should also be prevented from using local banks to hide money from their own governments.

The banks felt that secrecy, one of their most precious assets, was in danger, and they hastened to defend it. This is one of the key reasons for their unbending policy concerning accounts without heirs. The banks believed that providing information about these accounts would open the first hole in the secrecy dam, which could eventually collapse completely and bury with it huge portions of the local banking system.

The three-sided struggle for the deposits was fought by the banks, the Swiss government, and the Jewish people. The government did not have any practical means of enforcement against the banks. No citizen expects his government to get involved in a business dispute between banks and their clients. There are courts for this purpose. The case of Holocaust victims' deposits was unusual, however, as it touched on questions of policy and international law, well beyond the banks' usual field of endeavor. But, through decades of dealing with the deposits problem, Bern trusted the good faith and integrity of the banks because there was no reason to suspect them, and because the government, as a matter of practicality, did not want to, or could not supervise them.

The fundamental question of policy was the legal status of the accounts. Unlike many other countries, in Switzerland there is no general custodian who takes on trusteeship of property without heirs, and manages it for an unlimited amount of time until heirs are found. From time to time, documents concerning the deposits affair mention the cantons' right to inherit property without heirs, but there is no evidence that any bank transferred any deposit at any time to any canton.

The claim is sometimes raised that the victims' country is entitled to inherit; in that case Germany would become the heir of the Jews that it was responsible for killing. This of course is an unthinkable result from a moral perspective, which is where a factor usually not involved in legal verdicts comes into play: public morality. The law is the law and is effected while considering moral aspects, but its implementation is subject only to legal principles. But, how can normal legal rules apply to the Holocaust and its outcome, when it is one huge, blatant violation of the most basic human rights and morals? And if the Germans and their collaborators violated the law, should other people ignore or bend the law in order to assist the survivors? When we begin to cut corners due to moral considerations, who determines the limits?

These questions exemplify the legal labyrinth of the problem. But today, even the Swiss admit that they acted in a purely legalistic manner, without flexibility and consideration for the special circumstances of the Holocaust and its consequences, and that is the root of the ongoing crisis.[2]

The legal status of World War II assets was further complicated by the fact that Germany did not have an independent government after the war, and the Allies enacted their own laws in the zones of occupation. Among other things, these laws determined that the victors were entitled to appropriate all German property, including that in other countries. In contrast, accepted international law determined that property without heirs in a third country should be transferred to the government of the deceased. In any case, one thing was clear: owners and heirs have preferential rights over any other entitlement, and have the right to receive their property at any point, even if it has already been transferred to a third party.[3]

When handling of the problem of property without heirs began in Switzerland, the problem of German property was already pending between the government and the banks. The government asked the banks to locate

German assets, in keeping with the principles set forth in the December 1945 Paris Agreement. The banks were vehemently opposed, on the grounds that this was an invasion of their private business and a threat to banking secrecy, which would seriously injure the national economy. In the end, the Swiss Bankers' Association agreed outwardly to cooperate in locating German assets, but in practice instructed its members to maintain secrecy in their contacts with Bern.

After the May 1946 Washington Accord, the problem of property without heirs added to the confusion. As mentioned, Switzerland had promised in May 1946, to favorably examine making the property without heirs available for rehabilitating refugees of Nazi persecution, and in order to use this property, it first had to be located. The SBA heard of the Swiss promise only after the Swiss delegation returned from Washington, and immediately fought implementation of the agreement. The association was convinced that anyone wishing to locate the unclaimed property was asking to further puncture the secrecy dam, and therefore began to prepare every possible argument against the agreement prior to the expected cabinet debate.

Toward the end of 1946, there were already significant differences in the estimates of the scope of property without heirs. Robert Meier, a lawyer representing the office that handled the refugees, spoke of 40–50 million francs (179–223 million francs in current values). The banks provided conflicting estimates that all had one common denominator: they were very low. At that time, the Foreign Ministry also understood that it would have to pressure the banks so they would allow it to implement the Washington Accord concerning the deposits. As its first step, the ministry prepared a draft law, designed to force the banks to cooperate.

Under threat of publication of the draft, senior Foreign Ministry and Bankers Association officials met in August 1947. The SBA understood that they could not cancel the accord, and therefore made every effort to torpedo its implementation. They claimed that it would be necessary to receive confirmation of the death of the depositor, and proof of no legal heirs and no will. In addition, the banks representatives claimed that since both the Poles and the Allies claimed ownership of the assets, who would receive them? The banks also claimed administrative problems would be a burden.

Determining ownership based on client contact with the banks was another argument used by the SBA. According to the banks, many clients sever contact for various reasons, and therefore loss of contact is not proof that the client is no longer alive. SBA director general Albert Caflisch even estimated that 3–5 percent of the clients who had severed relations with the banks since 1939 died during the war. (As we saw in Chapter 1, the banks customarily used loss of contact with a client for ten years as proof of death.)

The head of the Foreign Ministry delegation, Franz Kappeler, demonstrated assertiveness and made it clear to the bankers that there were only two options: "Either the Bankers' Association conducts the investigation itself, or the government passes a law requiring the publication of the names of the owners of assets with whom the banks have had no contact since a given date." Caflisch vehemently opposed the second option, which he called a "stupid move," and announced that the banks would fight it in every possible arena, namely the cabinet, the Parliament, and even the press.

Later in his remarks, Caflisch even enlisted the Cold War in the aid of the banks and claimed the international situation required reexamination of existing agreements, in other words, the Washington Accord. Behind Caflisch's words was the fact that Switzerland's international status in 1947 was better than it had been two years earlier. Switzerland was now an important link in the Western balance of power against the Soviet Union, and had even agreed to participate in the Marshall Plan to rehabilitate Europe, which was a kind of test case in the question of identification with the Western bloc. The heads of the Foreign Ministry noticed that the Allies, worried about much more important matters, were losing interest in the problem of property without heirs. This resulted in the freezing of the draft law to publish the names of the missing depositors.

Nonetheless, there were those who did notice the Swiss silence, and were not willing to just let it pass by. In November 1947, the committee handling the preparations for the establishment of an International Refugee Organization contacted the Swiss Clearing Office and asked it to conduct the investigation to locate dormant accounts. The office, swamped with trying to locate German assets, was not enthusiastic about taking more tasks upon itself, and neither was the Foreign Ministry, which also opposed conducting the investigation.[4]

Five more years passed before the Swiss government took its first practical steps toward fulfilling its 1946 promise. In January 1952, the cabinet, at the request of the Foreign Ministry and the Ministry of Finance, ordered the preparation of a draft law concerning the handling of victims' property. It should be noted that the original initiative was not the cabinet's, but that of MP Philip Schmid, who was the first to note the difficulties that Holocaust victims' heirs encountered when they asked to receive the unclaimed property. The cabinet determined that "there is no way to justify leaving this property in the hands of its managers, just because the date for claiming it has passed."

Decisions, however, are one thing and putting them into practice is another. More than five years passed, until, in April 1957, Minister of Justice Markus Feldman submitted a proposal to the cabinet. He suggested enacting no special regulations for handling property without heirs, and granting only a "certain sum" to the local Jewish community, without admitting any legal obligation. Walter Eggenschwiler of the Foreign Ministry was opposed. In his opinion, this would appear as if the cabinet was making an empty gesture so that the banks could continue to hold onto property that was not theirs. Minister of Finance Hans Streuli claimed that the proposal was paradoxical: the government would pay and the private sector would keep the property it held.[5]

The initiative returned to the Parliament, where MP Harold Huber proposed, as early as March 1957, to obligate those holding property without heirs to register it, and set up simple procedures for officially determining the death of the owners (in order to make it possible to handle the assets as property without heirs). When the cabinet discussed taking a stance on this proposal, Markus Feldman revealed Bankers Association and insurance company figures from 1956.

The banks had located that year deposits belonging to missing owners amounting to 36,580 francs, and another 825,832.25 francs belonging to owners that might have been dead. The insurance companies reported four policies with missing owners with a total value of 2,698 francs, and another eleven policies of possibly missing owners totaling 24,314 francs (current values are four times higher). Feldman claimed that the registration requirement Huber proposed could cause financial damage, and hinted at a danger to banking secrecy. He had been won over to this position by two experts sent by the Bankers' Association for that very purpose. A Foreign Ministry official summed it up: "The Ministry of Justice has simply surrendered to the banks."

The SBA exploited this surrender in order to pressure the Foreign Ministry. Three senior ministry officials thus drafted a proposal to handle the accounts problem. The draft reached the SBA who sent its secretary-general Max Oertteli to meet with Foreign Minister Max Petitpierre. Oertteli stated openly, "After years of efforts, the Bankers' Association has finally succeeded in convincing the Ministry of Justice there is no need for legislation. I hope, that this draft law [by Foreign Ministry officials] will not again raise a question mark over the results of these efforts."

In the meantime, two more events took place that also affected the Swiss position. At the beginning of 1957, Professor Carl Ludwig of the University of Basel wrote a report on Swiss refugee policy in the years 1933–1945, and it was abundantly clear to the government that the report would be harsh and critical. As we now know, Switzerland turned 30,000 to 40,000 Jewish refugees away from its borders, which became a certain death sentence for most of them. Moreover, Switzerland initiated as early as 1938, the printing of the letter J on the passports of German Jews for identification and thus prevented them from entering the country.[6] The Ludwig report was discussed in Parliament in March 1958, and raised a storm.

The second event was the death of Minister of Justice Markus Feldman in November 1958. His successor, Friedrich Taugott Wahlen, had previously declared his desire to solve the problem of the deposits using a special law. In March 1959, Wahlen finally replied to the Huber proposal submitted two years earlier. His reply included principles for the proposed law, which would require reporting property that had belonged to foreign nationals or those without citizenship, about whom no reliable information had been received since the end of the war, and who may have fallen victim to political, racist, or religious persecution or other violence.

The Bankers Association and the Association of Insurance Companies tried in vain to wreck the proposal before it was submitted to Parliament, but did not succeed. Now the two organizations, but primarily the banks, because they had so much more to lose, focused their efforts on causing the proposed law that Wahlen submitted to the cabinet in July 1959, to fail. Massive bank pressure worked, and in June 1960, the Ministry of Justice informed the cabinet that "due to numerous difficulties" it was withdrawing its proposal.[7] It would be another two years before Switzerland finally ratified the law designed to fulfill the obligations it undertook sixteen years earlier.

We now move on to the third member of the three-sided triangle in the deposits' problem: Israel and the Jewish organizations. The first Jewish group to enter the picture was the Swiss Jewish Organization. In December 1947, the organization sent a memorandum to the Ministry of Justice drafted by three well-known lawyers, Paul Guggenheim, Charles Knapp, and Georges Sauser-Hall. The attorneys recognized the problem of handling the deposits, the need to change Swiss inheritance law, and the difficulty in conducting a thorough investigation at the banks and other institutions. They recommended legislation, in cooperation with the Foreign Ministry and Ministry of Finance, to solve the problem in a moral way, particularly if the steps taken by the Bankers Association proved fruitless.

Their memorandum mentioned that a prior investigation by the banks estimated that there were 500,000 francs in deposits (2.14 million in current values). The three lawyers emphasized that "The volume of deposits mentioned doesn't serve any function . . . only the fact that it is unthinkable that these assets should remain forever in Swiss hands in which they were deposited." Other Jewish organizations applied their own pressure—the Swiss branch of the League of Axis Victims, the American Jewish Committee (see Chapter 2), and more, but without result.[8]

Several years later, Swiss Jews again tried to resolve the problem. In March 1954, Minister of Justice Markus Feldman convened representatives of his ministry, the Foreign Ministry, the Bankers Association and the Jewish community "to hear both sides' claims for a last time, before the federal government finally determines its position concerning the steps necessary to solve the problem of property without heirs," according to a report by the Israeli consul in Bern, Shmuel Tolkowsky.[9] The Jewish representatives were Guggenheim and Georges Brunschvig. Brunschvig reported back to Tolkowsky, who then wrote to the Israeli Foreign Ministry:

The banks representatives made no claims against the government's moral obligation to seek a solution, which would satisfy those with rights to the property being discussed. According to them, their opposition was only directed towards breaking banking secrecy principle, which was a source of great revenues for the Swiss banks as the keepers of great sums of money smuggled into the country from countries in which hard currency was controlled.

Brunschvig and Guggenheim proposed legislation, the principle of which would be that holders of the property would report it to a "special trust company" that would invite claimants to approach it. Property for which no owners were discovered within a predetermined time period would be declared property without heirs. A certain percentage of the property would be set aside for future claims, and the remainder would serve "according to arrangements that must still be determined."

This meeting was one of the last steps taken by the Swiss Jewish community on the matter. Prominent in their absence were the leaders of the Jewish Agency and the Joint, the two bodies authorized to receive the property without heirs by the Paris Agreement of June 1946. The reason for their absence was that a few years earlier the two organizations had transferred responsibility for the property without heirs to the Israeli government. The official transfer was made in two identical letters sent by joint director general Mo Beckelman in November 1953 and Jewish Agency treasurer Giora Josephtal in January 1954 to Israeli Foreign Minister Moshe Sharet. The transfer was supported by the argument that Israel had a special interest in the matter because most Holocaust survivors lived in Israel, and the advantage of contact between the governments in Jerusalem and Bern to solve the problem. The Jewish Agency and the Joint asked Israel to use its good connections in Bern to conduct the rest of the negotiations on the fate of property without heirs.[10]

Israel's first act was to send Eli Nathan, a member of the Foreign Ministry's legal department, to Bern in March 1954, to carry out "initial steps in the handling of the matter of property without heirs.[11] Nathan arrived in Switzerland a few days after the meeting between Markus Feldman and the leaders of the Jewish community. He received the impression that "Switzerland had not appropriated the property for its own use, but will transfer it for welfare purposes, and it is Feldman's opinion that a law should be proposed to require those holding such property to declare it."

Nathan decided not to take any steps that would appear to be placing external pressure on Switzerland, since he had the impression that Bern intended to solve the problem of its own free will: "Direct negotiation is therefore something which must develop naturally over time, either if the Swiss government doesn't fulfill its promises to legislate the matter of property without heirs and there is a need to find a short cut by making a global determination of the volume of property, or if there is a need to determine the destination of the property after its volume is determined." In light of this, Nathan and Tolkowsky decided on a two-step plan to coordinate their actions with the Jewish community, and to submit to Bern a special message asking that Israel be included in the negotiations.

The Swiss response stated that the Ministry of Justice was preparing legislation on the matter, and that it was also necessary to change the law of inheritance in order to prevent the property from falling into the hands of Swiss cantons or Communist Eastern European governments. "This clarified to us that the Swiss had no intention of appropriating the property for themselves," Nathan reported to the leaders of the Foreign Ministry. "The Swiss admitted that there was opposition to the law from the banks, however they added that there was an explicit cabinet decision to implement the law, and if the Minister of Justice couldn't overcome the banks' opposition, he would have to return the matter to the cabinet to receive further instruction." Nathan was optimistic, and determined that as long as Bern acted honestly in legislating the law, Israel could suffice with tracking the process.[12]

Nathan's optimism turned into frustration very quickly, due to Swiss delaying tactics, and the banks low estimates concerning the volume of property. For example, Consul Tolkowsky reported on a meeting that he held in August 1956 with Foreign Minister Petitpierre:

I told the minister that it had been six years since I began the government's struggle on the problem, and for the last four years the Minister of Justice, and current president, Dr. Markus Feldman, told me year after year, that the government would bring out a law to solve the problem at the end of the year, but there has been no actual progress on the matter. The Bankers' Association persists in its opposition, and has succeeded in making government efforts be in vain.

For a long time, the legal department of the Foreign Ministry also endeavored to delay progress, claiming the Israeli government had no status in this matter. As I learned a few months ago from the Minister of Justice himself, the existence of certificates I provided more than a year ago to the legal department, in the presence of the assistant legal counsel for the Israeli Foreign Ministry [Eli Nathan], was hidden from him, which included proof the Israeli government is fulfilling the places of the known Jewish organizations [the Jewish Agency and the Joint] mentioned in the Paris Agreements. I further stated something that Minister Petitpierre apparently didn't know, that several months prior [in March 1954, as described earlier] the Association of Swiss Jewish Communities passed to the Minister of Justice a very interesting proposal which would have allowed the resolution of the problem in a fair manner for those entitled to the property, without harming the "sainted" banking secrecy.

I reminded the minister that Switzerland is not the only state in which the property without heirs problem existed, and as far as I know, all the other relevant governments have already found a solution to the problem. Only Switzerland hadn't managed to do so. In a few months, I will leave Switzerland on my way home. I am certain that my homecoming after seven years in Switzerland without announcing any practical progress on this problem, in which thousands of families in my country are interested, will bring no small amount of bitterness.

The report did not state Petitpierre's response, but his deeds in the coming years proved that he was not particularly moved that Tolkowsky was insulted.

Four years later, the representatives of Israel and Switzerland had been replaced, but the nature of the talks remained the same. In July 1960, the Israeli ambassador to Bern, Joseph Linton, met with Foreign Ministry director general Dr. Robert Kohli, to discuss the property without heirs. As we will see in Chapter 9, Kohli represented his government in the negotiations with Nazi Germany's central bank for the release of its frozen assets in Switzerland, just one month before the end of the war. Clearly, this matter did not come up in Kohli's conversation with Linton, which was lengthy and frustrating for him. Linton opened the discussion by saying:

We are a little disappointed that despite the late Minister of Justice Feldman's optimistic comments, to my predecessor and myself, and despite my efforts since that time, not a peep has been heard about the law of which Mr. Wahlen [Minister of Justice Friedrich Wahlen] spoke in Parliament in May 1959 as if it were ready and would soon be brought to the cabinet. My last memo wasn't answered, although it was delivered on the 14th of the month. The Jewish organizations in whose name we are acting, and who want to know when to expect positive results, are pressuring us.

I saw issuing the law as a first step toward discovering the scope of the property, and the possibility of locating heirs if there are any living. The second stage will be handling of property without heirs. Mr. Wahlen's unclear declaration in Parliament on this side of the problem didn't satisfy us. However, in the meantime, as we have already noted, it is our opinion that the Swiss government made a commitment in Dr. Stucki's 1946 letter, to make the property without heirs available to the three Allied powers, who have already decided it should be divided as follows: 5% to the International Refugee Organization for non-Jewish refugees, and 95% to the Joint and Jewish Agency for Jewish victims of Nazi persecution. Dr. Kohli responded that only a short time ago, they [the Foreign Ministry] had given their answer to the Minister of Justice, and I should approach that minister again.

Later in the conversation, Kohli raised a number of problems that would prevent ratification of the law. He noted opposition to the law from the Bar Association, as well as the banks, and expected the Minister of Justice would encounter difficulties in completing the legislation. He also referred to the need for an expanded administration to implement the law, in light of the fact that the agreement concerning German property had required the employment of 100 clerks. In Kohli's opinion, it was not justified to again employ a significant number of clerks "in light of the minimal value of the property." Kohli noted again the banks' low estimate concerning the volume of property, and added, "it is a pity such a law was not enacted immediately after the war in the right psychological atmosphere. Now, after so many years, the situation is much more difficult."

Linton, who had done his homework for the meeting, was not to be outdone, and reminded Kohli who was at fault for the red tape:

It was not the fault of the three Allied Powers, two Jewish organizations [the Jewish Agency and the Joint], and the Israeli government, that the necessary measures concerning property without heirs were not taken by the Swiss government in the years immediately following the war. All those concerned approached the Swiss government at that time, and the efforts continue until today. It is unimaginable that because the Swiss government did not act swiftly, the victims of Nazi persecution will not benefit from the property without heirs, which will remain at the disposal of Swiss banks, insurance companies and lawyers.

Linton threatened to bring the matter out in the open, and all Kohli could say in response was that he would arrange a meeting between Linton and Foreign Minister Petitpierre.[13]

The deposits' affair adversely affected relations between Israel and Switzerland, which reached their nadir in July 1961. Described in a telegram Ambassador Eliyahu Sasson sent to the Ministry of Foreign Affairs, it concerned a conversation between Sasson and Kohli following the visit of the Bank of Israel's governor, David Horowitz, to Switzerland, during which Horowitz had asked to track the dormant accounts. Kohli told Sasson "in the clearest, most decisive manner that his superiors saw the visit of someone as official as the Bank of Israel governor to Zurich and his conversations with the heads of Swiss banks concerning the property without heirs, as the intervention of a foreign government in internal Swiss affairs, and those superiors had requested that in the future such intervention be stopped by any means."[14]

Sasson responded aggressively to Kohli's remarks, which were the gravest available in the diplomatic lexicon. He stated that two Swiss ministers explicitly encouraged the president of the World Jewish Congress, Nahum Goldman, to pressure the banks, after which Sasson invited Horowitz to

Zurich. Kohli "pretended surprise," and said he would have to investigate this matter, which seemed to him "odd and unbelievable."

Kohli apparently thought that was the end of the conversation, and said he would summon Sasson to an additional meeting after he had clarified the information he had received, but Sasson thought otherwise:

It appears to me, that there is an intention to prevent Israeli representatives from continuing to handle the problem of the property without heirs. And here I comment that I am very doubtful that we will agree to this, as we are not acting out of mercy, but by rights of the power of attorney we received from the Jewish Agency in 1952 [should be 1954], according constantly appearing at the Swiss Ministry of Finance and other Swiss ministries.

Sasson added that Israel intended to submit its comments to Switzerland on the proposed bill (see Chapter 5), which was then in the advanced stages of preparation. Kohli was opposed: "Only Swiss nationals are authorized to submit comments to laws of their land." Sasson replied that Switzerland's good name demanded that it finally solve the property problem. Kohli commented that it had not yet been proven at all that the property without heirs belonged to Jews. Sasson kept his cool and replied, "The victims of the Nazi Holocaust were Jews and not Swiss nationals, and only Jews have rights to that property."[15]

In light of this diplomatic situation, where even the Israeli government could not motivate the Swiss government to act and Swiss ministers invited external pressure on the banks, it is clear that ordinary citizens did not have a realistic chance of receiving their property. During the course of the 1950s and 1960s, the Jewish National Fund (JNF) handled the matter, dealing with the restoration of Jewish property in several European countries. They accumulated some 900 requests from Israeli citizens concerning property held in Switzerland. The applicants were required to sign a contract authorizing the JNF to act to locate the property and accounts of other property in the manner it saw fit, in exchange for a "contribution" (essentially a commission) of a third to a half of the value of the property, with the exact sum determined individually in each contract.[16] Most of the applications came after the 1962 Swiss legislation concerning property and its return, which we will discuss in Chapter 5.

Many others appealed directly to the banks in the 1950s and 1960s, and were rejected outright. Several of these incidents have been prominently reported by the international media since 1995, as some of them spearheaded U.S. Senator Alfonse D'Amato's fight against the Swiss banks. D'Amato's staff discovered Greta Beer, a Holocaust survivor living in Queens, N.Y., who was the central witness in the first hearing the Senate Banking Committee held in April 1996 concerning the deposits. Another survivor, Gizella Weisshaus, was the first plaintiff in the $20 billion class-action suit filed in New York against the three major Swiss banks.

The survivors, especially the women, came across well on camera, and provided good copy for the media, particularly American television. On one side were the Swiss bankers, fluent in English, wearing expensive suits, and accompanied by legal advisors and image consultants charging hundreds of dollars an hour. On the other side were elderly women, some of whose manner of dress and speech patterns simulated extinct Jewish towns, and who still struggled with English even after many years of living in the United States. The contrast was so strong that the bankers' defeat in the battle for public opinion was certain.

More to the point, it should be noted that hardly any of the heirs who appeared before the media had real proof of the existence of assets in Swiss banks. The principal claim against the banks with the disclosure of their stories, however was their cold, bureaucratic attitude toward the applicants, most of whom were Holocaust survivors and the last remaining members of lost families. It is not hard to imagine how the Holocaust survivors felt, hearing, in German of all languages, that they were not entitled to receive any information whatsoever on possible property belonging to a father, uncle, or wife.

The banks not only avoided returning the money, they also cited confidentiality in their refusal to provide any information. A typical instance was the account of Franz Berliner, whose father was Herman Berliner, a Jew who was murdered in Auschwitz. Starting in 1951, Franz tried to locate his father's money. He had proof of his father's death and his own right to inherit his property, but he did not have documents relating to his father's account in Switzerland. Bern's Ministry of Justice, to which Berliner appealed, informed him that due to banking confidentiality, it would be very difficult to uncover information on the matter. This answer is not logical, since it is clear that he was entitled not only to information, but also to the money, should it be found. The ministry of justice directed Berliner to the Bankers' Association where he also did not receive a sensible answer.

In 1964, following ratification of the law requiring reporting property without heirs, Berliner repeated his appeal to the Foreign Ministry, citing his original request thirteen years earlier. This time Berliner received a business like answer in the shape of a standard form from the Claims Registry, which he was asked to complete and return. Several months later, Berliner received a letter that stated that the banks and insurance companies had not reported any property belonging to his father. Berliner hired a lawyer who approached the registry and asked that another search be conducted. The response was, "Being greatly overloaded, and in view of the many thousands of requests which we must attend to, we truly do not see why it is necessary to submit the same query via two different channels." The registry took no further action and Berliner received not a single penny.

Hug and Perrenoud summarize: "The Berliner case shows that even heirs with sufficiently validated claims could not rely upon complete assistance in their searches for presumed assets in Switzerland. It remains to be investigated whether this was the exception or the rule."[17] The expanse of testimony available today provides an indisputable answer to their question: it was the rule. No one in Switzerland, not the government and its agencies, and certainly not the banks, saw fit to assist the victims' heirs with any measure of goodwill beyond the formalities.

One case consolidated the problem of locating moneys after the war with the harsh Swiss policy toward Jewish refugees during the war. It is the story of the Sonabend family, who tried to escape from Belgium in 1942, through France and then into Switzerland. The father, Simon Sonabend, was an importer of Swiss watches, and thus already had both acquaintances and bank accounts on the other side of the Alps. According to his son Charles, his father left at least 200,000 francs in Switzerland in the 1930s (1.5 million francs in current values). The family was so wealthy that it could afford to pay the 125,000 francs (700,000 francs in current values) to the smuggler who promised to bring them to Switzerland.

The family reached Switzerland safely and Simon Sonabend decided to install his family in the city of Biel, one of the country's important watch-manufacturing towns. The family's peace and quiet, however, was short-lived. On August 15, 1942, just one day after they arrived in Switzerland, the family was arrested on charges of illegal immigration, and the authorities decided to deport them back to occupied France, a step that meant almost certain death. The parents and their two children were driven to the border, required to pay 6.80 francs for the taxi to the border, and despite their pleas, were deported to the part of France held by the Germans and not to the territory controlled by the Vichy government.

Tom Bower writes:

The Swiss policemen recorded that the routine deportation had passed uneventfully. Attached to their report was the receipt issued by the taxi driver. The file was placed in the archive and the family was forgotten.

The following day, in Belfort prison, Charles met his father for the last time. Together they prayed. Just before the eleven-year-old bid farewell, he was told of the valuables hidden in Belgium and of the bank accounts in Switzerland and New York.

In the meantime, the Swiss police gave Simon Sonabend's suitcase to his friend in Biel, who found inside, among other things, 200 francs, which he deposited in Sonabend's account in Biel's cantonal bank. Simon and his wife Lili were murdered, their son and daughter, Charles and Sabina, survived. The Sonabend children did not receive a penny of their father's money, and no one in Switzerland though it worthwhile to try and locate the heirs.[18]

Unusual testimony was provided by Elizabeth Trilling-Grusch who told of an attempt by her mother to use the family money in Switzerland during the Holocaust to try and save them, if only temporarily. She was the daughter of a wealthy family of textile manufacturers in Lvov, Poland, who employed many workers and held a distinguished position in the local Jewish community. During the Holocaust, the family suffered, as did all the city's Jews, from terrible hunger and Nazi abuse, and the mother was taken to forced labor in the Lvov ghetto. In an attempt to escape, the mother did something daring: "She told the superintendent that she was going to write him a letter, withdrawing 3,000 gold marks and that she was going to give him permission to do it. Now I don't know whether he ever did it, but I know that he denounced her and she was sent to Treblinka." In Elizabeth Trilling-Grusch's opinion, her parents' Swiss bank account contained about 300,000 francs or marks in gold, a sum equivalent (assuming it was francs) to 2 million francs today.

After the war, Trilling-Grusch, her uncle, and her aunt came to the United States. Her uncle wrote to the U.S. State Department concerning the account in Switzerland and received a reply that he should appeal directly to Swiss authorities. The aunt and uncle wrote to Switzerland and received a response expressing regret, but that banking confidentiality did not allow the distribution of details regarding accounts.

The banks asked for death certificates, although I am sure they knew what happened [in the concentration camps]. I lost everything—my family, my property. There were many hard times still to come.

It wasn't just the money. It's trying to prove to myself that my parents did exist. You know that it wasn't all wiped out, or without a trace. Another thing, it's justice in the sense that you know what you own is yours. I mean, it's just yours. It's not that I'm asking them for charity or, for anything that is not mine. It's a connection to my parents, it's a connection that I would like to be transmitted to my children since they never had grandparents in their lives. You know they would have had a part of something that belonged to my parents in their lives, because nothing is left of them—no grave, no memorial ceremonies. They went up in smoke.

Trilling-Grusch never even received an answer from the banks about whether her parents had an account in Switzerland. All she received, in her words, was "Fifty years of excuses, and that is just theft."[19]

Particularly moving testimony came from Estelle Sapir, the daughter of an affluent Jewish Hungarian family, who now lives in New York and subsists on an $800 a month welfare stipend. In a lengthy interview with the BBC, Sapir told of a dispiriting meeting with her father, a wealthy banker, in a concentration camp in France, where the family found itself at the beginning of the war:

He was on one side from the wires and I was on another side from the wires. I could not have kissed him and he could not kiss me. And he just puts his fingers out [through the wire fence], and I could kiss his hand. He told me, try to escape. If you escape don't worry for money, there's plenty of money in Switzerland for everyone of you. He says to me: take care of your mother, and try to escape, not go to Switzerland, they will send you back immediately. Go to Spain. Don't worry for the money you have plenty money in Switzerland. He told me: Geneva, Basel, Zurich and Lugano. He made me repeat this a few times, he says: you remember too I left some papers in the house? You go and escape, try to find these papers.

Sapir managed to escape, and after the liberation of Hungary, she returned to her family home, where she found the Credit Suisse documents that testified to her father's account with the bank. Her father had taken care to hide this information from prying eyes, and wrote instructions to approach "Dr. Basel," a clear hint that the account was in Basel. Another document indicated an additional Credit Suisse account in Geneva.

In 1946, Sapir traveled to Switzerland and asked Credit Suisse for her father's account. A bank clerk asked her for a number of details:

Ten minutes later she comes back with a file with the name Joseph Sapir on it. She says to me you wait here, somebody's gonna come talk to you. And five or ten minutes later a man comes out, very distinguished looking man, for me he looked old, but I was very young and he was maybe 35 years old or forty. And he asked me his first question: you have proof you're his daughter? I say Yes, I have my passport. And he says now you have his death certificate?

I was so surprised and I say: I never knew we would need this. I told them immediately my father died in a concentration camp and I never knew which one, but I knew he died in a concentration camp. I also told him that the British bank had already given money back to my mother. He [the bank official] was very arrogant, very cold. Finally he says to me: you have to have a death certificate. And I ask: how can I have a death certificate? He says: You have to go back to Paris and ask the French authorities to give you a death certificate. I was too stupid to answer immediately [that my father died in a concentration camp, so the French authorities could not issue a death certificate.]

I went back to the train going back to Paris the same day. I started to ask, but nobody saw my father dead. I went to the administrator for deportee prisoners from the war and there was a young man who explained to me that nobody had a death certificate. He told me: Your father died in Majdanek, and this was the first time I heard the name of the camp in which he died.

Sapir added emotionally that a father who knows he is about to die could not send his daughter to look for nonexistent money. After all, he would want to save his daughter.

Sapir returned to Credit Suisse and was asked again to wait and then asked again to produce a death certificate:

This time he asked in German and I answered in French. I don't want to speak German. I told them, this is impossible to have. Nobody has a death certificate. My father died in a concentration camp. I told them nobody saw my father die, and I became very very angry.

And I told them, you want me to recap [wake up] Hitler, Himmler, Eichmann, one from this you want me to recap, to bring him back to life, to give me a death certificate? And I started to cry. And we screamed real, real screams in the bank: how can I wake them up to give you a death certificate? You know he had money here. And I ran out of the bank, crying, screaming. People stopped me, Swiss people. Asked me in French and German: can I help you. I ran back to the hotel, paid the hotel, and went back to Paris.[20]

Many years later, at the height of the deposits scandal, an official representative of Credit Suisse publicly announced that the bank, then the largest in Switzerland, would have difficulty solving Sapir's problem, as the "account was closed several years ago and the documents no longer exist."[21] Only in April 1998, did the bank agree to compensate Sapir, and according to media reports, the bank paid her $500,000.[22] Sapir was not the only person who left a Swiss bank shocked in the 1950s. Many others applied and received the same answers: banking confidentiality, death certificate, proof of inheritance.[23]

Forty years late, the banks and the Swiss government finally admitted that their behavior toward Holocaust survivors was inadequate. On February 26, 1997, at the height of the international scandal surrounding Swiss actions during World War II, the Swiss Bankers Association convened a press conference in the Baur Au Lac Hotel, the most fashionable hotel in Zurich. In the hotel's banquet hall, dozens of Swiss, British, Israeli, and American reporters and television crews assembled. Seven senior members of the SBA sat on the stage, prepared to speak on a number of subjects, such as the Swiss economy (then suffering from a worrisome recession) and the banks' recommended policies. Except for the bankers, no one in the room, wanted to hear a single word about the economy. All the questions, some very pointed, concerned a single issue: the Holocaust victims' deposits affair.

SBA president Georg Krayer tried unsuccessfully to gain a little sympathy from those present. Some of his answers awakened even more pointed questions, and the general atmosphere was completely distrustful. But there is no doubt that Krayer told the truth when he admitted to errors the banks made in the decades prior to the storm of 1995–1997.

In the past fifty years, the Swiss banking community did not judge correctly the emotional aspect of the entire matter. The issue isn't the laws and the sums, but is very emotional. The development of the Swiss financial center spoiled us. And we thought 100 francs is not a large sum we should bother to look for, while in fact, it could be a very large sum indeed for those claiming it. The criticism of our behavior in this context is fair. We should have centralized the handling of this problem years ago, as is being done now, instead of the need to approach each bank individually. The fate of these people touches me deeply, and this gives me the strength to continue to handle the problem. Despite the attacks against us. In the past there were no questions, and now they are all coming up. This is the price for the fifty years of calm we had and did not make good use of.[24]

The Swiss government, which for decades treated the banks with kid gloves, also admitted their behavior was inadequate. Thomas Borer, then in charge of handling the affair at the Foreign Ministry, says that

The banks made a series of errors. I don't know if I would call it arrogance, but a bureaucratic-legalistic attitude. The attitude was: this is small money, and we have more important things to do than bother with some 100 dormant accounts. This was the attitude after World War II and in the 60's. They exhibited insensitivity to the whole question of handling the matter. [They didn't understand] that an entirely different attitude is necessary, than in instances where someone shows up and says, my father died in a car accident, and then the regular attitude is needed.[25]

Yet, Estelle Sapir and thousands of others went through years of frustration, trouble, and tears, before the banks and the Swiss government began to change their attitude. In the following chapters we will examine how the banks went from demanding death certificates of Auschwitz, Treblinka and other camp victims to the admission that all the applicants were telling the truth. We will also see how the Swiss government changed its attitude from complete confidence in the banks and promoting years of red tape in handling the problem, to discussing the issue at each weekly cabinet meeting. We will also discuss the change in the Jewish organizations and the state of Israel's policy from futile attempts to influence Switzerland to return property that did not belong to it and its financial institutions, to aggressive international pressure and utilization of all the existing tools to influence public opinion.

At the end of the 1950s, however, the point our story has reached, their aims were far more modest: to cause the banks to report the property and to try and locate the owners. In Chapter 5, we will see how even this minimal goal was not achieved and how the Swiss banks raised obstacles to their own government for decades longer.

5

"COLD AS ICE"
Evading the Law for Restoration of Property

THE FEDERAL PALACE in Bern is fancy and impressive, overlooking a wonderful view of the valley outside the city and the mountains on the horizon. The two houses of parliament occupy the building's central wing, and the Swiss government sits in the two side wings. Sharp-eyed visitors will notice that the parliament's address is Bundesplatz 3; no. 1 is the headquarters of the Swiss National Bank. The central bank is theoretically in the shadow of the parliament—at least that is the way things appear on the square—but the street addresses often reflect the real balance of power in Switzerland. The other two sides of the square house banks, and underneath the parking lot at the heart of the square is the central bank's gold vaults. Every parliament member and government official sees the bank buildings clearly and walks over the gold bars every time they go in and out of their offices.

This balance of power was preserved throughout the 1950s when the banks succeeded in nullifying every attempt to resolve the deposits without heirs problem. The 1960s, however, brought change, the source of which is unclear from a thirty-five-year vantage point. It appeared that the government finally managed to overpower the banks due apparently, at least, to the coincidence of a number of factors. First, the government never completely gave up on its intention to fulfill the Washington Accord and Bern Agreement commitment to locate the victims' assets and use them for refugee rehabilitation. To put it mildly, the government was in no hurry, but chose not to withdraw from the agreements.

Second, parliament members occasionally raised the issue, creating continuous public pressure on the banks. Third, Israel continued to apply incessant pressure and, in January 1960, the United States also began to apply pressure to resolve the problem. Fourth, the legislative process gained momentum after Israel captured Adolf Eichmann in 1960, and when world public opinion became aware of the horrors of the Holocaust.

Nonetheless, it does not appear that these factors are sufficient to explain the banks' relatively amicable 1962 agreement to a law they had torpedoed just two or three years previously. There are two possible answers for this, although neither is more than an assumption supported by circumstantial evidence. The first possibility is that the banks understood that the law was not such a great evil, as they would be able to sink it when it was implemented. As will be explained later in this chapter, the law that was ratified had many loopholes, and essentially left it up to the banks to determine if and how to implement it. For this reason, the banks could agree, unenthusiastically of course, to the obligatory reporting and transfer to the government of property without heirs.

Alternatively, we could assume that the banks did plan to appropriate Holocaust victims' accounts. For this purpose, they needed twenty years from the last contact with the client: ten years to define the account as dormant, and another ten years until they could close it, destroy the documents, and do with the money whatever they so desired. If this was in fact their plan, then 1959 was too early a date from their perspective: the war only began in 1939 and it was only in 1940 and 1941 that most European Jews came under Nazi domination. In contrast, 1962 was a far more comfortable date, as twenty years earlier, in 1942, the Holocaust was in full swing, and almost all the Jewish depositors were trampled under jackboots. This explanation is not anchored in direct proof, but fits well with the phenomenal change in the banks' position between 1959 and 1962.

Diplomatic pressure on Switzerland in the 1960s began as early as January 28, 1960, when Warren Blumberg, first secretary of the U.S. embassy in Bern, asked the local Foreign Ministry to act to resolve the unclaimed property issue. In July 1960, the Israeli ambassador, Joseph Linton, also appealed to Foreign Minister Max Petitpierre, who was then also serving as president. (The Swiss presidency is an annual rotation among the seven cabinet ministers.) Petitpierre was convinced and in October 1960, he said in a cabinet meeting that "Not only due to foreign policy considerations, but also for the benefit of those hurt by racist persecution, special legislation should be enabled" concerning the deposits, despite problems that have arisen in the past.

After another meeting with Linton in January 1961, Petitpierre, serving only as foreign minister, summoned Minister of Justice Ludwig von Moos to discuss the matter. On February 9, 1961, von Moos presented a bill to the cabinet, prepared with surprising speed by his ministry's director general, Edgar Mottier. On February 14, the cabinet approved the bill. The first draft was debated in the Ministry of Justice in April, and in June it was sent to the rest of the ministries for their comments. At the end of the month it was sent to the cantons, political parties, and relevant nongovernmental bodies to peruse. In light of the responses, changes were made in the draft, primarily in the law's application not only to victims of racist and religious persecution, but to victims of Nazi political persecution. An assurance of immunity from prosecution for the violation of banking secrecy of those who reported dormant assets was also added to the draft bill.

The cabinet approved the bill on May 4, 1962, and it was submitted to Parliament. In its prologue to the bill, the cabinet explained that the Bankers Association opposed the bill, arguing that it covered less then 1 million francs, and added that "It cannot be permitted that anyone suspect Switzerland of wanting to enrich herself from the victims of these terrible events." The bill was finally ratified on December 20, 1962. The government published the details for the implementation of the law on June 10, 1963, and the law took effect on September 1, 1963.[1]

The first clause of the law determines that

property of any kind located in Switzerland, whose last known owners are foreign nationals or without nationality who have made no confirmed contact since May 9, 1945, who are known or assumed to be victims of racist, religious or political persecution, must be reported within six months after this decision takes effect to the body determined by the government (Claims Registry), including all changes made since or at the time of the owner's disappearance.

The second clause defines property in a far wider manner, including cash deposits, gold and precious metals, collections, real estate, patent rights, copyrights, insurance policies, and securities. The third clause clarifies that the law applies to individuals, companies, partnerships, and institutions. The fourth clause states that "In case of doubt concerning the report requirement, the instance must be decided by the Claims Registry." The next clause describes the Claims Registry's working methods and emphasizes the confidentiality requirement imposed on the registry, which could not report to anyone but the property's owners or their heirs.

Clause 8 states that "If the original owners or their rightful heirs are not located within two years, the process for declaring the owners missing must be implemented without delay, along with its ramifications on property in Switzerland." The next clause determines that in such instances inheritance processes should be initiated according to Swiss law.

Clause 10 relates to lack of documentation: "If claimants cannot prove the credibility of their right to inherit, because the documents necessary for clear proof were destroyed or lost as a result of the war or acts of violence, or because authorized certificates are unavailable due to political circumstances, the inheritance should be transferred according to the decision of the custodian institution in charge of assistance" [appointed to assist the Claims Registry, actually indicating the various cantonal custodians].

Clause 12 determines the use of moneys whose owners are not located:

If the owner of property registered [with the Registry] did not leave an individual rightful heir, and left no instructions in the event of his death, the right of inheritance will be transferred to a fund established by the government. Use of the fund's money will be determined in cabinet decision, which shall consider the source of the moneys deposited in the fund. One tenth of the fund will serve [as reserves] to fulfill later claims. If someone declared dead or his legal heir or representative appears within five years after the transfer of property to the fund, the sum transferred to the fund will be returned to the claimant without interest.

Clause 13 determined that the penalty for violating the law would be 10,000 francs or incarceration for an unspecified time period.[2] In June 1963, the necessary regulations for implementation of the law were determined.

Seemingly, this was a comprehensive and intelligible law that would settle the deposits problem once and for all, even if it had been sixteen years since Switzerland first promised to "consider favorably using property without heirs to aid refugees from Nazi persecution." Actually, as lawyers in the Israeli Foreign Ministry immediately perceived, the law was full of loopholes.

Attorney Joseph Lador examined a draft of the law in April 1961 and wrote to his superiors that

a) according to the present Clause 1, the reporting requirement applies to the existence of a deposit in the event the depositors "are known or assumed to be victims of racist, religious or political persecution or other acts of violence." Arbitration of the question if these conditions exist, has not been conferred on the courts, but remains with the bank manager. In other words, the Swiss banks will be forced to report the existence of a deposit only if it is clear from the account's headline that the depositor is a member of this group.

b) in light of the fact that inheritance laws in all the Eastern European countries have been changed (the purpose of which is to limit the rightful heirs and enable the State to inherit in most cases), it is necessary to determine that the distribution of the inheritance will be made according to local instructions in effect at the end of the war, or possibly better still, at the beginning of the war.

c) the bill completely ignores the international commitment that the capital in question be transferred to the auspices of the Jewish organizations [the Jewish Agency and the Joint]. The bill in this matter mentions the existence of a special fund for appropriate use of the moneys (as far as we know, the Swiss government and Swiss Jewish communities agree on this point). On this matter as well, it is necessary that the bill be amended.

Lador's reservations, as we will see, were surprisingly accurate, as was the last sentence in his memo, which looks as if it were written in the late

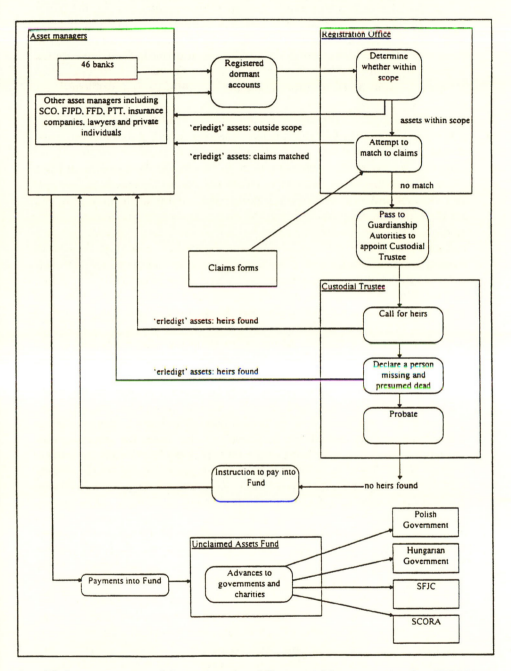

Simplified representation of the Registration Office's activities, accounting firm KPMG's table, presented to the Volcker Commission (Author's files)

1990s: "The Swiss are extremely sensitive about anything concerning their maneuvers and businesses during the war."[3]

The law, however was actually ratified with its faults, leaving the banks in charge of the decision about if and to what extent it should be obeyed, and without even determining the target uses of the unclaimed property in advance. The banks exploited the loopholes and the lack of government supervision, while the lack of clarity about what to do with the unclaimed property, despite Swiss promises made in the 1940s, caused problems later.

Implementation of the law was far from the traditional image of Swiss efficiency, despite the fact that the law was clear and allowed all concerned a one year pause between ratification by Parliament and entry into force, in order to prepare for implementation. What we are about to describe can be explained in one of two ways: either the Swiss bureaucracy simply is not efficient and its expertise is primarily associated with the private sector, or the officials concerned did not bother to implement the law prudently, and possibly even tried to cause its failure.

Holders of property without heirs were required to report it to the Claims Registry within six months of the law's having taken effect—by March 1, 1964. Holders of property reported assets at a value of 8,469,882.71 francs (27.6 million francs in current values), belonging to 961 depositors who felt they met the conditions of the law. As we have stated, the decision to report was entirely in the hands of the property holder; the government did not even conduct a random sampling to determine the credibility of the reports.

The banks reported 6.07 million francs of property (20 million francs in current values), much more than had ever been estimated before, but much less than the Jewish organizations believed. The Swiss Clearing Office reported that it still held 2.47 million francs (8 million francs in current values), apparently from German property. The insurance companies reported that they held 260,000 unclaimed francs (847,000 francs in current values), while private holders such as trust companies and lawyers, reported 670,000 francs (2.18 million francs in current values). Despite the fact that tardy reports constituted a criminal offense, no steps were taken against latecomers.

In total, the registry received reports of 9,989,897.15 francs (31 million francs in current values). Over the course of time, however, the registry decided that most of the money did not fall under its jurisdiction, as the depositors had not met the conditions under the law. In 1972, the registry still had 4,534,086.78 francs (11 million in current values). Over the years, the owners of 1,321,340.42 francs (3 million francs in current values) were identified, while 4,080,237.28 francs were designated for transfer to the fund established under the law. Actually, as we will see later, only 2,593,010.64 francs (5.2 million francs in current values) were transferred.[4]

Meanwhile, 7,000 claimants appealed to the Claims Registry concerning their relatives' property. In this context it must be noted, as we will describe later, that announcements of the possibility of appealing to the Swiss government were published so that only a few would read them, and were not published at all in Eastern Europe. Most of the applications were rejected, as the claimants could not supply the banks and the Claims Registry with the required proof. Later we will examine a number of instances that will verify the obstacles that the heirs encountered, not only from the banks, but also from the Swiss government.[5]

The first problems in implementing the law occurred as early as June 1963. In anticipation of problems, on June 10, the Swiss government had announced to the press the establishment of the Claims Registry, and the possibility of submittings claims. It did not advertise this to the public and left the work of disseminating the information to journalists, who did not always understand all the details. Prior to June 10, the Swiss and foreign press had published details of the law, but as the Swiss government did not bother to issue a detailed and organized press release, inaccurate details were also published.

It appears these reports also influenced Swiss diplomats, primarily in the United States, who, not surprisingly, did not know all the details themselves. The consulate in New York expected thousands of applications from American Jews while the embassy in Washington expressed fears that all the property would be returned and suggested creating appellate processes for the Claims Registry decisions and avoiding publishing lists of deposit owners.

Immediately following the official announcement in Bern, there was a flood of media reports on June 11–12. Swiss representatives in some countries discovered to their chagrin that they did not have reliable and complete information, and asked for urgent instructions from the Foreign Ministry in Bern, which arrived one week later on June 19. The representatives received the press release of June 10, and a summary of the law, but no explanation about how to proceed from there. The practical advice the Swiss diplomats abroad received was to tell applicants to wait until the end of February 1964. By that date those holding property in Switzerland were required to report it, and only afterward, the government claimed, would it be possible to answer property owners who applied.

The problems peaked concerning application forms for the claimants. No one in the Swiss government thought in advance that one form should be prepared, to make things easier for both the applicants and those designated to locate the property. Swiss representatives abroad pressed the Foreign Ministry to send such forms quickly. From their office windows, diplomats could see local citizens coming in to receive information. They wiped the sweat from their brows and prepared themselves for a tough day of meting out, "come back in half a year." But far away, in chilly offices with views of the Alps, Claims Registry officials were determined to first receive the reports, and then provide the forms.

The Swiss consulate in New York bombarded the Bern Foreign Ministry with requests for forms, press releases, and instructions, "so we can contradict the errors that appear regularly in the local press." The Bankers Association submitted a similar request, but only on March 13, 1964, did the Claims Registry deign to send the forms printed in Switzerland's three official languages: German, French, and Italian. No one considered the possibility that Jews in Israel, the United States, and Britain, the three largest concentrations of Jewish populations outside Eastern Europe, might not understand them and that maybe they should be printed in English, too.

Some Swiss representatives abroad, who had apparently already given up on the Claims Registry, decided to translate the forms into English, which caused more confusion, due to a lack of uniformity in the translations. In the meantime, the Claims Registry in Bern sent their New York consulate ten forms, with a request to use them frugally. The forms were sent by sea mail, and since he knew nothing of this, the consul in New York, Hans Gasser, wrote an enraged letter to the Foreign Ministry that he had only heard of the existence of the forms from a third party, and reiterated his request to receive accurate information on the procedures for handling applicants.

When Gasser received the ten forms in mid-April, he hastened to send a telegram to the Foreign Ministry, noting that he needed 1,000 forms, and again requested that they include all possible instructions. The Foreign Ministry was not impressed by the telegram, and sent just 200 forms to New York, along with a renewed instruction to save forms by distributing them only to those whose declarations appeared to meet the conditions of the law. The applicants were therefore asked to provide data on the date of death of the account owner, and the circumstances under which he had become a victim of Nazi persecution.[6] This created another obstacle; first, the applicants had to convince consulate officials that they had a chance to receive the money, and only then could they receive the form to begin the handling the matter.

In April 1964, Gasser wrote to his superiors that he had tried unsuccessfully for years to convince Bern to understand the pressures on the consulate concerning the deposits. According to Gasser, the consulate files already contained hundreds of applications since the ratification of the law. He noted that the consulate had previously responded to all applicants in writing, and had tried to convince telephone callers to try again at a future date. In other words, these applicants had not been recorded at all. According to Gasser, he could not continue to reject applicants without a practical answer, and therefore recommended the appointment of a staff whose only duties would be to respond to the applicants and relate to them "in a liberal manner."

In May, eleven months after the law was made public, the legal department of the Foreign Ministry made their long-awaited decision: "Due to political and psychological concerns, as well as the need to implement the process in the most economically feasible manner, free distribution of the forms is the most appropriate solution to the situation in the U.S." The Claims Registry sent another 500 forms to New York and fifty to Washington. The Foreign Ministry, however, continued to vehemently oppose providing the American public with any further information, and even succeeded in convincing the U.S. State Department to avoid publishing its own instructions.

The Swiss government itself was unsure that the banks were upholding the law. The director of the Claims Registry, Hans Weber, already saw signs in 1963 that the major banks were avoiding reporting deposits they held. UBS, for many years the largest bank in Switzerland, by October 1963, had already requisitioned 4,560 additional forms from the Claims Registry, after the bank used all 200 forms it had been allocated in less than one month. The exact number of requested additional forms hinted that they were responding to a real need, and not simply flooding the bank with thousands of unnecessary papers.

When Weber checked by telephone about why the bank needed so many forms, UBS's chief legal counsel, Dr. Kleiner told him, "Searches at the headquarters and at the branches have turned up a very high number of assets which likely will come into question [concerning the fate of the owners and the law's application to them]. These assets correspond to approximately the number [of owners of deposits] of forms requested." UBS was not exceptional. Swiss Bank Corp. asked for 5241 additional forms. Here again, the number was so exact, that it could not stem from anything but surprisingly exact information in the bank's possession. The Claims Registry sent a total of 14,186 forms for reporting property without heirs, most of them to the banks. Of the 400 banks then active in Switzerland, only forty-six bothered to report just 739 assets.

Weber still did not know how many assets the holders would ultimately report, but by November 1963, he was worried that they were unwilling to cooperate: "One cannot avoid the assumption that the managers of unclaimed assets simply were not ready to cooperate. How else could the enormous orders of forms by the largest banking institutions be explained, if not by the fact that considerably more unclaimed assets were present, than had at first been reported?" Weber asked, and left the answer a given.[7]

By April 1967, 1,055 assets without heirs had been reported to the Claims Registry. Of these, UBS reported 251. Credit Suisse, then the second largest bank in the country, reported 38 assets, while the cantonal banks and private banks found 269 instances. Swiss Bank, the third largest, reported 77. The insurance companies reported 60 cases, and the Clearing Office reported 65. A few hundred assets were found by various government bodies such as the Guardianship Office of Zurich, the Orphans Office of St. Gallen, the postal checking department of the General Headquarters of the PTT (Post, Telephone, and Telegraph), the Federal Department of Justice and the Federal Finance Administration. Another 62 assets were in the hands of private managers and companies.[8] In light of these figures, there is no doubt that the banks reported only a very small portion of the total number of accounts than at first appeared worthy of reporting. How did they do this?

Before the banks requested the thousands of additional forms, they had to begin locating the accounts to which the law could apply. The logical first step was locating dormant accounts, and later investigating whether it was a reasonable assumption that the owners of the accounts were victims of the Nazis. Therefore, when Swiss Bank and UBS ordered the forms, they were already past at least the first stage. Afterward, they expunged several hundred names wholesale, and reported only who was left. The deleted names were those the banks decided could not be victims of the Nazis.

It is possible their decision was justified, for instance, about account owners from America, but it is also possible that the banks acted arbitrarily.[9] For example, the banks could report according to the statistics for Holocaust victims from relevant countries. If the account belonged to a Polish Jew, the bank had no choice but to report it, as more than 90 percent of Poland's Jews were murdered, and thus there was a high likelihood that this was also the fate of the account holder. If the account belonged to a German Jew, however the probability dropped to 25 percent, the scope of the genocide in that country, and the bank could decide that there was a better chance that the person was not murdered by the Nazis, and that therefore there was no need to report the asset. What is clear is that the enormous difference between the number of forms requested by the banks and the actual reports they returned not only should have constituted a warning, as it did for Weber, but also should have led to concrete actions to investigate the credibility of the bankers' reports. But nothing was done. Despite the apparent indications that the banks did not uphold the law's instructions, Bern twiddled its thumbs.

The accounting firm KPMG, which examined the 1962 law and its implementation for the Volcker Commission, reached harsh conclusions in August 1997. It determined hundreds of banks that did not report dormant assets, assuming they had them, should be investigated. Most of the banks did not obey the instructions to report transactions made on the accounts after contact with the owners was lost (and thus they could chew away at them with commissions, until some accounts even disappeared). The accountants found that the principal criterion for reporting was the Jewish names of the dormant accounts' owners, while completely ignoring the fact that the Nazis also murdered those without strictly ethnic Jewish names. It was also found that most of the banks reported via their central branches, and it is therefore completely unclear how many other branches fulfilled the report requirement.[10]

These conditions attest to the possibility that the banks exploited the regulations for dormant accounts, closed the accounts, destroyed documentation, and appropriated the funds for themselves. This possibility seems perfectly reasonable in light of the details the banks themselves published in recent years concerning the scope of dormant accounts that they held. It can be theoretically assumed, according to the banks' percentage of assets transferred to the Claims Registry, that 75 percent of the assets located at first were held at the banks (of 1,055 assets reported, 739 were by banks). In other words, of the 14,000 forms requested after the preliminary investigation, about 11,000 were designated to report dormant assets at banks. The actual number reported, therefore, constitutes 7 percent of the total assets at first considered dormant. The rest were appropriated.

Some blame falls directly on the Claims Registry for the manner in which it instructed the banks and other property holders to interpret the law. In March 1965, the Claims Registry published "explanatory comments." It is very instructive that their comments were published one year after the deadline for reporting assets. They determined that the law was designed to apply to well-defined cases, and that wider interpretation "couldn't even be considered." The registry emphasized that assets belonging to anyone who disappeared under different circumstances should not be reported, and it gave examples.

Some of the instances were certainly logical, such as natural death, military conscription, or emigration. But the registry also removed from the law's application anyone who was killed in the war not under circumstances indicating Nazi persecution, for example, in bombings. According to the registry's logic, the property of a Jew killed in the bombing of Budapest who "didn't have the chance" to be sent to Auschwitz would not have to be reported by the banks, even if his entire family were murdered later. According to that interpretation, a Jew killed in the suppression of the Warsaw Ghetto Uprising is also not considered a victim of persecution, as it can be claimed, in a dry, legalistic manner, that he was the victim of military activity on the part of the German army, and not racist persecution.

The registry decided as well that it was not responsible for handling cases in which the client made contact with the bank after the end of the war. This determination immediately eliminated accounts whose heirs tried to locate them before 1962. Later in this chapter we will see an outstanding example of this policy. Anyone who tried to locate an account in the 1950s and failed due to the banks' harsh demands, could not find salvation with the Claims Registry. It became the petitioner's own fault for not waiting patiently until Switzerland deigned to fulfill its obligations and locate the accounts.

When the Claims Registry investigated the 1,055 reports it received, it strictly applied the rules it had published in March 1965. The registry announced that it was not responsible for the handling of 224 cases, all from various government authorities, as the depositors died of natural causes. (How these particular depositors died of natural causes is puzzling, unless the Registry wanted to leave those assets with the State.) The registry explicitly clarified that, in its eyes, death from natural causes included death from starvation or lack of medical attention. According to the rules, the law then applied only to those who died a violent death as the result of racist or religious persecution. This eliminated hundreds of thousands of victims who starved in the ghettos and concentration camps as a result of the inhumane conditions that prevailed there.

Just what was the fate of the assets that the registry refused to handle? Responsibility for them was returned to the managers, in other words, the banks primarily, who made no effort to locate the heirs or to consider those who appeared on their own. The banks, from their perspective, preferred the registry to handle the reported assets and were not enthusiastic about the appointment of a government guardian to handle them, for they still would have been responsible to the heirs.

Officially, the banks also preferred that the registry handle what they called "doubtful cases," although there is more than one hint that the banks appropriated the authority to decide about most of them. UBS, for instance, found several kinds of doubtful cases: the depositor's place of residence was behind the Iron Curtain (at that time, it was unclear what would be done with those moneys); lack of information concerning the depositor's citizenship and place of residence (a weird differentiation, as banks usually record a client's place of residence); lack of certainty about Jewish names (and naturally the banks were easy on themselves and reported only strongly Jewish names. Credit Suisse, for instance, enlisted the aid of a rabbi in locating Jewish names).

Finally, in December 1966, the Ministry of Justice determined the rule that was valid for the next thirty years: "In order to submit the claims of cases that do not fall under the auspices of the law, the involved parties must examine the existence of the alleged assets directly with the managers," in other words, the banks. The registry also returned to the managers the handling of 518 cases, 200 in which the heirs or owners were identified, and 318 it decided were not under its jurisdiction. Did the heirs receive their money? The Volcker Commission accountants said in August 1997 that they did not know yet; this became the key question that would have to be looked into later in the committee's investigation.[11]

After all the housecleaning, the registry still had 842 cases of property without heirs, which appeared to belong to Holocaust victims. Sixty-five percent of the bank accounts included in this category were current accounts, in which the banks charged fees but did not pay interest. In light of this, it is no wonder that more than half of the accounts contained only small sums of up to 1,000 francs. Other assets found at the banks, such as securities, were usually valued by the banks at zero. The value of jewelry found in safe-deposit boxes "raised misgivings," the Volcker Commission accountants note.

At the request of the Claims Registry and some of Switzerland's larger cantons in which most of the assets were located, Dr. Heinz Haeberlin was appointed the general guardian of these assets in July 1966. Some of the cantons, including Geneva, Bern, and St. Gallen, appointed their own guardians, and did not use Haeberlin's services. Haeberlin handled a total of 689 cases, in which 4,375,708.09 francs (13.2 million francs in current values) were reported.

The most important task facing the guardians was to locate the heirs, and Haeberlin appealed to the Red Cross Center and another group called the International Search Service. Afterward, he also asked for the assistance of the central Jewish organization in Switzerland and the Jewish welfare organization.

If the initial search failed, the guardians could publish advertisements to try and locate the heirs. But the Claims Registry policy regarding this was clear: "The advertisements will not include any account details and will be published only if there is no fear this will harm the claimants." Banking confidentiality prevented taking the simplest step: publishing names and a list of assets and asking potential heirs to contact the various guardians.

Haeberlin decided that it was not worth searching for heirs if the amounts discovered were too low. The amount was first set at 500 francs (1,865 francs in current values); in 1970 it was raised to 1,000 francs (2,670 francs in current values). Haeberlin did not consider the possibility that there were heirs for whom such a sum was worth the trouble. He considered only the Swiss perspective in allocating time and resources to locating heirs. He also ignored the fact that for decades the banks charged commissions on the accounts, eroding significant portions of their original value. In at least one instance, it led to a located heir not receiving his money. The "too small" sums amounted to 11,420.40 francs (297,000 francs in current values), and were transferred to the fund that received property without heirs.

According to Haeberlin's report, he succeeded in locating 132 heirs and paying them 1,671,277.05 francs (3.29 million francs in current values).[12]

Almost all the property was returned to heirs in Western countries, primarily in the United States and Israel. Haeberlin noted that even heirs who lived in the West sometimes had difficulty meeting the standards of evidence about their right to inherit, due to the difficulty in receiving documents from Eastern Europe. "In such cases," Haeberlin wrote in his summary report, "I used the means of affidavits under oath," a method that could have helped the heirs very much, if the banks had also adopted it.[13]

The greatest difficulty concerned accounts whose heirs lived in Eastern Europe. The banks claimed that handling these accounts could endanger the depositors, as authorities could accuse them of illegal possession of foreign currency, and might even try to force them to give up their inheritance. The Foreign Ministry did believe that most applications from Eastern Europe could be acknowledged, but its opinion was rejected. The Ministry of Justice decided that the Claims Registry would not be allowed to respond to representatives of Communist countries concerning specific accounts, would not publish applications for heirs in Eastern Europe, and certainly would not respond to the applications of citizens from those countries. Switzerland stuck to this policy until the end of 1995, years after the Iron Curtain fell.[14]

The obstacles created by the registry are some of the gravest aspects of the entire deposits affair. The measures were not taken by private banks, whose entire purpose is the achievement of maximum profit, but by a government body that was supposed to act in the best interests of its citizens.

The Claims Registry received 5,300 applications from account owners and heirs. Two hundred and eighty-three of the applicants could note in which bank the requested account was handled, others reported the codes used to identify owners, and in some cases, ownership was claimed for specific objects such as works of art and jewelry. The officials diligently examined the applications, but only in seventy-four cases did they find a match between the applications and the list of assets the banks and other property holders reported. It was immediately determined that ten of these cases were not connected at all with the 1962 law, and therefore the registry was not authorized to handle them. The applicants did not receive any information on the location of the property, because they probably argued banking confidentiality, (and we have already seen, this claim is invalid concerning legal heirs).

In the remaining sixty-four cases, the registry gave the applicants only general information concerning the assets. While the property managers, namely the banks, were supposed to decide whether to pay the applicants; the registry did not even bother to track the way the banks handled the matter. Furthermore, the Volcker Commission accountants found fourteen additional cases in which there was a match between applicants and the list of assets, but the registry declined to report them to the applicants for unspecified reasons.[15]

The case of Ernestine Steinhardt is one example of the way the Claims Registry behaved. The heir to the account was Steinhardt's niece, Herta Arbetz, a petite, friendly woman in her eighties residing in Tel Aviv. Steinhardt, a Vienna resident, deposited money in Switzerland in order to prove to the British Mandate authorities in Palestine that she was "a woman of means" and eligible to emigrate there. Near the end of the 1950s, after Steinhardt died in the Holocaust, Arbetz and her mother asked to receive the money. Herta Arbetz hired attorney Zvi Weigl, after her visit to Swiss Bank Corp. in Zurich did not yield results. Arbetz recalls that "They were as cold as ice and as the snow on the Alps. . . . The manager there only said two words to me, and all she wanted was to get rid of me."

Weigl officially applied to the bank, but in vain. The reason he was given was that there was no proof that Arbetz was the heir. "They made impossible demands," Weigl recalls. But in May 1964, when Weigl applied to the Claims Registry, he was told that the law did not apply to the Steinhardt account because the bank considered his original application and the customer's to be one and the same, and the law only applied to clients with whom contact had been lost. Weigl wondered, "On the one hand, the bank refused to recognize my client as the heir. On the other hand, my client was a good enough heir for the bank to avoid the legal processes."

Weigl appealed to the Israeli Foreign Ministry, who directed him to Georges Brunschvig, the well-known lawyer and veteran Jewish leader, who had begun to pull political strings in Bern. The contradiction in the Claims Registry and Swiss Bank's positions was clear to everyone, including Israel's ambassador to Switzerland, Shmuel Ben-Zur, who raised the case before the local Foreign Ministry in April 1965. The Claims Registry accused Weigl and Ben-Zur of raising "baseless, unilateral emotional arguments."

Israel submitted an official written application, Ben-Zur raised the question in a number of conversations, and finally even went to the trouble of going personally to the Bern Foreign Ministry in order to raise the issue directly with the minister, Willy Spuehler. Only then did the ministry appeal to the Bankers Association. The association's answer was there was no reason to hurry. Instead of expecting the Claims Registry to do its work, the association wrote to the Foreign Ministry, it would be better for Weigl to worry about finding the required documents to prove his client's right to inherit.

The association added that "Based on the investigation we conducted concerning the claimant and her representatives after the war, it is impossible to assume there are no reports of Ms. Steinhardt." In other words, as Arbetz claims Steinhardt died, we know what happened to her. The 1962 law covered accounts for which the owner's fate was unknown. The conclusion was that the law did not apply to this case. The Foreign Ministry accepted this position, although Arbetz's brother and uncle eventually received £1,000, the original sum deposited without any interest or linkage to inflation. The exhausted Weigl gave up any attempts to locate additional assets. Thirty years later, Arbetz summed up her experience: "I once believed the Swiss are the most honest people in the world. Today I don't believe them."[16]

The Steinhardt case was not the only one in which the Claims Registry knew the location of heirs, but still avoided transferring the money to them. Three additional Israeli citizens did not receive their relatives' property because they could not meet the demands of the Claims Registry. The three were among 900 Israelis who appealed to the Jewish National Fund (JNF) in the 1950s and 1960s, with requests for assistance in locating their relatives property in Switzerland, and were the only ones who received positive responses.

The most outstanding example concerns the account that belonged to Jacob and Erna Zimet, which their niece, Zilla Hass-Axelrad, tried to locate. She lived in their home in the 1930s, when she was already thirty years old, and knew that her uncle occasionally deposited money in Switzerland. In February 1964, Hass-Axelrod authorized the JNF to handle locating the property in Switzerland, and in December 1964, completed the official form for the Claims Registry. In August 1965, the Claims Registry announced the location of a few thousand francs in the name of Erne Zimet, but added that it needed to investigate "a few matters concerning the transfer of the inheritance, which will require some time."

JNF staff members attempted to hurry the Swiss. Attorney B. Grossman, who handled the matter in Jerusalem, wrote in December 1965 to Attorney A. Dayan, a JNF employee in Zurich, concerning the three cases in which property had been located—Zilla Hass-Axelrad, Moshe Katz and Egun Farkash:

I understand, that the Swiss authorities also have a tempo of their own, and that it is not so simple to change that tempo. However, this is deserted property that has stood more than twenty years with no possibility that those entitled to the property will exercise their rights. They have finally been given this opportunity, and efforts should be made that the current heirs be satisfied, and not that things should continue many more years so that only the heirs' heirs would be satisfied.

When nothing happened, Y. Holtzman, another JNF employee in Zurich, reported about a meeting held in December 1967 with Hans Weber:

I never encountered such negative and obstinate behavior. The manager relies on limited legal clauses in the law, and despite all my pathos, and my efforts to find a humane attitude in him, we stood before a wall that could not be budged. Dr.

Meldestelle für Vermögen verschwundener Ausländer
Service des avoirs d'étrangers disparus
Ufficio per gli averi di stranieri scomparsi

Bern
Berne   Monbijoustrasse 11
Berna

Ihre Anfrage vom
Votre demande du
Vostra domanda del

Anmeldeformular für Gesuchsteller	**Formule de déclaration pour requérants**	**Modulo di dichiarazione per gli istanti**
(Bundesbeschluss vom 20. Dezember 1962; Vollziehungsverordnung vom 10. Juni 1963)	(Arrêté fédéral du 20 décembre 1962; ordonnance d'exécution du 10 juin 1963)	(Decreto federale 20 dicembre 1962; ordinanza di esecuzione 10 giugno 1963)
Dieses Formular ist von den Gesuchstellern auszufüllen, die als Rechtsnachfolger eines in Art. 1, Abs. 1 des Bundesbeschlusses genannten Eigentümers auf seine in der Schweiz befindlichen Vermögenswerte Anspruch zu erheben wünschen. Beim Vermögenseigentümer muss es sich um einen ausländischen Staatsangehörigen oder um einen Staatenlosen handeln, von dem seit dem 9. Mai 1945 zuverlässige Nachrichten fehlen und von dem man weiss oder vermutet, dass er ein Opfer rassischer, religiöser oder politischer Verfolgung wurde.	La présente déclaration doit être remplie par les requérants qui, à titre d'ayants cause d'un propriétaire mentionné à l'article premier, premier alinéa, de l'arrêté fédéral, désirent élever des prétentions sur ses avoirs situés en Suisse. Le propriétaire doit être un ressortissant étranger ou un apatride dont on est sans nouvelles sûres depuis le 9 mai 1945 et dont on sait ou présume qu'il a été victime de persécutions raciales, religieuses ou politiques.	Il modulo deve essere riempito dagli istanti che desiderano far valere delle pretese sugli averi in Svizzera di un proprietario menzionato all'art. cpv. 1, del decreto federale come aventi diritto o lide di cui si è senza notizie sicure dal 9 maggio 1945 e si sa o si presume che sia rimasto vittima di persecuzioni razziali, religiose o politiche.
Für jeden Vermögenseigentümer ist ein gesondertes Formular auszufüllen.	**Une formule particulière doit être remplie pour chaque propriétaire d'avoirs.**	**Bisogna riempire un modulo separato per ogni proprietario di averi.**

1. Angaben über den Gesuchsteller — Indications sur le requérant — Indicazioni riguardanti l'istante

a)	Name (in Blockschrift) / Nom (en caractères d'imprimerie) / Cognome (in stampatello)	HASS geb. Axelrad
b)	Vornamen / Prénoms / Nomi	Zilla
c)	Geburtsdatum und Geburtsort / Date et lieu de naissance / Data e luogo di nascita	15.VII.1906 Gusztynek Bezirk Borszczow, Polen
d)	Beruf / Profession / Professione	Lehrerin
e)	Zivilstand / Etat civil / Stato civile	verheiratet
f)	Wohnort und Land / Domicile et pays / Domicilio e Stato	Haifa/Israel
g)	Strasse / Rue / Via	Azar 9 Neve Shaanan
h)	Verwandtschaftsverhältnis zum Vermögenseigentümer / Degré de parenté avec le propriétaire des avoirs / Rapporto di parentela col proprietario	Nichte (der Vermoegenseigentuemer war der Bruder meiner Mutter)
i)	Vertreten durch / Représenté par / Rappresentato da	KKL-Treuhand A.G.,Wuerich,wie auch die Rechtsanwaelte Paul J.JACOBI und Dr.B.GROSSMAN, beide Jerusalem
k)	Vollmacht vom / Procuration du / Procura del	28.12.1964

Form. Nr. 3 - 5590

Application form of Zilla Hass-Axelrad to the Claims Registry on December 28, 1964. (Central Zionist Archives)

Weber declared that until now there has been no case his office has completed in a positive manner, and the only cases concerning the property of foreign nationals whose traces were lost, which were concluded positively, were only those cases in which the heirs could prove the existence of the money in the banks, and thus conclude the matter directly with the banks.

The obstacles facing Hass-Axelrad and the other heirs appear in a letter sent to her in 1968, four years after she initiated her case. Hass was asked to provide the Swiss with a series of documents that were nearly impossible to acquire in the case of Holocaust victims: a Polish government death certificate for the victim testator (or at least a certificate from the Warsaw Jewish community); the death certificates for heirs prior to the current claimant; authorization that the testator died in testate; a document clarifying the claimant as the rightful or only heir; and the passport of the property owner.

This list raises a series of acute questions: When entire families were murdered, how could a regular chain of death certificates be created? Did someone really expect to receive death certificates for concentration camp victims? How could one provide notarization of a will that *did not* exist? And who could get the passports of Holocaust victims?

The handling of the Hass-Axelrad case went on and on. In March 1972, it became clear that she was entitled to 2,493.82 francs (14,000 francs in current values), and again she was asked to provide all the same documentation. Grossman replied that this was impossible in light of the fact that the Polish Communist regime had severed ties with Israel. In May 1973, the story ended from Hass-Axelrad's point of view. The amount to which she was entitled, which had inexplicably increased to 3,000 francs (6,300 francs in current values), was declared "property without heirs." Switzerland announced that it would transfer the property to the charity fund established under the 1962 law. In fact, as we now know, the Zimet account was one of those transferred to Poland in direct contravention of the 1962 law, in violation of Swiss promises to the JNF, and with full knowledge that there was a rightful heir to the account.[17]

The second case is the inheritance of Adolf and Elizabeth Denes, claimed by Egun Farkash. This case is an indication of the fate of other accounts in Swiss banks that were depleted by the commissions and fees that the banks charged.

Adolf Denes, Farkash's uncle, a bank manager in Hungary, was murdered in 1944 in Auschwitz. The handling of Farkash's case began in 1964, and in August 1965, Weber reported the location of a "small deposit" in the couple's name at one of the banks. As usual, lengthy and profuse correspondence began, with failed efforts by the JNF to speed up the Swiss end of the process. In February 1968, Farkash was asked to provide the same documents as in the Hass-Axelrad case. The JNF staff informed him that if he could not furnish these documents, he must provide "documents which prove the accuracy of your claims to the property in Switzerland."

In November 1968, the Ministry of Justice informed Attorney Weil, who represented the JNF that "The bank in question calculated the small value of the aforementioned property as against its costs, such that there remains no deposit today . . . therefore the matter should be seen as closed." This raised another set of questions: What costs are there for an account in which there were no transactions for thirty years? Who authorized the bank to conduct a valuation of the account and appropriate the funds for itself? There are no grounds for the assumption that this is a unique case. There is no doubt that there are other cases in which the banks appropriated the accounts of Holocaust victims under the guise of commissions, fees, and costs. As we saw in Chapter 1, Credit Suisse did just this.

The JNF tried to argue but in vain. In March 1972, Weil announced that the bank had already dissolved the account in which 225.60 francs remained (681 francs in current values) in 1966. The date should be noted: the bank acted after the account was located and Farkash's right to inherit the remaining sum was determined, at least preliminarily. Nonetheless, the bank acted unilaterally, and the Swiss government approved the action with its silence.[18]

In the third case, Moshe Katz claimed the right to inherit from Leizer Lehrer who was arrested by the Gestapo in Vienna in 1938, and was never heard from again. Katz said that among other things, Lehrer, his distant cousin, deposited $9,000 in Katz's name in a bank in Switzerland. In current values, this is $100,000. Katz approached the JNF in February 1964, and in August 1965, the Claims Registry announced the location of a "significant deposit" in Lehrer's name. Again, the need for further documentation was mentioned, which would require some time, and again there were complaints of Swiss red tape.

Katz was asked, like the others, to provide the same documents, and in December 1965, he replied with a mixture of pain, naiveté, and cynicism:

To your question as to whether I have a death certificate for the late Leizer Lehrer, that is impossible. Most of Polish Jewry died in concentration camps, and its ashes were scattered all over Poland. Nonetheless, if this is necessary, it is possible to try [to acquire a death certificate], although there is little chance. . . . In my opinion, if the Swiss authorities will insist, this will only be an evasive tactic, as it is clear that if the account holder were still alive, he would contact them and demand his property.

The correspondence between Katz and the JNF continued for a number of years, and when Katz asked what was going on, he was told that the Swiss had not yet completed the process. In the meantime, in February

1968, a surprising development occurred. Attorney Grossman informed Katz that the Swiss reported the appearance of other claimants for Lehrer's inheritance. Katz replied that it was impossible that someone was more closely related than he was. The Swiss continued to demand various documents and letters flew back and forth until Katz's death in May 1968.

His heirs tried to continue the case, which was becoming more and more complex, due to the need to prove to the Swiss that Katz had, in fact, died. Only in March 1972, did Weil inform the JNF that in May 1971, it had become clear that Lehrer's account contained 138,000 francs (352,000 in current values), but the Office of the Guardian for Zurich had decided that the heirs were represented by Solomon Lehrer of Antwerp. It was not clear how this had been determined, if these heirs had received the money, or if they had encountered similar problems. The Katz family doubted the Lehrer's right to inherit the property, but to no avail.[19]

Hundreds of Israelis appealed to the Claims Registry in the 1960s, primarily through the JNF, and all were rejected. One of them was then Minister of Welfare Joseph Burg, one of Israel's most prominent politicians. In June 1964, Burg filled out the standard form, noted his profession as minister and asked that property belonging to his mother, Zvia Burg, be located. According to Burg, his mother had deposited cash and jewelry in Switzerland, and was later killed in Theresienstadt on October 7, 1942, after being denied entry into Switzerland. In an accompanying letter on official stationery, Burg wrote, "I don't know how the objects were transferred to Switzerland. I remember two platinum necklaces with diamonds and a few rings of this sort, as well as a sum of money. I do not know details." Of course, the family received nothing.[20]

In an extraordinary closure, Avraham Burg, Joseph Burg's son, served later as chair of the Jewish Agency, and was one of the leaders of the campaign to restore Jewish property. At the beginning of 1997, Joseph Burg was himself appointed as one of the Jewish organizations' three representatives of the fund established by the Swiss banks to aid survivors of Nazi persecution.

The moneys that were located but whose owners were not, were left in the hands of the Claims Registry, which published announcements in Switzerland and abroad about the money. In October 1970, however, the Ministry of Justice decided not to publish announcements in Communist countries. The Ministry of Justice and representatives of the cantons of Zurich and Basel decided to transfer the money directly to the fund set up for unclaimed assets originating in the Soviet Union, Albania, Bulgaria, Hungary, Poland, East Germany, Romania, Czechoslovakia and Yugoslavia.

This decision was very significant in view of the fact that half of the assets reported to the Claims Registry originally belonged to citizens of those countries. At the end of February 1964—the deadline for the reports—and with 90 percent of the total reports the Claims Registry received, 9,469,882.71 francs were registered. Of this, 4,809,812.80 francs were deposited by Eastern European nationals: 1,100,876 francs by Soviet citizens, 981,191 francs by Czechs, 934,447 francs by Poles, 572,478 francs by Bulgarians, 460,522 francs by Hungarians, 365,637 francs by Romanians, and 238,456 francs by Yugoslavians. (Current values in this paragraph are 3.3 times greater.)

After much discussion between the Ministry of Justice and the Foreign Ministry, a policy that did not require legislation was chosen, under which assets of Eastern European nationals would automatically be considered "unclaimed," without having to go through the entire search process. This declaration enabled the immediate transfer of assets to the fund that was to receive all unclaimed assets. What was not disclosed was that this policy also enabled the transfer to Warsaw and Budapest of assets belonging to those countries' nationals, as part of the agreement between the Swiss government and the governments of Poland and Hungary.[21]

After resolving the Eastern Europe problem, the Claims Registry had 4,080,237.28 francs in assets (8.5 million francs in current values). (In this work, sums do not always tally because these procedures lasted years and were affected by inflation and changes in currency exchange rates.) About half the money was later written off in a manner insufficiently explained by the Hug-Perrenoud report and the Israeli documents, leaving 2,593,010.64 francs (5.2 million francs in current values). Of these, more than half were in bank accounts (primarily current accounts), about 40 percent were in securities, and the remainder were in gold, jewelry, insurance policies, and works of art.[22] The write-off could be explained by the appearance of more owners, although this is not explicitly noted in the Hug-Perrenoud report. This lack of clarity will apparently have to be resolved by one of the various committees examining the affair.

In any case, it was now time to decide what to do with the remaining money. The 1962 law made a general determination that "if the owner of property registered [with the Claims Registry] didn't leave a rightful individual heir and left no instruction in the event of his death, the money will be transferred to a fund the government will establish. The use of the fund's money will be decided by the cabinet, which will consider the source of the deposited money."

When the moment came to distribute the money, the fund held 2,815,338.61 francs. Of this sum, 6,974 francs were paid to a Romanian heir and 10 percent was set aside to pay future claims. In October 1975, after lengthy negotiations with the international Jewish organizations and the local Swiss Jewish community, the legal department of the Swiss Foreign Ministry ordered the following distribution: 1,685,019.07 francs to the Jewish community, and 842,509.54 francs to the central office for refugees (current values are doubled). In the next years, a few more small sums were paid to heirs, securities held by the Claims Registry were sold, and, in 1980, the remainder was distributed at the same ratio of two-thirds to the local Jewish community (435,050.75 francs), and one-third to the refugee office (217,525.37 francs). (Multiply by 1.6 for current values).[23]

In 1975, Israel and the Jewish organizations expressed disappointment at the small amount of money: "It is unnecessary to state that we were unsatisfied with the fact that only a small portion of the assets were considered worthy of transfer to Jewish hands," wrote Jewish Agency CFO Yehiel Michel Giladi.[24] Another problem was the fact that the Jewish community in Switzerland asked to distribute the money itself, according to the recommendations of the Jewish Agency and the Joint. "The money was given by those who didn't own it, to those who didn't deserve it," World Jewish Congress's Israel Singer today defines the situation.[25]

In the end, 400,000 francs were transferred to an agricultural school in Israel for the purpose of building a dormitory for children studying there under the auspices of the Jewish Agency. The rest of the money (35,000 francs) also went to other schools in Israel, and documents indicate that the Joint eventually transferred its portion of the funds to Jewish Agency projects in Israel. From the point of view of the Jewish organizations, the story was over.

6

"WE GO TO WAR"
A New Generation Takes on
Righting the Wrongs

IN THE 1970s, the heads of the Swiss banks could breathe a sigh of relief. The 1962 law released them from the burden of handling Holocaust victims' accounts, and, more importantly, from the need to respond to hundreds of annoying applicants who nagged bank officials with trivial questions about a few hundred francs that some dubious relative might have deposited forty years earlier. In retrospect, many senior bank officials probably would have been willing to admit that the law they had so opposed had actually worked in their favor. For the price of less than 7 million francs, they had bought themselves a certificate of integrity and the right to hold on to all the rest of the money.

The certificate of integrity was not granted by the Swiss Bankers Association, but by the Swiss government itself. The SBA instructed its members to inform new applicants concerning the deposits that the 1962 law released them from all responsibility on the matter, and that the heirs' right to demand the return of money had now expired.[1] Meanwhile, the Ministry of Justice wrote a standard response to all those who petitioned them that the matter was affected by a statute of limitations, and "thus, we regret we are unable to help you in this matter." The Ministry of Justice directed the petitioners to the banks, saying they will provide you with the desired information if you are able to show, on the basis of legal documents, that you are the heir of the missing foreign or stateless person."[2]

In light of these conditions, it is no wonder that the petitioners continued to encounter an insurmountable wall and that some received no answer at all. Hannah Greenberg remembered that her father had told her three things the last time she saw him in the Warsaw Ghetto. She was four years old and was about to be smuggled to a hiding place in a Polish village. Her father told her, "Remember you are Jewish, remember you have family in the Land of Israel, and remember that after the war you must collect your dowry which is waiting in a bank in Switzerland." Her father, Arom Kestenberg, died in Buchenwald in April 1945, just one month before the end of the war. In 1964, at the height of the implementation of the 1962 law, Greenberg tried to claim the money, and was answered in the same way as Hass-Axelrad, Farkash and Katz: please provide a will and a death certificate. She gave up. After eighteen years, Greenberg sent letters to the 600 banks then operating in Switzerland. She did not receive a single reply.[3]

Jacob Friedman is one of the few people who can still testify that they deposited money themselves in a Swiss bank. In 1937–1938, Friedman, then seventeen years old, was sent by his father, Martin Friedman, from the Romanian city of Timisoara to Zurich to deposit money in one of three local banks. This was a lengthy undertaking—the train ride took a day and a half in each direction—as well as dangerous. Foreign currency smugglers in Romania could expect ten-year jail terms. Friedman went on this mission once every two to three months, traveling each time with an envelope containing 22,500 francs (153,000 francs in current values). A number written on the envelope indicated one of his father's numbered accounts in Zurich.

When the young Friedman reached the Zurich train station, he got on a streetcar and traveled to Anwend Street, the home of a family friend Chiel Riger. From there, Friedman headed to one of the three banks in which his father had numbered accounts: UBS, Wohl-Landau, and Swiss Bank Corp. In the evening, Riger called Martin Friedman and confirmed the deposit. In total, Jacob Friedman says, he made eight deposits. If each was a regular sum of 153,000 francs, these accounts have a current value of 1.22 million francs. Martin Friedman was sent to Auschwitz on May 28, 1944, the Jewish Pentecost (Shavuot). In the 1970s, Jacob Friedman and his wife Margarita tried to locate the accounts. The banks' response: without the numbers of the accounts, it was impossible to locate the money.[4]

An extraordinary case relates to the account of Joseph Blum held in UBS. Although Blum was not a Holocaust victim, as he passed away before the war, his heirs were Holocaust survivors, who tried in vain to obtain their money. This is an interesting and unusual case, since the heirs knew the exact number of the account and the date it was opened, and were still told in the 1970s that they could not receive their money. The story is therefore all the more indicative of what those who could not give an exact account number were told, and these were the vast majority of the petitioners.

Joseph Blum, a vodka manufacturer from the town of Prostiev, Czechoslovakia, opened account number 21300 in UBS's central branch in Zurich on May 5, 1938. As a protection against forgery and theft, it was agreed that the bank would honor only those instructions in which a period appeared after the letter B in the name Blum. Thirteen days later, Blum passed away. His son and daughter, Louisa and Heinz, who were registered at the bank as co-owners of the account, inherited it.

In 1940, after the Gestapo raided the family home, Louisa, who had married in the meantime, understood that no written notes should be left that would enable anyone else to get their hands on the account in UBS. She destroyed the bank documents, and wrote a few vital details in the form of initials in a cookbook that she hid. Louisa and Heinz were arrested and transported from Theresienstadt to Bergen-Belsen to Auschwitz, but miraculously survived. The two could not get into the bank account at UBS, as the cookbook had disappeared, and Louisa only found it in 1971, when the notes in the cookbook enabled the receipt of another bank account, one that their father had opened in the Anglo-Palestine Company (now Bank Leumi) in Israel.

In contrast, an unpleasant surprise awaited them in Switzerland. In February 1971, UBS replied to Louisa that "Using the few details you provided, we have conducted another search for your father's account, opened after 1938, but, regretfully, without success." The bank made it clear that further details would probably not change the result, "as the requirement to maintain books is legally effective for just ten years after the last entry." This was further proof that the banks methodically destroyed documents for dormant accounts.

Louisa Blum did not give up, and sometime later received a different and weird answer from UBS: "After a lengthy examination of the documents remaining in our archives concerning accounts opened no later than December 13, 1941, we found that account number 21300, in the name of Mr. Joseph Blum, Miss Louisa Blum and Mr. Heinz Blum, was opened on May 5, 1938. It is therefore entirely clear to us that this account was paid out before the end of 1941 and added to other accounts." The bank added that it was impossible to determine the exact date the account was closed, "as all documents referring to accounts paid out before 1941 were destroyed a long time ago, along with all relevant correspondence." UBS summarized: "No claim whatsoever can be filed, and the matter is closed from our perspective."

Their answer is puzzling. If the documents were destroyed, how did the bank know the account was opened and later closed? What does "added to other accounts" mean? Is the bank claiming Blum had other accounts there? And, of course, the main question: who ordered the account's closure? Joseph Blum died two weeks after he opened it. His children did not close it. Forgery is unlikely in light of the special identification required of those signing instructions to the bank. Is this an unusual case, or is this what UBS did with other accounts when it thought there were no heirs?

All the family's attempts to receive further information from the bank were fruitless, and they clearly never saw a penny of the money, whose current value (without interest) would be about $200,000. Interestingly, at the beginning of 1997, at the height of the storm surrounding the deposits affair, the bank remembered the case and offered 100,000 francs, but the family rejected the offer. In 1999, the bank announced to the family that the offer was cancelled. As of this writing, the case is still pending, along with all the question marks surrounding it.[5]

Israel and the Jewish organizations no longer wanted to deal with the matter of the deposits that caused so much trouble for twenty years. Attorney and Holocaust survivor Amram Blum, who was Israel's general custodian for twenty years, recounts that "When I took office in 1973 and started to stir the matter up a little, the Israeli Foreign Ministry told me that I was preaching to the pope and the matter had already been handled and closed. It could be that they had reached the conclusion that there was not much money, and that it wasn't worth straining relations with Switzerland for this."[6]

In 1988, Akiva Lewinsky, whose actions are controversial among the interested parties, entered the picture. At a Jewish Agency rally in February 1988, Lewinsky was completing a term as the organization's treasurer when then president Raya Jaglom of WIZO (a worldwide Jewish women's volunteer organization), raised the problem of the deposits in Switzerland. Jaglom did not have any real information on the matter, and it appears that she was responding to the reports and rumors that have always surrounded the affair: there is a problem, a lot of money may be left, something should be done.

Handling of the issue was delegated to the Swiss-born Lewinsky, because of his financial experience, because he was a senior member of the Conference for Jewish Material Claims Against Germany and handled property issues, and because his friends were looking for respectable employment for him. Lewinsky says:

I thought it was almost impossible, because it was clear to me what problems there would be to prove the connection between the property and the people fifty years later. . . . I said I was willing to try, without promising results. I started to investigate if anyone knew anything about property of his own or of his parents. No one remembered, and those who did remember, didn't remember accurately. We reached a dead end, I was about to give up, but I decided I could not surrender.

Among other things, Lewinsky made indirect contact, via mediators, with some of the banks. "I suggested they make a gesture," he recalls, although he will not say what sum was discussed. "The answer was, 'If we agree to something small, that will be an admission of guilt, and we are unwilling to do that.' And that's how it was torpedoed." In practice, Lewinsky's work amounted to the collection of information on the fate of Jewish accounts, and random contact with bank branch managers for the purposes of receiving more specific information.[7]

The renewed struggle against the Swiss banks was led by three Jewish dignitaries—Israel Singer, Edgar Bronfman, and Avraham Burg. Israel Singer, the secretary-general of the World Jewish Congress, plays a key role in the Swiss deposits story. He is a unique character: ordained as a modern Orthodox rabbi, he is a lawyer and owner of vast real estate holdings in places as far-flung as Miami and Nigeria. He is articulate and able to completely confuse a listener with a torrent of details and subjects—sometimes exaggerated—that he squeezes into a single conversation. Singer adroitly exploits the media for the purposes of the World Jewish Congress, and is a tough negotiator. He disdains notes and the handling of everyday matters.

When asked about the current struggle, Singer talks a great deal about World Jewish Congress president Edgar Bronfman's power. A colorful and unusual leader, Bronfman, along with his brother Charles, heads Seagram, a $15 billion international holding company. *Forbes* magazine estimates Bronfman's personal wealth at $3.3 billion, which allowed him during the crisis to tell the Swiss bankers, who were offering a $250 million settlement, "Don't do any favors. I'll give the money myself." Most important, with capital like that, Bronfman has an open door to people at the highest levels of the United States, including the Oval Office.

Bronfman is easily angered, and "starts cursing so even I need a translator," says an activist who knows him well. Bronfman says that he manages Seagram's dictatorially, and that is how things get done. He is unwilling to have the wool pulled over his eyes and does not accept wasting time as a negotiating tactic. For all intents and purposes, he sees the negotiations with the Swiss as a business negotiation. As we will see, in one meeting with the Swiss, Bronfman was truly enraged by what he saw as the banks' "dragging their feet," stood up, left the room, and literally slammed the door. From that point on, the talks moved at a much faster pace.

Bronfman became president of the World Jewish Congress in 1980. He took a dormant organization and made it combative. Bronfman led the movement against Kurt Waldheim when his dubious World War II past was discovered. Although claims about Waldheim's active involvement in war crimes were never proven, Bronfman's success was reflected by the nearly complete boycott of Waldheim while he was president of Austria (1986–1992). Bronfman and the World Jewish Congress fulfilled an important role in opening the gates of the Soviet Union for Jewish emigration to Israel with the collapse of the Communist regime. However, in the mid-1990s, the organization needed a new cause célèbre, and the property affair in general, and Switzerland in particular, came along with perfect timing.[8]

The third member of the group leading the campaign in the deposits affair is Avraham Burg, chair of the Jewish Agency between February 1995 and June 1999. Burg is possibly one of the most complex figures in the affair. He is religious, but has opinions that anger many in the Israeli religious community. He is the son of Joseph Burg, the historical leader of Israel's right-wing National Religious Party, but has very left-wing political opinions. An intelligent, charismatic man, he is quick to use his sharp tongue, sometimes reacting in an extreme way for the sake of making headlines. Burg is the person who saved the Jewish Agency from bankruptcy, but still has trouble explaining to most of the Israeli public why the Agency is needed when a Jewish state already exists.

Zvi Barak, then co-chair with Singer of the World Jewish Restitution Organization, has played an important, though not leading, role in the struggle against the banks. From the first day the Jewish organizations decided to devote their time to the matter, Barak has been on the front lines. "If Singer is the good cop and Burg is the bad cop, Barak is the worst cop," a source describes their characters. Barak is "the worst cop" in the good sense. An unrelentingly aggressive man, he pushed the Swiss into the corner allowing his colleagues to compromise just a little less, which is a lot more than they would have achieved without his extreme actions.

The triumvirate of Bronfman, Burg, and Singer set the tone in the campaign against the Swiss banks. All three share two important characteristics: they belong to a generation that was born or came of age after the Holocaust, and they are not afraid to make a scene when they believe there is a need. As none were born in Europe, but in the United States and Israel, they are free of the mentality that characterized—for better or worse— European Jews, who lived for hundreds of years in constant fear of losing their lives and their property. Naturally, these Jews and their leaders are more accustomed to pleading than demanding, and using lobbyists more than the media.

Bronfman, Burg, and Singer think and act differently from the previous generations. In their opinion, the Jewish people have rights just like any other people, and they are obligated to demand them. Their attitude is that no one does any favors for the Jews by treating them in an egalitarian manner: they claim this is proper behavior and does not deserve any special thanks. If people do not understand this, it has to be explained more than once, then so be it.

Another important factor in the current struggle is that now some time has passed since the Holocaust, which has allowed a campaign for restitution to emerge in a more forceful way. Survivors snatched from the flames often had difficulty explaining to themselves why they remained alive, and felt an understandable aversion to dealing with questions of money, homes, securities, and jewelry. With Europe littered along its length and breadth with the bodies of Holocaust victims and physical and emotional wounds still bleeding, could any of the survivors think about what happened to their father's Swiss bank account? They were also troubled by the much more pressing question of learning to survive, living in barren camps, emigrating to Israel or some other country, and rebuilding their lives. They did not have the financial means to begin a campaign for the restitution of their property while the attention of the Jewish organizations was justifiably focused on refugee rehabilitation and the struggle to establish the State of Israel.

Nonetheless, post–World War II Jewish leaders had to deal with the matter of the looted property, as they knew that the question, as difficult and cynical as it was, was critical to rehabilitating refugees and establishing a state.[9] The discussions, however, primarily revolved around claiming reparations from Germany as part of the overall payment for the loss of property, and not claims for the return of private property held in other countries. The Jewish organizations became aware of the deposits in Switzerland at the end of the 1940s, and were very active on this matter in the next decade. After the 1962 law the organizations let the matter drop, for they did not foresee any better solution.

In the mid-90s, the picture changed from this point of view also. The state of Israel was a fait accompli, and the Mideast peace process seemed to be leading toward a long-term footing. The opening of the gates of the Soviet Union did place a new and heavy burden on the Jewish organizations, particularly the Jewish Agency, but these problems were close to resolution by the middle of the decade. When the Swiss banks affair first exploded in 1995, the heads of the World Jewish Congress and the Jewish Agency were free to take on a new battle, which certainly did not hurt their public image, to say the least.

There were a few more points that aided the renewed campaign. In the United States, documents pertaining to Operation Safehaven—conducted by the United States and Britain near the end of the war to locate German assets—were being declassified in the mid-1990s. These documents, as we will see in Chapter 9, include massive and valuable data about relations between Switzerland and Germany during the war, particularly the vast financial aid Bern granted to Berlin. They also contain important details concerning Jewish property in Switzerland. Their great importance for the deposits affair will soon become apparent.

The fall of the Iron Curtain also had a great deal of significance in the struggle against Switzerland. The collapse of Communism set off the handling of the Jewish property problem, focusing on the possibility of getting back some of the property in Eastern Europe that had been looted first by the brownshirts, and later nationalized by the robbers in red.

Singer first heard about the deposits problem from his many acquaintances in Switzerland. His wife Evelyn comes from a Swiss family and still holds Swiss citizenship. Evelyn's parents met in the office of attorney Georges Brunschvig, a leader in the Swiss Jewish community, who had a prominent role in the negotiations with the Swiss government in the 1950s.

Singer recalls a conversation from the early 1970s: "Brunschvig handled a number of transactions for me. I was a guest in his home. He told me about the deposits, saying 'If sometime you want to do something really interesting, go find out what happened to the Jewish money.' "

Another person who told Singer about the deposits problem was Max Kimchi, "a banker from a bank called Kimchi-Landau who told me there are billions of dollars buried here. . . . I liked Kimchi very much. He used to get up at noon and say that his American clients didn't get up any earlier than 7–8 A.M. New York time, so why should he get up before noon Zurich time? He showed me a warehouse in 1972 in which Jewish art treasures were stored [stolen goods transferred by Germany to Switzerland]. That stuck in my mind and I said to myself that one day I would handle that."

That "one day" came in the last years of the Communist regime. In 1987, Singer received the first clues about the property in Switzerland from East Germany of all places, then still under the rule of Erich Honecker. The reason for this was that "they wanted us to go elsewhere and leave them alone, something like: go after the real thieves," Singer explains. The notoriously brutal and infamous Stasi (the East German secret police) had collected a vast amount of information about everything and everyone, including the accounts of Jews in Switzerland, even from before World War II. This information began to make its way to Singer, some of it purchased with Bronfman's own money.

In 1993, with the Iron Curtain in the past, Singer was one of the initiators of the World Jewish Restitution Organization (WJRO), of which he is still co-chair. The organization's president is the president of the World Jewish Congress (Bronfman) and the Jewish Agency chair (in 1993, Simha Dinitz, then Burg), is a co-chair. The WJRO includes the ten key Jewish organizations in the world that have an interest in the matter. As a formality, Bronfman and Burg acted on the Swiss matter in the name of the WJRO, but in practice, the matter is handled by the World Jewish Congress and the Jewish Agency.

On visits to Eastern Europe after 1993, as part of his WJRO work, Singer occasionally heard more about the accounts in Switzerland. Among other things, Singer was informed about a document from one of the Eastern European spy agencies that mentioned 17,000 accounts belonging to Polish Jews that were transferred to Switzerland. "I had old angers, I had old 'accounting' with the Swiss, due to what I had heard years earlier," Singer says. After that, he began to work intensively. In 1993–1994, in truth, the work mainly focused on collecting information, with plans for practical action when there was enough data.[10]

In the meantime, a surprising development occurred in Switzerland. On September 11, 1994, the Swiss newspaper *Sonntag Zeitung* published a general article about property without heirs in Swiss banks, virtually without mentioning Holocaust victims. In the reporter's opinion, there were 2 billion francs (then $1.4 billion) in "orphaned" accounts. "Foreign heirs and others try to trace the treasure, mostly without success," the article stated. The article's closing paragraphs were amazingly accurate.

Banking experts estimate that most of the deposits gathering dust in Switzerland belong to foreign concerns. On the one hand, these are dubious businessmen, who intentionally sever contact with a bank for years. On the other hand, there are many foreign heirs feeling around in the dark, since the deceased account owners often hid black market money, without leaving traces.

The chances to uncover these assets are slim, and the Bankers Association doesn't make it any easier. The depositor's travel habits can often hint at the location of the bank managing his money. But in the case of assets that presumably belonged to Jews or missing persons, whose post–World War II fate is unknown, and the existence of which the grandchildren and great-grandchildren raise again and again, the bank's behavior borders on the truly cynical.[11]

Among those who read the article was Otto Piller, then a senior member of the Upper House of the Swiss Parliament who later moved to a senior position in the Ministry of the Interior. "This was always an important issue for me," Piller says. "Our banking system has a very good reputation, and for these two reasons I submitted a motion in Parliament. It was important to me that if there was money without heirs in the banks, not necessarily that of Holocaust victims, that they should inform the government of that. I didn't have any real information, but I was sure there was such money in the banks."[12] In the motion Piller submitted in 1994, he asked the government:

What is the current legal status that enables the banks to act in this manner? Does the government know the scope of the assets acquired by the banks in this manner? Are such procedures routine, sporadic or possibly even without the knowledge of the Supervision of Banks? If the Supervision of Banks is not regularly and completely aware of such cases, is the government willing to change the legislative basis, in order to ensure that supervisory institutions will be notified in the future of such cases? Doesn't the government believe these assets, which have allegedly become "property without owners," should become state property in the future, and not the property of the banks?[13]

The Swiss government's answer was mostly evasive and accepted the banks' position. Nevertheless, it uncovered the beginning of talks between the government and the banks concerning a comprehensive investigation of the problem of deposits without heirs, an investigation that would quickly become one of the peaks of the crisis. In actuality, the SBA final report from that investigation in February 1996 completely changed the face of the struggle, brought it to the American arena and more or less determined that the banks would be defeated.

When the government answered Piller's motion, however, no one dreamt of these dramatic developments. According to the government, as long as a bank did not provide legal notification of the cancellation of its relationship with the client, it could not begin counting the required ten years before acting according to the regulations covering dormant accounts. There is a contradiction here: If the client-bank relationship is canceled, then the account is closed, and cannot be declared dormant. If there are no dormant accounts without such cancellations, then what are dormant accounts?

The government added, "Reality indicates that legal heirs of bank clients residing abroad often know only of the existence of a deposit in Switzerland [and not the specific details] and must therefore investigate at all the banks in which such a deposit could exist. The banks charge the cost of such investigations to the interested parties. However, the Supervision of Banks does not officially know of banks' methodical appropriation of foreign deposits, or refusals to give deposits to known legal heirs."

In other words, the Supervision of Banks heard about cases in which the banks appropriated moneys for themselves or refused to return them, but could not substantiate the rumors. A superficial investigation would have revealed to supervision officials what was found with great ease in the coming months by journalists from all over the world, that the banks created insurmountable obstacles for claimants.

The Swiss Federal Council responded to Piller's motion in the following way:

Therefore, the government cannot be a partner to the fears expressed in this motion. Nonetheless, the government believes that, in the interests of Switzerland as a banking center, it would be worthwhile to simplify the investigations of people entitled to search for deposits in Swiss banks. Therefore, the Supervision of Banks, unrelated to the abovementioned motion, has launched talks with the Swiss Bankers Association. These talks will not emphasize enforcement of Supervision, but solutions to problems of individual rights.[14]

In January 1995, Singer tried to move the process along. He was summoned to a meeting of a Bern Parliamentary committee, at the close of which the banks announced the establishment of an internal committee to examine the procedures for handling dormant accounts and whether such accounts exist.[15] It then appeared that there was no chance that this new investigation would be more successful than those conducted decades earlier. Furthermore, the banks could now brandish the 1962 law, and claim that they had already done everything they could, and finally, bury forever the entire affair.

At that time, Rolf Bloch, the president of the Federation of Swiss Jewish Communities entered the picture. He had noted the reports following Piller's motion, the government's answer and the parliamentary debate, and approached the Bankers Association in February or March of 1995. "I only asked to direct their attention to the possibility that they had dormant accounts," Bloch says. "I told them they must set new operative guidelines based on the assumption these were Jewish accounts, which had to be handled in a special manner, and that death certificates and the like would not be available. I told them, 'this subject had to be handled more sensitively.' "

Predictably, the SBA told Bloch that everything had already been settled according to the 1962 law. Bloch responded by reminding the bankers that the banks were to set aside the deposits originating in Eastern Europe, and that it was now possible, with the fall of Communism, that new heirs would appear and claim the deposits. "I had no concept of the scope of the problem," Bloch admits. "It was a matter of principle, and not about the sum. The Bankers Association response was, 'We understand there is a problem, and we will try to consider what you have said. We will look and see.' "[16]

This sleepy picture—an internal bank investigation with no outside oversight and a declaration that Holocaust victims' accounts would probably not be found—began to change in April 27, 1995. On Israel's Holocaust Memorial Day, I published the first comprehensive investigative report of the affair in *Globes*, Israel's financial daily, which led some of the central Jewish activists, primarily Burg, to deal with the matter. According to what these activists have said publicly a number of times, the report was also a catalyst to putting the matter on the public agenda, which, in retrospect, was extremely important.

The *Globes* article was based on two primary sources—Israeli Foreign Ministry files and a field investigation at the Swiss banks. The documents published in this report were presented in Chapter 1, as well as the answers I received concerning the retention of documentation in Swiss banks. The article covered the phases of the deposits' affair, from when it was first put on the agenda in the 1940s through the 1962 legislation and its implementation.

The most important findings concerned the banks' treatment of claimants, as revealed in October 1994, when they were asked to provide information about potential accounts of deceased relatives. My investigation was conducted in the Geneva branches of the three major banks, along with the Warburg Bank and the Julius Baer bank, under the assumption that Jewish depositors might have chosen them because of their Jewish ownership.

Typical of the banks' requests were those stated by two representatives of UBS. They asked for a letter from all the deceased's heirs authorizing the Geneva branch to conduct the necessary investigation: "The signatures must be properly notarized," the bank emphasized. They also demanded a payment of 300 francs, "to cover our costs in conducting the investigation in all the bank's Geneva branches." Parenthetically, they stated that as the bank does not maintain older documents, there is no possibility of locating accounts more than ten years old.

UBS suggested making contact with one of the officials responsible for assets in its Geneva branch. In a meeting with him, he noted a few legal requirements: presentation of original documents (succession order, power of attorney, etc.), as well as a valid international writ from an Israeli court (known as an Apostil) verifying each document, as notarization would be insufficient. The official also explained that the ten-year limit that appeared in the letter from the bank applied only if the account was closed, but if the account was still open, the documents were kept indefinitely. Also, since UBS's Geneva branches are a subsidiary of the entire group, events could only be investigated in that city. In order to search for an account throughout Switzerland, it would be necessary to appeal to the head management in Zurich. Other banks noted that such investigations would cost 1,000 francs.

Interviews at the six banks revealed a number of important things. First, most banks buried the heirs' requests for information in a sea of burdensome legal demands. Power of attorney, signature verification and Apostils are not just trouble, they involve a substantial financial outlay. Second, the investigation fees alone were enough to deter many petitioners. Was it worth 1,000 francs to find out if the account existed, without knowing anything about its size or the possibility of obtaining the money? In the 1990s, there are about 400 banks operating in Switzerland. Was it worth spending 400,000 francs on an attempt to find information, before receiving even a single penny? Many heirs probably gave up at that point. Third, the ten-year limit remains the biggest question mark and greatest stumbling block in the entire affair.

My investigation also covered the official position of the Swiss government and the SBA as of October 1994, which were essentially identical and unambiguous: the banks obeyed the 1962 law. Both bodies confirmed that the Bern government did not examine whether the banks reported properly, but did say there was no doubt that the reports were complete.

Dr. Giacomo Roncoroni of the Ministry of Justice's commercial department said, "The banks transferred much more money than they originally reported possessing, which is a sign they transferred everything. I do not believe they robbed the depositors. It is hard for me to see who can be blamed for anything today: we did everything possible at the time. Nonetheless, anyone who wanted to cheat, could always have done so."

Attorney Silvia Matile-Steiner, the SBA's legal secretary, said, "I cannot imagine that the banks did not report. They had no reason to intentionally

Union Bank of Switzerland

Schweizerische Bankgesellschaft
Union de Banques Suisses
Unione di Banche Svizzere

Rue du Rhône 8
P.O. Box 2950
1211 Geneva 2

Telephone 022 388 11 11
Telex 422 861

Direct Dialing   022/388.67.45

REGISTERED AIR MAIL

Mr. Itamar LEVIN
39, Bloch St.

IL - 64681 TEL AVIV

Our ref.	Your letter of	Your ref.	Date
ANSU ZBI.			7th October 1994

Dear Sir,

We acknowledge with thanks receipt of your fax dated 6th instant.

In reply, please note that no enquiries can be taken on before having provided us with :

- a letter signed by the heirs of your grandfather, authorizing the **Union Bank of Switzerland in Geneva** to carry out the necessary inquiries and to inform you about their results, their signature having to be duly **authenticated**

- a sum of **Sw.Fr. 300.--** to cover our charges concerning the inquiries which will be made through all branches of the Union Bank of Switzerland in Geneva (no investigation can be made prior to ten years ago which is the term for keeping our files according to Swiss Law, i.e. prior to 1984).

Upon reception of this letter, we invite you to contact us by phone (tel. 022/388.67.45), in order to fix an appointment with Mr. HARDER, in charge of the Bank's estate department.

We thank you in advance and remain

Yours faithfully,
Union Bank of Switzerland

Union Bank of Switzerland's letter to the author concerning inquiries into Holocaust victim's account, October 7, 1994. (Author's files) hide accounts from the government. We have a long-time reputation to defend, and if it were discovered that a bank cheated, that would be very serious for its reputation." In response to the question whether she thought there was a place for some gesture from the banks, as Akwa Lewinsky had tried to convince them to do, Matile-Steiner said, "The banks believe that they did everything they could in the framework of the 1962 law, and they have no reason to give more money."

The *Globes* report led to passionate responses from two people, MK (Member of Knesset) Avraham Hirschson and Avraham Burg. Hirschson has been involved for many years in documenting Holocaust history and is the initiator of the annual March of the Living youth walk from Auschwitz to Birkenau. Hirschson pushes hard to promote the issues close to his heart, and although his remarks are not always the most accurate, they do make the boldest headlines, a legitimate consideration for a politician.

The day the investigative report was published, Hirschson asked then Knesset Speaker Shevach Weiss, a Holocaust survivor himself, to urgently place the subject on the agenda. "The article about the unconscionable appropriation of Holocaust victims money by Swiss bankers, presents additional questions concerning the measure of fairness the Swiss relate to themselves, particularly in all matters concerning the moneys managed by them," Hirschson wrote to Weiss. "Taking the property of a helpless person is horrible, but all the more serious, when the helplessness is the Jews led to the slaughter by the many-headed Nazi monster. This affair requires urgent Knesset attention, which must issue an unambiguous call to arms to both the Israeli government and Switzerland, to act immediately to correct this horrific wrong."[17]

Within a few days of the report, Burg met with then Prime Minister Yitzhak Rabin and the issue of the Holocaust deposits came up in conversation. Burg recalls:

In 1994, when I wasn't at the Jewish Agency yet, Israel Singer told me he was traveling to Switzerland, as we have been friends for fifteen years and speak often. I came into the picture a day or two after Holocaust Memorial Day, after the *Globes* article, when I was in Rabin's office and he asked what the story was. I told him, "Listen, there is something here, and for some time now Jews have been talking around this point, and I believe there is something here."

Rabin told me, "This is very interesting. Do this, because it is the mission of your generation, the one our generation didn't manage to handle. Go with the international Jewish organizations and talk to Edgar [Bronfman], because it cannot be the role of the State of Israel since we have other interests with Switzerland." I spoke with Israel that day and sent e-mail to Edgar. Until then, it had been a glove with no fist, because we had not yet gone to the public, and I told Israel, "for this, we go to war." The whole way, Israel and I have shown a completely unified front, although we don't always agree. In this context, I am far more extreme than he is, more aggressive. That's why I told him, "we go to war."

In Burg's opinion, the decision to launch an open, public campaign was a "promotion," and he explains it this way: "I imagine the entire thing as a campaign to topple a wall. Bronfman is the end of the battering ram, but there are also a bunch of guys holding the ram and banging it into the wall. Israel didn't go to the media, and I don't know why. When I entered the picture, a certain dimension of aggressiveness entered the picture. I felt that without an international effort, we would not vanquish the Swiss. The media is one of my tools, and I do that everywhere."

Burg also does not deny that the Jewish Agency's image, and therefore his own, was one of his motives for getting involved in the affair. "I stated explicitly in one forum that the Jewish Agency must handle this for three reasons. First of all, it had been involved in compensation and reparations and the various property matters, and that is an ongoing responsibility. Secondly, I felt that there had been those from within the Jewish Agency who handled the affair and failed. And thirdly, a fighting Agency is better than a sleepy Agency, and this is a good subject for a battle."[18]

In the meantime, the Swiss press had become interested in the developing affair. The findings of the *Globes* investigation were widely reported by the local Swiss media, which were already aware of the problem to some extent due to some public attention at the end of 1994 and the beginning of 1995.

On May 7, 1995, the Parliament convened in Bern for a celebratory session to mark the fiftieth anniversary of Germany's surrender. Then president Kaspar Villiger used the opportunity to ask the forgiveness of the Jewish people for the Swiss initiative that led to the stamping of the letter J in the passports of German Jews. According to him, "This was an unforgivable move" that stemmed from anti-Semitism, fear of immigration, and the desire for closer relations with Germany.[19] The Jewish organizations took note of his remarks and identified Villiger as someone it was possible to talk to about the deposits affair. Burg and Singer both voiced the same sentiment: "If all the Swiss were as decent as Villiger, we would have much easier lives."[20]

Ten days later, on May 17, the Knesset debated a motion proposed by Hirschson based on the report in *Globes.* Hirschson reiterated the principal findings and stated, "I call on the Israeli government to act immediately in every accepted and possible channel to convince the Swiss government to do everything necessary to locate the accounts and transfer these moneys to the State of Israel." According to him, these funds could help those disabled by the Holocaust, currently granted "mere crumbs in the government budget."

Then Minister of Finance Avraham Shochat's reply was the first official government remark on the affair in more than thirty years. Shochat briefly reviewed developments on the subject and then set Israeli government policy:

The total sum declared by the Swiss banks as belonging to those persecuted by the Nazis was a ridiculous, small and naturally unrealistic 10 million Swiss francs. Most of the money, 8 million francs, was transferred to heirs who demanded it and some to Jewish institutions and the State of Israel.[21] As far as we know, the investigation at the Swiss banks did not include numbered accounts, safes, and corporate accounts of companies owned by Jews in which Jewish property was held. . . . It is clear that the Swiss banks announcement that the scope of these accounts amounted to 10 million francs was not credible to anyone who dealt with the matter.

Concerning the restoration of property in Eastern Europe, there is coordination between the Israeli government, the World Jewish Congress, the Jewish Agency and WJRO, which is operating in Eastern European countries. These concerns will consult and coordinate an effort to clarify the problem of the Swiss government. The government of Israel was recognized in the past, both by the government of Germany and other governments, as having a valid claim to Jewish property and Jewish property without heirs. Based on this recognition, I will recommend to the Foreign Minister [Shimon Peres] to push the Swiss government to take renewed action on the entire subject. At this time, we at the Ministry of Finance and Foreign Ministry will study the subject."[22]

The debate in the Knesset was very important not only because it placed the subject on the government's agenda, but because it brought the subject to the attention of the global media. A June 1995, article in the Israeli English-language weekly *Jerusalem Report* was also of great importance as it helped direct the attention of the foreign journalists in Israel to the matter. It was the first article to tell the personal stories of heirs who had failed in their attempts to receive their relatives' money, stories that would receive a great deal of attention in the next few years.

The foreign press began to discover the affair in the spring of 1995. After reports in Switzerland and in London's *Jewish Chronicle* immediately following the *Globes* investigation, some of the most important newspapers in the world began to cover the affair. The U.S. magazine *Business Week* wrote an article on May 22, 1995, while on June 21, the story made the front page of the *Wall Street Journal*. The influential newspaper wrote that the banks were hiding behind banking confidentiality and refusing to respond to petitioners. The reporter felt that the bank's attitude raised a strong sense they had something to hide. According to the *Journal*, two leading banks, Swiss Bank and UBS, now recognized that they could not reject all the claims and that they had property belonging to Nazi victims. The *Journal* felt that this time, as opposed to the past, the banks would not be able to dodge the matter so easily.

The international press played a central role, and it is therefore important to note the central media outlets that covered the matter. This also demonstrates the international interest that brought about heavy pressure on Switzerland.

7

"IT'S THE PRINCIPLE"
The Beginning of a Frontal Assault
on the Banks

THE NATURE OF historic events, which develop over time, is such that it is usually difficult to pinpoint their beginnings. It is usually possible, however, to mark milestones in the process, events that significantly change the situation. In the affair of the Jewish deposits in Switzerland, June 16, 1995, is such a date.

This was the day when Avraham Burg first participated in a meeting of the executive committee of the World Jewish Restitution Organization (WJRO). As the recently appointed chair of the Jewish Agency (having taken over the position just four months previously), Burg replaced Simha Dinitz as the co-chair of WJRO. Originally, the June 16, meeting had been scheduled to discuss the matter of property in Eastern Europe, but Burg raised another question, asking, "What are we going to do about Switzerland?" It was decided to name Israel Singer and Zvi Barak, the joint chairs of the management of WJRO, to examine the problem and report back to the next meeting of the presidency.[1] Jewish activity, which until then had focused on gathering information, now moved on to the next stage.

Barak and Singer began to look for someone in Switzerland with whom they could negotiate and encountered quite a few closed doors. Finally, with the help of Maram Stern, the World Jewish Congress representative in Brussels, a meeting was scheduled on July 5 with Jean-Paul Chapuis, general manager of the Swiss Bankers Association (SBA), and his deputy, Heinrich Schneider. The meeting was pointless. The bankers held the meeting to tell Singer and Barak that they were only willing to talk with the president of the Swiss Jewish community, Rolf Bloch.

On July 17, Singer and Barak returned to Bern and approached the supervisor of banks, Kurt Hauri. The pair was disappointed to discover that Hauri was not a powerful commissioner, but a fairly weak Ministry of Finance clerk, particularly in light of the fact that the banks are subject to cantonal supervision on most matters, and not bound by Hauri's federal supervision. Singer asked whether Hauri believed that there was a problem with dormant Jewish accounts, a rhetorical question, since the Jewish leaders were already convinced that a problem existed, as Singer explains:

I knew there was such a problem because I had already read the Washington Accord. I knew there was a problem since I had already seen the first documents from the "Safehaven" files. I knew there was such a problem as I had already seen evidence of money transfers between Poland and Switzerland. I knew there was a problem because I had already talked with a number of people who had handled the matter in an unofficial capacity. I had a lot of evidence that there was a problem, and when I detailed the evidence for Hauri, he also knew there was a problem.[2]

The painstaking, methodical gathering of information began to bear fruit.

Singer and Barak, who spent the next few years flying dozens of times between New York, Zurich, and Tel Aviv, returned to Bern on August 16 for another meeting with Hauri. In the interim, Hauri had managed to study the matter a little, and not only acknowledged the problem, but was also willing to handle it aggressively. "He told us that we had to talk to each bank separately as well as the Swiss Bankers Association, since according to Swiss law, a bank must act appropriately and fairly," Singer recalls. "Hauri said that if a bank does not act appropriately and fairly, he could revoke its license. Hauri was the first person in Switzerland to handle the problem seriously and fairly. His threat to revoke licenses was the only reason that the banks were even willing to talk to us."[3]

During their visits to Switzerland, Barak and Singer also met with representatives of what were then the three major banks, Union Bank of Switzerland (UBS), Swiss Bank Corp, and Credit Suisse. Union Bank of Switzerland and Swiss Bank Corp. have since merged into United Bank of Switzerland, also known as UBS. They also met with the SBA legal advisor, and with two representatives of the central bank. The pair heard the same answer from all of them: no case, nothing to talk about, everything was closed according to the 1962 law; the same answers that had been given to the press and to the heirs. Meanwhile, the two men met with Rolf Bloch, who succeeded in setting up a meeting for Burg and Bronfman with then Swiss president Kaspar Villiger. When the bankers learned of this, they also agreed to meet with Bronfman and Burg, after their last planned meeting with the president. Both meetings were scheduled for September 14.[4]

On September 11, 1995, the heads of both the WJRO and the European Jewish communities met in Brussels to discuss the ongoing matter of restoration of Jewish property in Europe. On the periphery of the meeting, the heads of the Jewish organizations prepared for the meetings in Bern. Bronfman, Burg, Singer, and Barak were rather worried, as essentially they had no hard proof to present to Villiger and the heads of the banks.

Another problem arose as they prepared for the meeting, when the participants received a surprise message from the offices of the Swiss president

that Villiger was unwilling to meet with Burg, as Burg had begun to publicly attack Switzerland and threaten a boycott. Singer turned to Burg and
said, "There is a problem, they don't want you." Burg, with a sharp eye
toward the press, immediately took the golden opportunity and responded:

Israel, go back and tell them that if they are making that selection, I will show up
at the front gate of the Federal Palace and stand on the steps. Press from all over
the world will be there. If the president doesn't receive me, I will hold a press
conference and announce that Switzerland is continuing the selection of Jews, in
those words. They should tell the president that if this is what he wants, that's fine
with me, since the Swiss didn't accept my grandmother as an immigrant forty years
ago. What do I care? That's just fine.

Singer understood with the same speed, that contact with the Swiss could
not be blown up before it had even begun. He sent a fax to the president's
office in Bern noting that if Villiger did not meet with Burg, he would not
meet with any of the Jewish representatives, the meeting would be off and
he could read about it in the newspapers. "Bronfman and Singer don't
come without Burg. No Burg—no meeting." Within hours the announcement came from Bern that Burg could participate in the meeting.[5]

The next day, September 12, 1995, the banks had a surprise for the heads
of the Jewish organizations the banks held a press conference and published
the preliminary report of the committee (established under pressure from
the government and the Parliament on January 25) that examined the
whole issue of dormant accounts. The crux of the report was that in a
dozen banks 893 dormant accounts had been discovered, at a nominal
value of 40.9 million Swiss francs, and that most of the accounts did not
belong to Holocaust victims. From this point, new procedures for handling
accounts without heirs would be established. The SBA's ombudsman's office would set up a central liaison office to service the petitioners, which
would nullify the need to approach each bank individually.

When the law of 1962 was implemented, the SBA stated "It must be
assumed that the banks carefully examined the accounts in which there
were no transactions for quite some time. There is no other indication."
That statement sounds rather ridiculous now. The SBA added that the
banks also reported to the government the accounts of citizens of Eastern
Europe, as "place of residence was not the issue. What was important was
the possibility that the client was a victim of the Nazi regime." Again, the
facts known today refute this claim.

The association determined that "The basis exists to believe that no dormant accounts remain that belong to individuals despite contradictory al-
lusions in the media." It claimed that it was impossible for accounts to
remain without owners, since if that happened, a custodian was appointed

for the account. Be that as it may, how could the SBA explain the long talks held by Switzerland with the Allies on one side, with Israel and the Jewish organizations on the other, and further still, with Hungary and Poland, on the fate of accounts without heirs, and the question of who owned them?

The next paragraph of the preliminary report includes an outstanding inaccuracy: "The estimated numbers and sums of unclaimed assets published in the media are extremely exaggerated. While the assets were reported according to law in 1962, they were quite close to the previous estimates by the Swiss Jewish Association," apparently the local community. First, Swiss Jews had no earlier estimates of their own concerning the sums involved. Second, the sums discovered in 1962 were much higher than the banks had assumed.

From that point, the SBA moved on to its foregone conclusion: "There is no need to reopen the 1962 law." Nonetheless, the SBA agreed to admit that the concerns of dormant account heirs were "important and justified." In order to solve the problem without damaging bank confidentiality, and without bureaucratic red tape, the SBA decided to establish a Central Liaison Office, which would pass on the requests of "legal and identified heirs" to the banks. Nothing was said about the question of who would determine the "legality and identification" of heirs, and what the heirs would have to do should they not receive recognition. The SBA decided that the liaison office would handle the inquiries of heirs who had not established their claims only if they were related to *dormant accounts not associated with the Holocaust period* (emphasis mine.)

After reviewing the steps made until that point concerning the accounts and the relevant legal background, the SBA determined the actions that the banks would be obligated to undertake in the future. They were asked to locate and mark the accounts for which there had been no transactions and no contact with the owners for at least ten years. The banks would not be allowed to close those accounts unless the administrative costs were not covered. They could not publicly search for the owners in order not to harm their reputation. And finally, "the banks must safeguard the interests of the client whose account was dormant."

This is a very edifying ruling. First, it clearly indicates that until 1995 the banks regularly closed dormant accounts; otherwise there would have been no need to instruct them to stop doing so. Secondly, they were allowed to continue closing dormant accounts, if expenses ate up all the money in the account, despite the fact that with a dormant account the bank should not have any expenses. Third, how were the banks supposed to look for heirs after ten years without publicizing their search? Fourth, since these regulations took effect on January 1, 1996, the banks still had enough time to close out the dormant accounts that had not yet been liquidated, and destroy relevant documents.[6]

By September 8/1995, a dozen of banks had been able to search for and report the assets in question. Among them are Big Banks, large Cantonal banks, large private banks and banks specializing in managed accounts as well as some regional banks, all of which today represent about half of the banking industry in Switzerland. The interim result is shown below:

Accounts and Custody Accounts Opened before 1945 and dormant since 1985 or longer	
(Interim Results)	
Number of accounts and custody accounts: (accounts with news from customers or heirs between 1945 and 1985 included only partly)	893
Total amount as of today:	Fr. 40'900'000.--
Distinguished according to domicile of client:	
- Eastern Europe	Fr. 6'800'000.--
- Germany/Austria	Fr. 2'300'000.--
- Switzerland	Fr. 6'100'000.--
- other countries (F, I, GB, USA etc.)	Fr. 25'700'000.--

Bankers Association publishes dormant accounts of both swiss and non-swiss nationals dating from the period before 1945
06/1997 29.10.1997

(bc) From 29 October 1997 a list of dormant accounts of Swiss bank customers will be available free of charge from all branches of the big banks and the cantonal banks. In addition, a second list of accounts held by non-Swiss nationals can be obtained from ATAG Ernst & Young. All the banking relationships concerned have been shown to have been established before 9 May 1945. Claimants to the assets in question can submit their claims, free of charge, until 31 March 1998.

At the time of going to press, 123 banks in Switzerland had identified a total of 74,496 dormant accounts of Swiss nationals, of which 86% represent less than CHF 100 and 97% less than CHF 1,000. 3% of the accounts hold assets in excess of CHF 1,000. One hundred and sixty five accounts, 0.2% of the total, represent assets of over CHF 10,000.

In September 1995 the Swiss Bankers Association announced that 893 dormant accounts—belonging to both Swiss and foreign citizens—were found in banks representing half of the banking industry in Switzerland (above). In October 1997 it admitted that the number of dormant accounts belonging only to Swiss citizens was over 74,000 (below). Author's files.

There are prominent men here who insist that the Italian holdings here and in the United States are much larger than those held by Germans. In any case, German corporations like the I. G. Farben Industrie, unlike the Reichsbank, do not seem short of Swiss francs. The former recently paid out Swiss francs 1,000,000 to meet their bank obligations in Basel.

Italian accounts are, in great part at the Banque Fédérale S. A., including those of high-ranking Fascists, it is said. The Italian holdings are not comparable with those of France, but there are still many such accounts here, despite Italian measures to repatriate such capital, according to a Swiss banker thoroughly familiar with the subject.

SOME OF THE BANKS INVOLVED

There will be found below a list of twenty-four banks at Basel said to be carrying German accounts, but the amounts thereof as given are submitted with the usual reserves:

Estimated Value of German-owned Accounts Swiss francs	Name of Financial Institution
nil	1. American Express Company
10,000,000	2. Basler Handelsbank
2,500,000	3. Basler Kantonalbank
---	4. Crédit Industriel d'Alsace et de Lorraine
5,000,000 (German Jews)	5. Dreyfus Söhne & Co.
5,000,000	6. Ehinger & Co.
10,000,000	7. Eidgenössische Bank A. G.
2,500,000	8. Gutzwiller & Cie., E.
5,000,000	9. La Roche & Co.
10,000,000	10. Lüscher & Co.
500,000	11. Münch, R.
5,000,000	12. National Bank of Switzerland
1,000,000	13. Röchling & Co.
5,000,000	14. Sarasin & Co., A.
10,000,000	15. Schweiz. Bankgesellschaft
10,000,000	16. Schweiz. Bankverein
15,000,000	17. Schweiz. Kreditanstalt
1,000,000	18. Schweiz. Spar- & Kreditbank
5,000,000	19. Schweiz. Volksbank
1,000,000	20. Zahn & Co.
3,000,000	21. Basellandschaftliche Hypoth kenbank
3,000,000	22. Genossenschaftliche Zentral
3,000,000	23. Handwerkerbank
2,000,000	24. Zinstragende Ersparniskass
114,500,000 TOTAL	

American consulate in Basel's report to the secretary of state on German assets in financial institutions in Basel, January 18, 1945. (U.S. National Archives; World Jewish Congress)

Anyone who thought salvation would come from the Central Liaison Office, announced by the Bankers Association with such pomp and circumstance, was proven wrong later the same day when the president of the association, Georg Krayer, described in a press conference in Basel what actions would be taken. According to Krayer, the office would require that the petitioners "declare credibly" that the claimed account existed or may have existed. They would be required to provide the name of the account holder, and prove their entitlement with official documentation. The inquiring parties would be required to prove that the account holder had been dead for more than ten years, or had been considered dead for a similar period of time.[7]

Krayer expected that the office would begin operating during the first half of 1996, and that use of its services would involve a "small fee." He admitted that the goal of establishing the office was not only to assist heirs, but also to discourage international criticism of the banks concerning Holocaust victims' accounts, and that the media publicity had pressured the SBA to change its position and decide to reexamine the issue.

Krayer's words could only be interpreted in one way: the Central Liaison Office would demand the same proof that the banks themselves had demanded. Inquiring parties would have to prove that the account holder was dead by presenting a death certificate; they would have to prove their right to inherit by producing a series of wills and death certificates for two generations; and moreover, they would have to prove that the account existed. Their declarations would not suffice, unless they were "credible" and supported by documentation. Nothing had changed.

At the same press conference, the heads of the SBA also presented the results of the investigation to locate dormant accounts conducted at a dozen banks, including the three major banks. The criterion for this investigation was different from that activated by the 1962 law. Now, the banks examined not only the accounts of potential victims, but any account opened before May 1945 in which there had been no transactions for at least ten years. The SBA noted that not all the banks could investigate the entire period since the end of the war, since they had not transferred all account information to computerized databases when they were created in the 1970s. In addition, the SBA reported that fees and taxes had been collected from all the accounts, and that they were credited with interest. It is now known that the second part of their claim was untrue, as the banks themselves participated in 1998 in the committee to determine the real value of the discovered accounts.

The investigation uncovered 893 accounts, valued nominally at 40.9 million francs: 6.8 million francs belonged to Eastern European depositors, 2.3 million francs to clients from Germany and Austria, 6.1 million francs from Swiss account holders and 25.7 million francs from depositors in the United States, France, Britain, Italy and more. Based on this distribution,

Krayer stated that it was possible that most of the money did not belong to Holocaust victims.[8]

The heads of the SBA were sure that this report would end the affair: We checked, this is what we found, we will help petitioners. Case closed. They still did not understand that the Jewish organizations primary demand was to prevent just this situation, in which the banks took on all the roles: investigator, investigatee, supervisor, decision maker and reporter. For a very long time, the banks thought this was just another round of standard inconveniences, which arose once every few years. They thought it could be warded off quite well using the methods of the past: admitting little, promising investigation, wasting time. But two days later, they were about to discover, if not completely understand, that they were dealing with other types of Jewish leaders, and other types of claims.

On September 14, 1995, Bronfman, Burg, Singer, and Barak entered President Villiger's office in the Federal Palace in Bern. Despite the chilling incident at the beginning of the week surrounding Burg's participation in the meeting, this meeting went quite well from the Jewish organizations' point of view. Villiger stated that he recognized the principle that no bank should profit from money that did not belong to it and that had remained in its hands due to crimes committed against the rightful owners.

On a practical level, Villiger was less effective: "I will support you morally, but Switzerland has a free market. This is a problem between private banks and their customers, and you should therefore solve the problem with the banks." In the balance of power that existed between the government and the Swiss banks, Bronfman and Burg could not expect more than that.[9]

From the Federal Palace, the Jewish representatives went to La Grande Société, a prestigious club-restaurant close to Parliament and the Bankers Association offices in Bern. A cold reception awaited them there. According to the original plan, representatives of the banks and the Jewish organizations were to meet during lunch, but Krayer had other intentions. The experience awaiting the Jewish representatives was so surprising and offensive that it was emblazoned in Burg, Singer, and Barak's memories, all of whom describe the episode identically.

When Bronfman, Burg, and their colleagues entered the prestigious restaurant, they saw the table set for a meal in the next room. After shaking hands, Krayer said, "Before we eat, we will go to the lobby." About twenty people from both sides were squeezed into the room, in which there was not even a single chair. The only furniture was a podium, which Krayer approached. Beside him stood his deputy and the owner of the Julius Baer bank, the Jewish banker Hans Baer, and SBA general manager, Jean-Paul Chapuis, and his deputy, Heinrich Schneider. A battery of the banks' lawyers was also present.

Krayer usually appeared grumpy and angry, and this time was no different. The president of the Swiss Bankers' Association took a six-page document from his pocket and began reading it in rapid English, including the date printed at the top. Most of the document's contents were what the Jewish participants later described as "cursing and humiliating Burg," without actually mentioning his name. Krayer sharply criticized those who conducted the negotiations via the press and publicly embarrassed the banks, and emphasized that "it will be impossible to negotiate if you go to the press." After scolding Burg, Krayer moved on to the practical side as all those present remained standing. He described 839 accounts holding 40.9 million francs and offered that money to the Jewish representatives, despite the fact that only two days earlier the banks had claimed that most of the money did not even belong to Holocaust victims.

During the entire episode, Bronfman was becoming more and more furious. He was unaccustomed to being treated so impolitely, hearing his colleagues slandered, and finally, as he himself would later refer to it, being offered a bribe. Burg and Singer began to whisper to each other in Hebrew, preparing a response to Krayer's speech-attack-offer tirade. Burg whispered to Singer in Hebrew, "Make sure Edgar doesn't explode, because that is exactly what they want—to blow up the whole business." Bronfman looked at Burg and Singer and whispered to Singer, "What do we do?"

Singer drew on the accepted custom used by the Japanese during negotiations which he had heard from his father-in-law, and said to Bronfman, "Tell him, 'I heard you.'" When Krayer finished speaking, Bronfman was furious, but managed to control himself. "Are you done?" he asked Krayer. When he received affirmation, and was asked what he thought of the speech, he said, "I heard you." Krayer insisted, "But what do you think?" Bronfman said, "I heard you, I will consult with my colleagues and give you an answer."

Krayer was shocked. He had expected two possible answers, but not this one. If he had received acceptance or rejection, a discussion of the offer of 40.9 million francs to the Jewish organizations would have been opened, thus forcing the negotiations from the start to focus on money. But Bronfman essentially rejected Krayer's entire approach, and set the tone that would accompany the negotiations the entire way: "It's not the money, it's the principle."

Bronfman was still furious about the impolite manner in which had been treated by the bankers. "What is this? Don't the Swiss offer chairs?" he asked angrily. The bankers did not know what to say. And then Singer said, "I don't really care about the chairs, I care that you aren't giving us a place at the table," a play on words that hinted at the one-sidedness with which the Swiss tried to conduct the negotiations. Krayer and his colleagues were left flabbergasted.

At that point, Bronfman took control of the meeting. Instead of playing into the bankers' hands and rebuking them for the insult, and perhaps even ending the meeting right there and then, Bronfman said, "Let's talk about it over lunch." This essentially made Bronfman the host at a meal organized by the Bankers Association in its private restaurant. Hans Baer did try to regain the initiative by saying, "Let's sit down to eat," but Krayer and his colleagues had lost control of what happened during those hours, which set the tone for relations between them and the Jewish organizations.

During the meal, the atmosphere thawed slightly, and Krayer again declared, "We will return every penny that belongs to Jews." He repeated the question of how much money the Jewish organizations wanted. Burg replied, "The money doesn't interest us, the principle interests us, and the process must be entirely transparent."

"They fell into the trap," Burg later analyzed. "The bankers came with the strategy of buying us off with money. I suppose they said to themselves, 'we'll suggest 30 million, they'll demand 100, we'll compromise on 80.' But we told them, we don't want money, we want the principle, and for that principle we want the transparency, and for transparency, banking confidentiality must be lifted."

During the meeting, Burg added, "Gentlemen, let's begin a process in which we define how we return home to our public, and how you return home to your public, so that everyone can satisfy his people. We won't break the banking system, and you won't deceive us like thirty years ago." Burg explicitly chose the word deceive and even explained to the Swiss exactly what he meant: "How is it possible that four months ago the matter was closed forever, and suddenly you discovered $32 million? Have you not deceived us?"

The Swiss response, correct in and of itself to that question, is that the two investigations were different. In the 1960s, the banks looked for, or at least they were supposed to look for, only accounts of possible Holocaust victims, while the 1995 investigation encompassed all dormant accounts. But that did not interest Burg, and the general public did not notice the difference. Only later did the bankers understand that what had appeared to them as a brilliant exercise to finish off the issue was yet another investigation that had boomeranged, and now served their opponents' claim that they were once again misleading the public.

Bronfman pressured Krayer to determine a schedule for the investigative process, and the Swiss finally agreed that by the end of 1995 a mechanism would be established to ensure the transparency of the investigation. This was to become a critical point in later developments. When the Swiss violated their commitment to cooperate with the Jewish organizations, the turning point in the crisis occurred in the form of the transfer of the struggle to the American arena. It is possible to imagine that under the pressure of the events of that meeting, Krayer agreed to Bronfman and Burg's conditions, but when he reconsidered them later, he understood their significance and recanted. A joint, forthright investigation meant waiving the banks' exclusive handling of the issue and negating their principle means of covering up the problem of the accounts.

Just before dessert, Krayer again spoke about the ombudsman's investigation. He promised that the work of the ombudsman, an employee of the SBA, would be supervised by Leon Schlompeff, the former Swiss president, who was then the president of the Ombudsman's Fund, in other words, a direct connection to the banks. Bronfman, the head of a liquor company, replied,

I don't know this ombudsman, I don't know who he is. If it works, I accept. If it doesn't, you'll hear from me. For me, the ombudsman is like a bottle of wine. I look at the bottle and it looks good. But it has to be opened, the color examined, the wine must be smelt, tasted, and only then do I decide if I will drink it. And believe me, I understand these things.

At the end of the meeting, the Jewish organizations and the banks agreed to two courses of action. The first was the ombudsman's investigation, and the second was the establishment of an unofficial joint committee that would determine the overall investigative procedures for the affair, with the goal of establishing a joint council that would supervise the process. Singer and Barak were appointed to the committee from the Jewish side, and Krayer and Baer from the banks' side.[10]

Immediately after the meeting, the Jewish representatives were satisfied. Bronfman went to rest on his yacht and Burg, Singer, and Barak returned to Zurich in a black Mercedes 600 supplied by the Bankers Association, complete with chauffeur. The mood was good, and Singer said, "That meeting brought us to $100 million." Burg was even more in the clouds, and responded to Singer, "That meeting brought us up over $1 billion."[11]

In retrospect, Burg admits that agreeing to the ombudsman was a mistake, which allowed the Swiss to buy more time. "We were naive. Essentially, we climbed in through the window because the door was blocked. The ombudsman was a window. In retrospect, we know that the ombudsman became what I would almost call the system's 'contraception.' In my opinion, the Swiss thought they would just tie everything up with the ombudsman."[12]

At this point, it is worthwhile to skip ahead to discuss the work procedures of the ombudsman's office in order to better understand what angered the Jewish organizations. The ombudsman began work in January 1996 (for the results of his work, see Chapter 10). The man in charge, is Hanspeter Haeni, has served as SBA ombudsman since September 1995, and his principal responsibility is handling public petitions concerning the banks.

Haeni's salary is paid by the ombudsman's public fund, which is financed by the banks themselves, a possible conflict of interest. A routine complaint investigation against a specific bank is one thing, whereas an investigation into thousands of inquiries tied to hundreds of banks that is likely to severely damage the entire system's credibility, is quite another matter altogether.

Another problem was that there was no real difference between Haeni's methods and those used by the banks themselves, but there was one significant improvement: Petitioners could now send their inquiries to one address, instead of having to inquire at dozens, or even hundreds of banks. Instead of paying multiple 300–1,000 franc fees, they would be charged only once. At first, Haeni charged each petitioner 300 francs, but after the Jewish organizations objected the fee was decreased to 100 francs, and was not collected at all from those who declared they had no means to pay it.

The investigation itself, however, despite Haeni's declarations, was not very different from the banks' own investigation. In February 1997, Haeni stated that

We accept almost every claim as credible, and there are no inquiries we refuse to handle due to lack of documentation. In the past, inquiring parties had to make their case before each bank separately, and I can certainly understand the feelings of someone asked to produce a death certificate for a Holocaust victim. I do not believe those petitioning me are lying, but they cannot know exactly what happened to the accounts in the long time since they were told of the accounts existence.[13]

In his first report, in November 1996, Haeni expanded the description of his methods. At the beginning of his report, Haeni stated, "I have one single principle in my position as Contact Office in the search for dormant accounts: everything that can be returned to the legal owners must be returned. And I would never have taken on this task if I had not been convinced that all the institutions involved were totally unanimous on this point." A few minutes later, Haeni outlined his position on the issue most distressing to the banks: confidentiality.

According to the legal regulations of banking confidentiality, information can be imparted only to representatives and legal heirs of past customers. We verify this entitlement based on the appendices to the questionnaire sent to inquiring parties. Therefore, in contrast to the common misconception, banking confidentiality is preserved.

As soon as the entitlement is determined, the petitioner can note a number of names under which he believes the account was opened. The Central Contact Office then transfers a list of all the names [to the banks]. It includes other details, which could help identify the clients relations. The banks must compare the names on the list to the list of clients whose relationships with the bank have been defined as dormant and report to us appropriately.

Haeni continued to detail the primary difficulty in locating accounts, at first blaming the media and the Jewish organizations for creating inflated expectations. "Almost all the searching parties assume that money will be found for them. The reports—unrealistic to any unprejudiced eye—of billions being held up by the banks have led to additional expectations and further pushed up the idea held by inquiring parties about the sums that could be found." Later on, Haeni even claimed that the media interest in the affair was sometimes inversely proportioned to those who spoke in public with knowledge of the situation.

Later in the report Haeni touched on the real problem—documentation. "Documents concerning a client relationship that has ended are kept by the banks for ten years, and are then usually destroyed. In simple terms, this means that if an account holder or his representative withdrew the money, in other words, the account was closed, there is no trace after ten years. Therefore, the bank cannot again prove that the relationship ended appropriately."

Haeni also delineated a third problem: "Along with the problem of documentation, as a result of the historical distance from the events, stands the personal involvement of the inquiring party. What is history for one person, is immeasurable pain for many of those inquiring."

His response to these difficulties was simple: they were not his problem. He reiterated that his office served only as a mediator and as a center for the inquiring parties and the banks. In a meeting with reporters in February 1997, when the results of the investigation had already been criticized and appeared very disappointing, Haeni stood by his belief in the banks: "There is official supervision of the banks, and I have no reason to assume that they cheat."

Haeni's remarks require rebuttal. The most important point they raise is that he had no means—and no intention—of investigating the credibility of the banks' reports. On the contrary, he declared his wholehearted belief in the banks. Haeni did not believe the press or the Jewish organizations, and chose to believe the banks—caught in inaccuracies, to say the least, for decades.

Haeni's remarks that he investigated every claim were true, but nearly insignificant. His investigation was no more than a superficial and clerical examination of the forms, and not an in-depth probe. The only thing that Haeni and his staff examined thoroughly was the inquiring parties' legal right to the account they claimed. In other words, Haeni said he believed the claimants, but carefully examined that no one tried to damage banking confidentiality.

It is true that the ombudsman's mandate was only to serve as a liaison office, but as such, there was no need for Haeni to express any opinion on the credibility of the banks' reports. If he wasn't supposed to ascertain that the banks were telling the truth, on what basis did he give them a public certificate of integrity? And if he was supposed to examine their responses, why did he avoid doing so, even going so far as to publicly declare that he had no intention of taking any action?

As Haeni believed the banks, he did not bother to respond to the biggest problem: documentation. He spoke of the possibility that the owners or their representatives withdrew the money and the accounts closed, and then the banks destroyed the documents after ten years. But that is not the case when dealing with Holocaust victims' accounts. Here we are dealing with the question of whether the bank itself could close a dormant account. Haeni did not say a word about that and his silence is puzzling. Since he took the trouble to defend the banks from hostile and misleading media reports, it could be expected that Haeni would also rebuke the claims of the closure of dormant accounts. Does the fact that he did not do so indicate that such a procedure was implemented?

The proof required from inquirers was a problem in and of itself. Let us examine the questionnaire that Haeni sent to thousands of petitioners and see what it demanded, as determined by the SBA:

Any person addressing an inquiry to the Contact Office must: show that an account, custody account or safe-deposit box still exists, or could exist, with a Swiss bank; supply the name of the person for whom the account, custody account or safe-deposit box was maintained; show that the bank client (testator) has been deceased or has been presumed dead for at least ten years.

If anyone had any doubt about what that meant, the list of requested documents stated that it was worthwhile to submit

copies of the inquiring party's official identity papers (passport, identity card), birth certificate, death certificate of the bequeather if such exists, the legacy document or an equivalent document, will or decree due to death, documents concerning property in Switzerland (bank documents, keys, account numbers, etc). If any of the above documents are missing, please give reasons.

Haeni may have understood the impossibility that Holocaust survivors and their heirs faced when asked to present a death certificate, but his demand was the same as the banks'. While the form raised the possibility that it would not be possible to submit such a document, it categorically demanded a will and legacy document, and those who did not possess them had to provide reasons why they did not have them. This is the same cold-hearted, legalistic demand that characterized the way the Swiss handled the inquiries. There was a lot of public sympathy for the heirs, and Haeni even understood the fact that for many of them this caused "immeasurable pain," but in writing, the demands remained unchanged.

Another problematic point was swallowed by Haeni's remarks and those of the chair of the ombudsman's fund, Leon Schlompeff. They admitted that they cooperated only with the Swiss Jewish community, and not with the international Jewish organizations. This was a continuation of the policy taken from the first day by the SBA, which had a declared preference for talking to moderate Rolf Bloch—a distinguished local industrialist and large client of the banks—rather than to the aggressive and dispassionate Edgar Bronfman and Avraham Burg. It is interesting that the banks continued this way through November 1996, the date of Haeni and Schlompeff's press conference, despite the fact that during the entire year they saw quite clearly that the real struggle was conducted by Bronfman and Burg, and that only they would participate in negotiations and a possible agreement.

Schlompeff revealed in November 1996, that the liaison office enjoyed a valuable relationship, in his words, with Rolf Bloch and Michael Kohn, former president of the Jewish community, then serving as the vice president of the European Jewish Congress, an affiliate of the World Jewish Congress. Haeni also reported that

Right from the outset I have placed particular importance on support from the Jewish organizations. The brochure and questionnaire were discussed with the Swiss Jewish Society [the Jewish community]. We explicitly point out in an accompanying letter that the Jewish Organizations are also available in the event of any difficulties. We are not talking here about technical assistance, as the procedure is actually very simple. What I would like is that Jewish Organizations are informed about the process and thus establish some basis of trust. With this thought in mind, I contacted the World Jewish Congress a few days ago in order to find ways of bringing this support into reality.

Haeni's remarks are extremely edifying. Only a few days before the publication of his first report, when it was already clear to him that the results were likely to arouse criticism from the World Jewish Congress (WJC) and the Jewish Agency, he called the WJC in order to begin overtures for possible cooperation. Considering that approach, it is no wonder that in retrospect Singer returned to Bronfman's analogy of the wine and stated, "After a year we discovered that this ombudsman is sour wine."[14]

The Arthur Andersen accounting firm, which examined the ombudsman's work for the Volcker Commission, also found many shortcomings. The most important flaw is the problem of Haeni's dependence on the banks, or as the accountants put it diplomatically: "It is possible he is not entirely independent." They also noted that the ombudsman's work was limited to administrative tasks, and he was not allowed to supervise the banks' reports. About the banks' guidelines, the accountants stated that they eased the requirements for inquiring parties, but did not require the banks to search for dormant accounts. They even noted that until implementation of the ombudsman's procedure, the banks acted "entirely legalistically," without considering the special circumstances of Holocaust victims' inquiries.[15]

Already by the end of 1995, long before Haeni's "sourness" became clear to them, the Jewish organizations did not trust the ombudsman as the primary channel for carrying out the investigation. This was also because he was a salaried employee of the banks and because his mandate was limited to technical and administrative assistance to those currently inquiring. The September 1995, understanding between the heads of the Jewish organizations and the Swiss Bankers Association included the establishment of a joint council for examining the entire affair. This issue was at the center of debates in the unofficial committee established that month.

The committee held three meetings between September and December 1995, and made no progress. The general feeling on the Jewish side was that the banks were again using delaying tactics. In one of the meetings, for instance, two and a half hours were dedicated to an argument about whether victims' heirs would also be required in the future to present the account owners' death certificate. The discussion led nowhere.

When Singer and Barak raised the issue about looted property deposited in the banks during the war, the response was, "there is no such thing; there is no looted property here." It is possible that their remarks meant that such property no longer existed as it had all been returned according to the Washington Accord, but the Jewish representatives understood it as a blanket denial—there is no looted property and there never was any. The banks' claim was, of course, untrue, since Switzerland entered negotiations on the Washington Accord only because it had a huge volume of looted property.

When Singer and Barak raised the question of Switzerland's wartime refugee policy, the answer was that the matter had already been investigated and there was no need to discuss it again. Singer responded by saying that according to documents he had, 30,000 Jewish refugees were deported. The Swiss asked, "What documents?" And Singer responded, "The Safehaven documents." That was the first time that Singer revealed the documents from the American operation to locate German property, which ultimately played a decisive role in the coming months in destroying Switzerland's international image.

Barak and Singer were beginning to feel uncomfortable. On their visits to Switzerland, they always received the same two rooms in the country's leading hotel, the Bel Vieu in Bern, located next to the Federal Palace. What is the likelihood that the same guests invariably receive the same rooms regardless of the date of their arrival or the length of their stay? One of them asked, half in jest, if it was conceivable that the rooms or phone lines were bugged.[16] Even if it was a joke, it certainly indicates something of the lack of trust between the two sides.

Meanwhile, Singer created a "side channel" with Hans Baer, the vice president of the SBA. This was not due to Baer's being Jewish, as the family assimilated and cut off ties with the Jewish community and Israel in the 1980s. The reason was something else entirely. Baer had spent many years in the United States, as a youth and as an adult, was familiar with the American system and was supposed to understand the damage that it would cause the banks if the deposits affair crossed the Atlantic Ocean.

Singer and Baer used to meet in a Manhattan bar not far from the offices of the World Jewish Congress on Madison Avenue. Their talks dealt primarily with the joint committee the two sides were supposed to establish in order to investigate the deposits affair.[17] But Singer quickly felt that this channel was also leading toward a dead end. Jewish or not, half American or not, Baer was first and foremost a Swiss banker, and his interests were identical to those of his colleagues: investigate as little as possible, as slowly as possible, and as secretly as possible. Singer's goal, of course, was entirely the opposite: investigate as much as possible, as fast as possible, and as openly as possible.

Just three months after Bronfman, Burg, Singer, and Barak left the meetings with the president of Switzerland and the bankers full of optimism, it became clear to them that almost nothing had changed. The ombudsman had not yet begun his work, and, in any case, the Jewish organizations had no great expectations from him. The banks promised cooperation and provided bureaucracy. President Villiger was about to complete his term of office and return to the Ministry of Finance, and his moral support was not worth much in practical terms.

Essentially, the talks had returned nearly to where they had been thirty to forty years previously, with one prominent disadvantage from the Jewish perspective: the banks could flourish the 1962 law as proof that the problem had been solved. But now there was one big difference between the situation in the 1990s and the situation in the 1950s: the Jewish leaders were not willing to give up, and this time they had very powerful weapons.

Thomas Borer, then head of the Swiss Foreign Ministry's Task Force, with Ruth Runder, daughter of Paul Grueninger, at the inauguration of Grueninger Square in Ramat-Gan (Israel), June 1997. (Photograph by Tamar Matzafi)

Rolf Bloch, president of the Federation of Jewish Communities in Switzerland. (Photograph by Ariel Jerozolimsky)

Edgar Bronfman, president of the World Jewish Congress. (Photograph by Ariel Jerozolimsky)

Zvi Barak, former co-chair of the World Jewish Restitution Organization. (Photograph by Ariel Jerozolimsky)

Paul Volcker, chair of the Volcker Commission. (Photograph by Ariel Jerozolimsky)

Avraham Burg, chair of the Jewish Agency (left), and Israel Singer, secretary-general of the World Jewish Congress, at a press conference in Jerusalem, January 5, 1997. (Photograph by Ariel Jerozolimsky)

Then Swiss president and foreign minister, Flavio Cotti, with Abraham Hirschson, chair of the Knesset's Committee for Jewish Property Restitution, in Jerusalem, May 1998. (Photograph by Ariel Jerozolimsky)

8

"THE JEWS WERE BETRAYED"
The Battle Moves to the American Front

AVRAHAM BURG AND Israel Singer are old friends. Both families come from Vienna, and they have known each other well since the beginning of the 1980s. Despite their differences in character and style, they have a few things in common that have helped them greatly in the campaign for Jewish property, namely, aggressiveness, sharp tongues, and a willingness to confront others. Burg and Singer understand each other's every gesture, and do not need to consult much with each other. This was true in a conversation between the two after the third—(and, in retrospect, last)—meeting of the Jewish organizations and Swiss banks' joint committee, on December 18, 1995. Singer laconically reported to Burg, "It's not working." Burg received a similar report from Zvi Barak.[1] Singer and Burg began to plan altogether different measures.

When it became clear to them that the negotiations were not serious, they changed their strategy completely. No more aggressive public declarations while negotiating secretly in good faith, but an open, all-out battle. Singer began planning for the possibility of the collapse of the negotiations with the Swiss, and prepared what he calls the "shelters." The strategy was to move the campaign battle to the United States, an arena Burg left to Singer, who acted with Bronfman's backing. In just one month, between the end of December 1995 and the end of January 1996, their weapon was ready, and just in time, too, since just one week later (February 1996), the Jewish organizations' trust in the Swiss banks came crashing down.[2]

The threat to the Swiss banks from the United States was very significant, both financially and in terms of their image. In 1996, thirteen branches of six Swiss banks operated in the United States, led by the three major banks, Credit Suisse, UBS, and Swiss Bank Corp. In 1994, Swiss banks loaned American businesses $38 billion. The banks employed 6,000 people and paid federal, state, and municipal taxes in the amount of $100 million. In addition, the Swiss banks managed hundreds of billions of dollars in investments in American stocks and banks for their clients.[3]

As some of those involved in the affair have said, a banker has no more important asset than his reputation. If serious claims against the banks are raised by senior members of the U.S. administration, it could cause vast, long-term damage. After all, what was the struggle about? It was about the return of money deposited in the banks by the victims of the most horrible crime in the history of humanity. The idea of a bank not returning money deposited with it is enough to shock any potential customer. The thought that a bank exploited genocide to get rich illegally arouses public outrage. In the United States, where there is a great deal of interest in World War II and the Holocaust, the banks could find themselves in a crossfire that would seriously damage their business. And when well-known figures with political and personal interests join the struggle, the banks have an even bigger problem. And this is exactly what Bronfman and Singer did.

On December 25, 1995, Singer and Bronfman met with Senator Alfonse D'Amato, the then chair of the Senate Banking Committee. From their perspective, he was the right man, in the right place, at the right time. In 1995, D'Amato represented New York, a state with a large Jewish constituency. As chair, he set the agenda for a powerful Senate committee—not just any committee, but the most appropriate one to handle this affair. He could open hearings under the pretext that the Swiss banks' U.S. subsidiaries are subject to local supervision.

Moreover, at the time, D'Amato needed an important undertaking that would earn him favorable headlines. His committee had dealt for a long time with the Whitewater affair, in which President Bill Clinton and his wife, Hillary Rodham Clinton, were investigated, but that engine was running out of steam. The American public was not terribly interested in the couple's real-estate dealings from years prior to Clinton's becoming president. D'Amato was not doing well in the polls and running significantly behind potential competitors in the next elections, to be held in 1998. An affair like the problem of the bank deposits was an answer to his prayers. Public opinion would always be on his side—the Swiss banks versus the Holocaust survivors, to him, the results were obvious. He could force the administration to act, and with a little luck, he would also find enough stories to make the evening news over and over again.

It is therefore small wonder that D'Amato, who has very sharp political instincts, immediately asked, "Can you give me examples?" On January 3, 1996, Singer and Bronfman gave D'Amato a New Year's present: two Holocaust survivors, Estelle Sapir and Mrs. Blau, who came to his office. D'Amato heard firsthand about their treatment by the Swiss banks, and was excited that both resided in Queens, his home borough of New York. D'Amato wanted to call an immediate press conference with the two women, but Singer restrained him, saying, "Not yet, we are still in talks with them [the banks]." D'Amato agreed and held off.

In the meantime, Bronfman and Singer were operating on a second front: the state and city of New York. The pair contacted Alan G. Hevesi, New

York City's comptroller, and Carl D. McCall, New York State's comptroller. Among their other duties, the two are responsible for investing state and municipal pension funds. The city's $70 billion pension fund consigns about $1 billion daily in overnight deposits (moneys that move between accounts receive a special interest rate due to their large size) in Swiss banks. In addition, Hevesi was then the president of the U.S. Comptrollers Association, which includes 500 local government comptrollers, who collectively manage $30 trillion in pension funds. Hevesi and McCall were capable of doing serious damage to the banks if they decided to use even a little of their power. Hevesi is the grandson of a former Chief Rabbi of Hungary; McCall is a friend of Bronfman's with higher political aspirations.

In a meeting with the comptrollers in January 1996, Bronfman and Singer convinced them to prepare a draft letter to the Swiss banks. The draft stated that the comptrollers were very interested in the World Jewish Congress and WJRO activities, that they had recently met with Bronfman and heard that the talks were not progressing effectively; and that they were interested in meeting with the bankers. Hevesi and McCall were willing to come to Switzerland for a meeting, and hoped the bankers would agree to present all the figures to them. The implied threat in the letter from Hevesi and McCall said it all.

Despite his political ambitions, McCall did not forget that he owed his allegiance to the current governor, George Pataki, and told Bronfman and Singer that they would have to speak with Pataki. Singer said, "We already spoke to him."

At the end of January, Singer's daughter married the son of banker Gary Pairgain, Pataki's college roommate. Only three non-Jews attended the wedding, two of whom were George Pataki and Alfonse D'Amato, political allies for many years.

In spite of the tumult of the surrounding wedding, Singer found a few minutes to speak with Pataki and briefly explain the Swiss affair to him. "Look what kind of man I am," Singer mocked himself, "doing business at my own daughter's wedding." Pataki's immediate response was, "Have you spoken to Alfonse?" Singer responded, "We spoke with him." Pataki immediately wanted to know who "we" meant. Singer told him, "Edgar and myself." Within a few minutes Pataki and Bronfman were talking about the affair. With Jewish wedding songs playing in the background, Pataki and D'Amato found each other in the hubbub and D'Amato announced, "I am going to hold hearing in my committee."

Even Singer did not think he would have to use the "shelters" so quickly. On February 5, 1996, he found out that the Bankers Association was about to publish a report that would determine once and for all whether the volume of property without heirs in all the banks was the sum published in the partial report of September 1995, about 40 million francs. Singer saw the publication of the report as a blatant violation of the September 1995, agreement that all measures in the affair would be coordinated between the banks and the Jewish organizations. He immediately phoned SBA headquarters in Basel and asked for the president, Georg Krayer. Instead, the association's director general, Jean-Paul Chapuis, took the call, trying to calm Singer by saying it was an internal association report that would be delivered only to association members, and not made public.

One day later, on February 6, the World Jewish Congress representative in Brussels, Maram Stern, called Singer. Stern said he had heard from a senior official in the European Union that the Bankers Association was planning a press conference to publicize its report. Singer called Basel again, this time reaching Heinrich Schneider, the deputy director general. Schneider said that they would never publish a report, due to its confidential nature, and further, the association did not discuss such things in public. It later became clear that while Singer and Schneider were talking, the press release was already prepared and set for distribution.

When Singer woke up at his usual 5:00 A.M. on February 7, 1996, his voice mail had a message from Maram Stern that the banks had published the report—in Brussels and Basel it was already 11:00 A.M. It stated that an examination of fifty-one banks that had operated in Switzerland at the time of World War II revealed 38.7 million francs (then worth about $32.1 million) in 775 accounts in which there had been no transactions for ten years or more. The report ended by stating, "The rumors of much greater deposits belonging to Holocaust victims, are therefore completely groundless." The survey of the banks had served the purpose defined by the association for its members in June 1995: "To show that the speculation concerning large sums still in their possession, is nothing more than rumor and innuendo." Upon publication of the report, the association did not bother to explain where 118 deposits worth 2.2 million francs had disappeared, after already reporting them in November 1995, but at the moment, that was not the important point.

Singer exploded with rage. Not only had the banks broken their five-month-old promise, not only had they defined the position taken by the Jewish organizations as groundless rumors, but the deputy director general of the association had lied to him just the day before when he claimed the report would not be published.[4]

Singer didn't hesitate because of the early hour, and phoned the World Jewish Congress's executive director, Elan Steinberg. "Kill them," he instructed. "Publish the document on Lecca." Singer had found documentation in the Safehaven files a few months earlier about a Swiss bank account belonging to a Romanian officer, Radu Lecca, who was in charge of the destruction of the Jews in his country. Singer kept the information to use as a secret weapon in case of a particularly serious crisis.

The document's most immediate import was its severe blow to the public image of the Swiss banks—as the holders of money Holocaust victims paid as bribes to a reviled war criminal.[5]

At the more reasonable hour of 9:00 A.M., Singer called Bronfman at Seagram's New York headquarters. Bronfman heard from Singer about publication of the report and saw red. "Fuck them, kill them, they are a bunch of bastards," he yelled into the telephone. Singer responded, "We are already in high gear. We are calling Alfonse and Pataki and Hevesi."

In the next few hours Singer's office became a war room. The American media was full of the Lecca story, and almost no one noticed the Swiss report. The banks tried to deny the document, claiming that Volksbank did not exist. The denial tangled them in another lie. True, Volksbank does not exist today, but during the war it definitely existed, and is now part of Credit Suisse.

The New York arena took on an important role that eventful day, which irreversibly changed the face of the struggle for the restoration of Holocaust victim's property. Singer called Hevesi and McCall, and they sent the letter to the banks that had been drafted a few weeks earlier, which included the veiled threat to remove New York City and State deposits in Swiss banks. Singer also to wrote to Swiss MP Verena Grendelmeier with whom he had made contact a few months earlier, and who had expressed a willingness to act in Bern toward legislation that would require the banks to allow an independent investigation of the affair.[6]

In Jerusalem, Burg learned of publication of the report via the Internet. That morning, when he saw the Bankers Association's press release, for a moment it looked to him like a positive development. "Since the meeting in September 1995," Burg recalls, "I believed we needed to demand they publish the list of account holders located at the banks. When I saw that announcement, I thought they really meant to publish names." Burg waited patiently for a reasonable hour to call New York, not knowing that Singer had been up and working for hours.

"I asked him, 'Israel, Did you see it?' And he said to me, 'yes, Maram woke me up in the morning and it's awful.' I said to him, 'What's awful?' Singer answered, 'They're pulling the wool over our eyes.' I said, 'Israel, what do you mean wool?' He said, 'You don't get anything! Six months are lost, and they don't plan to move at all. We must go to war.'" Only then, Burg admits, did he understand the seriousness of the SBA's announcement and agree wholeheartedly with Singer's actions.[7]

The most important conversation of the day was between Singer and D'Amato, who also reacted angrily, saying, "I'm convening hearings." D'Amato summoned his legislative aide, Greg Rickman, that very day, charging him with finding the necessary documents about the whole dormant accounts problem before the hearings. Rickman, whose red mustache stood out on Capitol Hill, is the son of a Holocaust survivor. His uncle had tried to locate an account in a Swiss bank that had belonged to a relative who died in the Holocaust, and had been asked to present the death certificate, the same demand that angered so many claimants, and that stood between them and their relatives' property. Rickman later became a key behind-the-scenes player, providing D'Amato with a large portion of the ammunition that would destroy Switzerland's neutral image over the course of the next several months. On February 21, 1996, D'Amato announced that he was holding hearings, designed to estimate the volume of assets in Swiss banks that belonged to Holocaust victims.[8]

The KPMG accounting firm that had examined the Bankers Association report for the Volcker Commission presented a series of findings in August 1997, casting a heavy shadow on the banks' credibility. The accountants found that the SBA's announcement that all the Swiss banks had been examined in the review was not true. Later, an accountant appointed by the SBA determined that the SBA report was correct. KPMG says in response that the accountant dealt only with a mathematical examination of the figures in the report, and did not examine the methods by which the banks reported. The most serious finding was that the banks did not report instances in which they closed dormant accounts, donated them to charity, or appropriated them for the banks.[9]

It is important to emphasize that KPMG did not note the most important fact concerning this review by the Bankers Association, that the findings were refuted over the coming months by the association itself. In July 1997, the association published a list of 1,800 names, two-and-a-half times the number of accounts reported in February 1996. This was just the tip of the iceberg. In October 1997, the SBA admitted that its members located more than 65,000 dormant accounts, primarily owned by Swiss nationals. The 1996 review had the pretense of finding all of the accounts, which even included a significant number of Swiss-owned accounts. It is now therefore completely clear that the review did not reflect the reality, and covered only a small fraction of the real number of dormant accounts, to say the least.

Over the next few weeks of the winter of 1996, it seemed as if the battle was calming down, as there were no headlines, no practical steps taken against the banks, no negotiations, and D'Amato's hearings seemed like a distant dream. Even the unusual declaration by then UBS general manager Robert Studer did not stir any real response from the Jewish organizations. On February 25, 1996, Studer told reporters that it was "absolute gall to say we hadn't checked our figures properly. Repeating fictitious numbers over and over again doesn't make them accurate. Our figures are accurate, and you can trust us."[10]

Actually, the fate of the battle was determined in those weeks. The resolution occurred in the quiet halls of the National Archives in College Park,

Maryland. Chief archivist Michael Kurz, Israel Singer, Elan Steinberg, and Greg Rickman sat and pulled out file after file of the thousands stamped Safehaven. Some of the files, which had been classified, were declassified by court order. Almost every file revealed testimony of looted property—mostly gold—that had been smuggled out of Germany and into Switzerland. Interspersed was testimony of Jewish property deposited in Switzerland. In just a few weeks, the overall picture became clear to them: Switzerland was giving Germany valuable economic aid as the Germans were slaughtering a third of the Jewish people.

On March 27, 1996, D'Amato had enough information to raise the issue on the Senate floor. A short time before, Rickman and Steinberg had found documents in the National Archives from the Société Général de Surveillance, an investment company that held 182 accounts of European clients, many of whom had Jewish names (see Chapter 1). That day, D'Amato published the documents and spoke about them to the Senate.

After a few remarks that reviewed the history of the Swiss deposits, D'Amato made a frontal assault on the banks, which became his trademark in the next two years:

For the Swiss though, the matter was simple. They did all that they could to avoid any type of examination of their banking system, despite clear evidence of the very deep cooperation [by the banks] with the Nazis. The Swiss hid behind their 1934 Banking Secrecy Act, claiming that they could not divulge the identity of their account holders. This is quite ironic in view of the fact that the 1934 Act was designed to protect the identity of the account holders from the Nazis. Now they were using this same law to shield the assets from the survivors and the victims' rightful heirs.

D'Amato described the 1962 Swiss law, recent developments, and said that he came into the picture when the Bankers Association report about finding $32 million in dormant accounts was criticized. "The Committee will try to discern if the searches were comprehensive enough to find assets," he announced.

From there, D'Amato went on to describe the Société Général de Surveillance document of July 12, 1945. D'Amato explained that this document would test the credibility of the searches conducted by the banks by cross referencing its names with those the banks uncovered. "To start, I would like to know if these accounts are among those found in the postwar, 1962, and 1995 searches, and if not, where is the money now?"

D'Amato appended the document to the record and moved on to the numbers. The record documented deposits valued at $2,441,552 in 1945, ($20,401,741 in 1995 terms), if the calculation is based only on inflation in the United States. Current values could also be calculated using another method, D'Amato continued, according to cumulative annual interest of

3%, 4%, or 5%. These calculations yielded amounts of $10,878,065, $17,843,518, and $29,035,096, respectively.

As you can see, these amounts are of an incredible magnitude. If they are accurate numbers, there is a real problem and the Swiss banks have a lot of questions to answer, and I plan to pose questions to them today. I plan on actively pursuing this matter until we achieve an authoritative, accurate and final accounting of all assets that numerous Swiss banks continue to hold from this time period and to which the survivors and rightful heirs are entitled.[11]

On March 22, 1996, prior to D'Amato's hearings, the World Jewish Congress and the Jewish Agency published an ad in the Israeli press: "Do you have information on Holocaust-era deposits in Switzerland? We need your help!" Bronfman and Burg personally appealed to the "public at large to offer any information on accounts and other valuables deposited by or for Jews in Swiss banks during the 1930's and 40's" that could be used to help D'Amato.

The ad led to dozens of responses from Israeli citizens and during the course of the struggle hundreds of letters have accumulated. Some looked like identical copies of letters from the 1950s and 1960s. Now, however, a new mood prevailed: to conduct an uncompromising, concentrated, and organized battle, and not leave the applicants to deal with the banks alone.

One letter from Beer Sheva read:

I have letters from 1939–1941, from my parents who were in Germany to myself, a refugee in London. They wrote that they sent money to a bank in Switzerland as payment for travel to Brazil. I notified the Swiss authorities of this and they [the ombudsman], along with the questionnaire they sent me, demand 300 francs for the investigation. The money has been sitting there for 55 years. In other words, the Swiss want to make money off me again. I ask you to act that my murdered parents' money should be returned to me before I close my eyes. I am unwilling to beg to retrieve what is rightfully mine, and to take insults from the Swiss. The demand for 300 francs in payment for an investigation into my parents who were killed in the Holocaust is an insult, and humiliates their memory.

A letter from Ramat-Gan read:

Before the Sukkot holiday in 1934 my late father traveled from Breslau in Germany via Switzerland and Yugoslavia to Palestine, with the aim of checking into the possibility of emigrating. On his way there, my late father managed to deposit in a Swiss bank or financial institution in Zurich 1000 pounds sterling in gold sovereigns. My father took seriously ill and the emigration was delayed. My father died of this illness in the fall of 1938 and the emigration never took place. . . . We, my sister and I, do not know in which financial institution in Switzerland this money was deposited. Moreover, we know that before his death in 1938 our father left money and valuables with a loyal family friend who transferred it to the same bank or financial institution. That friend died forty years ago.

A letter from the Tel Aviv suburb of Kfar Shmaryyahu read:

In 1934, due to Nazi race laws, my parents moved from Berlin to Tel Aviv. In 1938, my mother visited an uncle in Berlin and pleaded with him to leave Germany. The uncle, an officer with the German army during WWI who had received the Iron Cross Class A, said the Nazis wouldn't dare touch anyone with Germany's highest military decoration. When he was asked by my mother how he would make a living, he answered that he had deposited his money in a Swiss bank, and since he was rich, he had nothing to worry about. He had no children. After the war, we learned that he, his wife, and all his relatives died in the Holocaust.

When the Swiss government opened an office for the location of Holocaust victims' accounts in Swiss banks, we petitioned the [ombudsman's] office, completed the required forms, and the office instructed the banks to search for my mother's family's bank accounts. On September 6 we received an answer. No account in the name of our family members was found. In my opinion, this is impossible. The uncle was reliable, of sound mind and body, and I have no doubt that his money is still in a Swiss bank. . . . The banks will do everything in their power not to return the money. This is a huge sum. If the bank paid just 5% annual interest, then the original sum has increased 18 times over in sixty years. No bank would rush to return such sums.

At the beginning of 1996, D'Amato had asked the Jewish Agency for information about the deposits affair. The agency replied in a long memo written by Eli Nathan, WJRO's legal counsel. The note began with a review by Burg of the talks between the Jewish organizations and the Bankers Association, and listed WJRO's demands that still awaited a solution: cooperation in determining the procedure claimants would follow; employment of an independent accounting firm to supervise the banks' examination process; inclusion of representatives from all the Jewish communities, not just the Swiss Jewish community in the examination process; what would be done with the victims' moneys and looted property that remained without heirs; and involvement by well-known Jewish figures in all stages of the process.[12]

It was no coincidence that Burg raised the demand to involve representatives of the international Jewish organizations in all stages of the examination. This question had continued to be a bone of contention in talks held between the organizations and the banks since September 1995. The banks insisted that they were only willing to involve representatives of the local Swiss Jewish community, whose position throughout the crisis was more convenient for the banks, which was why they were willing to include them in the examination process.

On April 16, 1996, just one week before the date set for the first hearing in the Senate Banking Committee, the banks tried to win public favor by formally announcing their willingness to include three representatives of the Swiss Jewish community on a seven-member independent committee to examine the affair. In addition, the SBA announced that it was requesting the Swiss government to examine the steps taken by the banks since 1962 concerning the compensation of Nazi victims for property, "emphasizing transparency and credibility."

Burg replied vehemently that "The idea isn't new. There is no limit to Swiss gall—what the banks are unwilling to do as part of quiet negotiations, they do via the media. What I have learned until now about conducting negotiations and banking is that things are done in a quiet and orderly manner. Nonetheless, when we receive the Swiss offer in an orderly fashiono, we will consider it." The World Jewish Congress's opinion was similar,[13] and as we will see in the following chapters, the banks were forced within a month and a half to agree to the involvement of Jewish Agency and World Jewish Congress representatives, and not the local community, in the independent committee investigating the affair.

Preparations for the hearings were in high gear. On April 21, two days before the hearing began, the Israeli government joined the effort, although indirectly, which was characteristic of the way it handled the entire affair. Then Prime Minister Shimon Peres sent a letter to Burg clarifying "the State of Israel's categorical position on the matter." According to Peres

The State of Israel will never renounce the trusteeship placed in its hands by those who can no longer speak for themselves to press their claims for the world and its peoples. . . . The State of Israel granted the Jewish Agency and the international Jewish organizations the authority to ensure justice be done, to ensure that not a single agora [penny] proved stolen will remain in the wrong hands. The State of Israel firmly stands behind every effort to bring justice and restitute the property to their legal owners; to locate the property of individuals who were brought to their deaths in the furnaces of Europe, which was left without owners, and return it to their heirs who survived the inferno. To restitute all that was robbed in opposition to the natural laws of justice.[14]

In the meantime, the World Jewish Congress was looking for ways to enlist U.S. President Bill Clinton in the struggle. No one but Singer or Bronfman would have imagined that there was any point in trying to interest the world's busiest and most powerful politician in this kind of problem. But Singer thinking politically, thought that Clinton should be enlisted, particularly in view of his conflict with D'Amato about the Banking Committee's investigation of the Whitewater land deal.

The opportunity came in March, while Singer and Bronfman were traveling in Brazil. Bronfman's secretary called to update him on a few matters, one of which was a request from Hillary Rodham Clinton for Bronfman to hold a fundraising luncheon in his Manhattan apartment. Bronfman was not enthusiastic about the idea, primarily because it would involve no small amount of bother, but Singer immediately recognized the opportunity: "Are you nuts? The First Lady!"

The luncheon was set for April 22, just one day before the start of the hearing. Hillary Clinton sat at the head of the table, surrounded by a dozen billionaires. That morning, and Singer promises it was just a coincidence, *New York* Magazine published another report about Radu Lecca's account at Volksbank. Bronfman handed the magazine to Hillary Clinton and asked her to read it. After the First Lady read it, she asked her host, "Swiss banks—can you do something about them?" Bronfman told her, "Yes, Mrs. Clinton. With your husband's help, I believe we can." A few hours later, Bronfman and Singer were invited to meet with Clinton the following afternoon, after the hearings.[15]

That day, Greta Beer came to Washington from her residence in Queens, New York. The next morning, April 23, Mrs. Beer went to the Hurt Building at the foot of Capitol Hill and entered D'Amato's office. She was met by Greg Rickman who led her into D'Amato's large inner office. It was not long after that that D'Amato and Beer left together for the nearby Senate. As they approached the hearing room, a serious-looking D'Amato put a gentlemanly hand on Mrs. Beer's back and promised the many journalists awaiting him, "The committee will do everything to reach the truth."

From the other side of the corridor the representatives of the Jewish organizations entered the room. Bronfman, Singer, and Barak looked tense and drawn for battle. A few minutes later, the delegation from the Bankers Association arrived, headed by Hans Baer and Heinrich Schneider. The pressure on them was evident on their faces, and Schneider barely agreed to say a few words to the media.

The large room was crowded to capacity. D'Amato took his place at the center of the committee members' semicircular table. Baer was invited to sit in the front row alongside Bronfman and then Under Secretary of Commerce Stuart Eizenstat. The banks' representatives sat in the second row, and tried, relatively unsuccessfully, to hide their nervousness. Singer and Barak, who had pulled the strings for the preceding several months, sat close to the committee members' table, as if they wanted to supervise the entire process closely.

At 10:00 A.M. precisely, D'Amato began the proceedings.

Good Morning. This morning the committee meets to take up an important matter that has implications that go back to World War II, the Holocaust, and it involves more than money, more than millions and tens of millions and maybe hundreds of millions and maybe more than that. But it involves the systematic victimization of people.

It involves not just one person that we will hear of and from—Greta Beer, who is a Long Islander from Queens, Long Island, Jackson Heights, New York—and her fight and that of her mom to attempt to deal with victimization that has continued, that started in oppression with the Nazis, with the shroud of secrecy which was initially intended to give protection to the Jews of Europe who sought refuge in Switzerland, a banking system set up so as to protect them from seizure. She and her mother went from city to city and from bank to bank back in the '60s in Switzerland looking for accounts that her father had placed in trust with the Swiss banks. That trust was broken. And because of that broken trust, she and her family have been forced to deal with the evasions and the excuses over 50 years.[16]

In those few sentences, D'Amato set the tone: The banks violated the trust their clients placed in them, the most serious charge that can be made against any bank. From this point on, Hans Baer and his colleagues were on the defensive, a position they could not overcome, not only on that day, but for the months to come. D'Amato added that he was very worried by initial findings uncovered by his staff: "Relying on bank secrecy laws, the Swiss banks have refused to publish the names of owners of accounts that they've identified. It's rather ironic that these secrecy laws originally acted to shield assets of the Holocaust victims from the Nazis are now being used as a sword against those victims and their families."

D'Amato gave the floor to Beer, who presented her background. She was born in northern Romania, and her father, Siegfried Belicdisc, was one of the country's leading industrialists. He traveled a great deal in Europe, and on his trips deposited money in local banks. He opened numbered accounts and often told Greta and her brother about them. "He used to say, 'Don't worry, kids, you have nothing to worry. You'll be provided for. The money is safely deposited in Switzerland.' " In 1940, her father fell ill, and the family moved to Budapest for his medical treatment.

About four years later, when her father's condition worsened, Greta asked him to sign a power of attorney so that her mother could act on his behalf. Beer showed the committee the power of attorney. It was only one line, and written on a scrap of paper. Greta had asked her father for the numbers of the accounts, but her father hesitated. He died a few days later, without ever giving his family the account numbers. After the war, Beer and her mother moved from country to country in Europe until finally reaching the United States.

Beer's brother remained in Europe, and when her mother fell ill in the 1960s, her son invited her to rehabilitate in the Swiss city of Montreau. The trip also offered mother and daughter the opportunity to approach the banks in an attempt to locate the unclaimed accounts. "We went from bank to bank. My mother—they didn't allow me to go in—but [only] my mother, who was the widow of Siegfried Belicdisc."

The two continued to pound the pavement—going from bank to bank until they finally gave up.

How come Swiss banks perpetuate the same things we thought was *tempe posoti*, a thing of the past. And now the Swiss banks perpetuate the same things towards people who have suffered in one way or another, and who had believed [in the banks] and had to do with a broken trust. The only thing I can say, I do hope, Senator D'Amato, that the Swiss banks will see the light—and so many people have died in the meantime—and will see the light to correct what has been done—[for] so long.

Our collective mission here is nothing short of bringing about justice. We are here to help write the last chapter of the bitter legacy of the Second World War and the Holocaust.

What today's hearing is about is respect for human rights and the rule of law—nothing less. I am not here to talk about whether there's only $32 million remaining in the Swiss banks belonging to Holocaust victims and survivors or, as may be closer to the truth, several billion. Nor am I ready to endorse those who say the records were purposely destroyed and the money confiscated.

Bronfman continued and aggressively attacked the report published by the banks in February 1996, saying its figures defied credibility:

"Trust us," they told the victims of the Holocaust, "we looked into our records and our own vaults, and that's all we could find." One of the documents already uncovered and released by your own investigators, sir [Bronfman addressed D'Amato in mentioning the Société Général de Surveillance document] suggests that at a single Swiss financial institution the present value of deposits may be clearly that much alone.

As a businessman, I often deal with bankers, and I know the most important asset any banker can have is his reputation, the trust of his customers. If we cannot have faith in the integrity and trustworthiness and the honor of the banker to protect our deposits, to give a faithful and accurate accounting, then we must go elsewhere. Dealing with Jewish people must be for the Swiss bankers an issue of trust.

Bronfman demanded a complete and credible accounting of the banks' assets during the Nazi period, both those deposited by Jews and by those who stole from the Jews.

Swiss institutions cannot be permitted to come back and say once again that they will create such a process, but that they want to be the ones who appoint the auditors. Their repeated failure of integrity over 50 years has forfeited for them such a privilege. There must be an arm's length process that is credible to the entire world. . . . Many Jews in Central Europe and many others in those countries saw the Nazis coming and made the trip to Switzerland because they thought their assets could be held safely there. They put their faith and their trust in Swiss neutrality and in the integrity of that nation's banking system. It appears they were betrayed.

Another witness whose presence was more important than his actual testimony was Stuart Eizenstat. As we will see in Chapter 9, Eizenstat later had a central role in dealing with Switzerland's wartime actions. The appearance and testimony of the then Under Secretary of Commerce at the Senate Banking Committee hearings symbolized the U.S. administration's commitment to handling the problem of the deposits.

Turning to the Swiss bank institution issue, this could prove a source of assistance for an aging destitute population in Central and Eastern Europe and perhaps their heirs. These survivors have been largely uncompensated since the end of World War II. To provide a possible source of assistance for these persons, as well as to ensure moneys are returned to rightful owners, it is important the U.S. government facilitate the development of a just, transparent and non-discriminatory process for their resolution. The Clinton Administration is committed to do just this.

According to Eizenstat, the U.S. chargé d'affaires in Bern, Michael Polt, was officially pressing the Bankers Association to create an open and transparent process for locating the remaining accounts. Polt also expressed "special concern" about the $250 payment the banks charged claimants, and clarified that the U.S. embassy would continue to follow developments. Among other things, the embassy was in contact with the Bankers Association after the February 1996 report, and heard its explanations.

After Eizenstat spoke, D'Amato conducted a discussion with the committee members, Greta Beer, Bronfman, and Eizenstat. D'Amato opened with a direct attack on the SBA February report, claiming that the investigation had been "absolutely inadequate in terms of the database and the manner in which the data was collected." He also mentioned one of the most difficult problems they faced, the question of accounts opened by trustees, which probably could not be traced. Bronfman said that the real investigation would have to be conducted by an independent accounting firm, and include not only the banks. Eizenstat put an even finer point on that issue. He demanded that the accounting firm examine not only the banks' methodology in dealing with the problem, but also the specific handling of the problem at each of the banks.

Bronfman was asked by Senator Barbara Boxer (D. Calif.) about the location of the $32 million, the figure that had so angered him two months earlier. It appeared that Bronfman had not yet calmed down: "Without any factual backup," Bronfman replied, "my instinctive judgment is that they said in 1962, here's some money, now go away. And they're trying to do that again in 1995. Here's a lot more money, and please go away and leave us alone."

After all the attacks, Hans Baer's situation was clearly very poor. The banks had sent him to the hearings for a number of reasons. His English is eloquent, he lived in the United States in his youth, he had conducted secret negotiations with Israel Singer, and he is Jewish. Baer began his testimony by noting that he owed a debt to the United States and the State of New York—D'Amato's constituency—which granted refuge to his widowed mother when Switzerland faced the danger of Nazi invasion.

On the point at hand, Baer said his testimony was to respond to the painful "accusations that have appeared recently in the press that suggest that the SBA is not sensitive to the interest of Holocaust victims or their heirs who believe they have claims to funds still remaining in Swiss banks."

Baer declared that "The SBA and its members share your deep concern and that of the World Jewish Congress about this all-important issue. We are committed to resolving all outstanding questions about assets that may have belonged to victims of the Holocaust in a sensitive, equitable, open, accurate and professional manner."

He reviewed the steps taken by the SBA, and focused primarily on the establishment of an independent committee later known as the Volcker Commission, which would be authorized to employ an independent accounting firm and other experts in order to investigate the methodology for the identification of accounts. Baer also mentioned the appointment of the ombudsman, whose job it was to receive and collect the claimants petitions to trace accounts. Baer promised that

All identified funds that could have belonged to Holocaust victims that remain undistributed [to heirs] after the claim process is completed will be distributed to charitable organizations. After consultations with the [planned] independent commission and various Jewish groups, it will be determined which charitable organizations should most appropriately receive every last dollar.

In conclusion, Mr. Chairman, let me reiterate the desire for the SBA and its members to resolve the matter fairly and expeditiously in accordance with standards of the Swiss banks and the Jewish community. Our single purpose is to put in place a plan that will sensitively, openly and effectively resolve this matter once and for all. We believe we have done this with the plan I've outlined [the independent commission, the ombudsman, and the distribution of funds]. We hope that all sides will let the process work, and will withhold judgment till the results are in. We are deeply concerned, for example, that speculation in the media that the amounts involved vastly exceed what has been identified to date may only serve to disappoint and harm those whom this process is meant to benefit.

Baer also declared the banks' desire to cooperate with the Senate Banking Committee and Eizenstat, and send interim reports to the committee about the progress of the investigation.

Baer's additional written testimony was far more detailed, and touched on, among other things, a key question: the fate of the documents about each account. It is important to remember that he represented the SBA position at the beginning of 1996, before the evidence began to pile up about the destruction of documents (see Chapter 1).

Then, as now, Swiss banks had to maintain accurate records of their clients' accounts. Specifically, the most important account records, including the identity of the customer and the documents establishing an account are maintained indefinitely for existing accounts, including dormant accounts, and for at least ten years after an account is closed—a period, I am told, that is longer than that required in the United States.

Swiss banks maintain "dormant accounts" indefinitely. (Some Swiss cantons have procedures that permit banks to donate amounts in long-dormant accounts to charitable organizations. However, this in no way relieves the bank of its obligation to pay the dormant assets to its client if he presents himself after the donation was made.) This certainly had benefited many of our clients in the former Soviet bloc who could not (and dared not) seek access to their funds from the late 1940s until 1990.

Baer also touched on the question of why so many claims had been refused.

I can tell you from personal experience that, unfortunately, many claims are supported by almost no information. It is crucially important to treat all potential claims seriously and sensitively and to work with claimants to substantiate their claims, as the Ombudsman is doing. However, a responsible institution cannot simply pay someone an indeterminate amount based on little more than a hope that there is an account somewhere in Switzerland belonging to some relative.

The members of the Senate Banking Committee who may not have read Hans Baer's written testimony, and even if they had, probably did not notice its subtleties, knew only one thing: they had to attack him. Public opinion was clear and unambiguous: for Greta Beer, against Hans Baer. D'Amato led the charge, and asked Baer about the 1962 law. Baer admitted it was possible that not all the property had been located. D'Amato then asked about accounts opened by trustees. Baer thought the independent commission should cover that issue. D'Amato asked about German assets in Switzerland. Baer only said a few words about freezing them. In response to another D'Amato question, Baer declared that the banks continue to manage dormant accounts, and do not appropriate for themselves the moneys in those accounts.

At the conclusion of the hearings, Hans Baer approached Greta Beer, shook her hand warmly, and exchanged a few words with her. Greta Beer remained seated, her right hand in the banker's hand, her left had gripping her handkerchief. In a photograph taken at that moment, Greta Beer looks very agitated, and the handkerchief creates the impression that she is about to burst into tears. Even if that is not the case, the picture, worth a thousand words, created a clear perception.

After the hearings, Singer, Barak, and Baer met again. Afterward, Bronfman, Singer, and Barak went to the White House for the private meeting between Bronfman and Clinton. Bronfman reminded Clinton of the importance of the Jewish vote in the upcoming elections, and particularly emphasized in the size of the Jewish constituences in electorally important New York and Florida. Clinton replied, "I am convinced of the morality of your claim and shocked by it, but I don't want to do anything that will harm our relations with Switzerland." Bronfman responded immediately, "There are not too many Swiss voters in New York or Florida." Clinton got the hint. "Naturally, that is not my consideration," the president of the United States contested. "This is a moral issue."

Clinton immediately summoned his then chief of staff, Leon Panetta. In Bronfman's presence, Clinton instructed Panetta to consider legislation that would punish bankers who did not cooperate with the U.S. government in investigating the matter. In order to remove all doubt, Clinton clarified that he would cooperate with D'Amato concerning Switzerland, despite Whitewater. Finally, Clinton instructed Panetta to publish an official announcement, expressing the president's support of the World Jewish Congress's efforts to locate Holocaust survivors' accounts in Swiss banks.[17]

The following day, April 24, 1996, Greg Rickman, Steinberg, and Singer met in the archives in College Park, Maryland. The results of their work would shock global public opinion, and bring Switzerland to a dramatic policy change in the deposits crisis.

9

"OPENING IN THE WALL"
Neutral Switzerland Served Nazi Interests

IN FEBRUARY 1997, the cover art on *Time* magazine was a swastika made of gold bars, illustrating an article that dealt almost entirely with Switzerland. Within four months, CNN's Web site posted an item about the discovery of more dormant accounts in Switzerland. It was accompanied by an illustration with a swastika at its center, along with a pile of gold coins. The caption read, "Swiss banks."

In the eyes of the Western world, particularly the American press, this was a portrait of Switzerland: an accomplice of Nazi Germany, almost to the point of identifying Bern with Berlin. This image is overwrought, distorted, and unfair, but is based on a series of reports published since mid-1996, each correct unto itself. Switzerland was never Nazi, but certainly sinned through close economic cooperation with Germany throughout World War II.

Did this cooperation actually lengthen the war, as then Under Secretary of State Stuart Eizenstat claimed in his May 1997, report?[1] If so, then Bern bears an indirect, but apparent responsibility for the deaths of thousands of soldiers and citizens, including many victims of the Holocaust. Due to the lack of comprehensive research on the financing of the German war effort, however, the accusations cannot be proved or disproved.

Almost everything reported concerning Swiss-German relations since mid-1996 was perfectly well known to historians for many years. The most prominent example is Professor Arthur Smith's book, *Hitler's Gold*, published in 1989 (2nd ed. 1996) which included most of the information concerning the Swiss purchase of German gold.[2] Very few of those handling the matter of Holocaust victims' deposits, both politicians and journalists, however, knew of the previous research concerning Swiss-German relations. Therefore, many of them truly believed that they had made new discoveries, and published them with great fanfare, mostly in the United States and Britain.

Since reporters and politicians are not professional historians, they often fall into the trap presented by archives that can contain dozens and hundreds of relatively worthless documents for every one important piece of paper. This is particularly true of intelligence or diplomatic archives, the two principal sources for documents about the victims' deposits. Intelligence agents and diplomats have a tendency to write down everything they learn and everything that occurs to them. An inexperienced reader, can easily mix up facts and assessments and proposals and decisions, which apparently happened in some of the current reports on Nazi gold.

This instance is a clear example of the distance between the Ivory Tower of the academic world and the public world. Academics such as Arthur Smith researched and unraveled important facts, but could not find a way to bring them to the attention of decision makers or the general public. It was only under the right conditions—Senator D'Amato's pressure on Switzerland, the World Jewish Congress's demands for an investigation, the opening of classified documents, reports in the media—did the matter make headlines.[3]

What was the importance of the gold trade between Germany and neutral countries, primarily Switzerland? It enabled Berlin to convert gold looted across Europe into hard currency that could be used to purchase raw materials and vital goods, also primarily acquired from those same neutral countries. This critical need, from the German perspective, stemmed from the embargo implemented by the Allies, which did not allow Berlin to purchase anything outside of the Reich and the occupied territories. This was Switzerland's importance—the country provided a crack in the wall of the embargo; in a war in which, in the words of author William Shirer, military might was greatly dependent on economic power.

The Germans themselves recognized Switzerland's significance in real time. In a top secret memo from June 1943, Minister of Propaganda Joseph Goebbels was asked by the Ministry of Economics to avoid any mention in the press of the Swiss gold reserves, "most of which stem from us." The ministry emphasized that Switzerland was the only country trading in gold with Berlin, thus enabling Berlin to acquire foreign currency. In January 1944, the Reichsbank (the German central bank) clarified what would happen if Switzerland were to stop gold trading with Germany: "We would no longer get Swiss francs for military and other non-commercial matters: our gold would therefore be worthless for all purposes of interest to us."[4]

Germany looted everything available all over Europe, especially monetary gold that belonged to the central banks of occupied countries, namely, Holland, Belgium, and France. In contrast to other looted property like works of art, crops, or machinery, gold was easily converted and used for any purpose.

No one knows the exact sum of the loot. The Eizenstat report determined that Germany stole gold worth $579 million ($5.2 billion in current values) from eleven countries. Of that sum, Switzerland purchased $398–414 million in nominal gold ($3.55–3.7 billion in current values). Two-thirds were transferred to Switzerland's account in the Swiss National Bank (central bank) in Bern as partial payment, for the raw materials, electricity, and weapons that Germany purchased from Switzerland. The remainder was transferred to other countries' accounts in the central bank, in exchange for goods they sold to Germany.

The international committee of experts appointed by the Swiss government in 1997, known as the Bergier Commission, reached a similar conclusion in May 1998. The committee determined that the extent of the theft from the central banks was $483.2 million ($4.3 billion in current values), and $82 million from individual victims ($730 million in current values). The Swiss central bank purchased $387.8 million ($3.45 billion current values), while the commercial banks purchased $56.3 million ($501 million in current values). The acquisitions by the commercial banks were made until October 1941, when the central bank decided to handle all the trade itself as part of its financial policy. Swiss Bank Corp. had a strong lead in the commercial banks' acquisition of gold from Germany, with $34.9 million ($311 million in current values).[5]

The big question is whether Switzerland knew the gold was stolen. The clear answer is in the report released in September 1996, by the British Foreign Office. Foreign Office historians found that Switzerland must have known no later than early 1943 that it was buying stolen gold. By then, Switzerland had already bought more than $200 million in gold from Germany, the entire volume of Germany's prewar gold reserves, according to official Reichsbank reports. Since the Reichsbank figures were public domain, and since Switzerland knew perfectly well how much gold it had purchased, there could only be one conclusion: Bern knew the source of the gold with certainty, and kept on buying it.[6]

There is also direct evidence that the Swiss central bank knew the source of the gold. In the fall of 1943, the bank's governor, Ernst Weber, wrote to the Ministry of Finance, expressing the hope that "the gold dealings with the Reichsbank won't cause the bank problems, as it is impossible to deny that some of the gold originates in occupied countries." In another letter to the Ministry of Finance, the central bank stated that "according to international law, an occupying power is entitled to confiscate gold." The ministry replied, in a manner that makes the Swiss government a full partner, that it trusted the central bank implicitly, although the government would prefer that the transactions be "more modest" in the future.[7]

Furthermore, the Bergier Commission found that in June 1942, the central bank even considered resmelting the gold it purchased from Germany, for fear it would be difficult to sell. This was after the Belgian government in exile published a list of property looted in Brussels. The numbers etched into the gold bars could have identified them as stolen property. In this case, the central bank clearly knew that stolen property was involved, but continued to buy it. At the end of 1943, the head of the bank's legal de-

COPY
cb

15 December 1945

STATEMENT BY MR. EMIL PUHL.

I arrived in Switzerland on 15 March 1945, and left on 19 April 1945. I was on a mission to the Swiss National Bank, but for the first time in the history of negotiations of this sort between the Swiss National Bank and the Reichsbank, the governments participated in the actual meetings. The German side was represented by two officials of the Legation in Bern, and the Swiss Government was represented by Dr. Kohli, of the Swiss Political Department, who was advised by Mr. Hotz, of the Department of Commerce.

The situation upon my arrival was that all German accounts (including those of the Reichsbank and of German subsidiaries in Switzerland) had been blocked by the Swiss Government. I began negotiations by asking that the Reichsbank accounts be freed, since they represented the monetary reserve of a central bank, even though the blocking of German accounts had taken place for political reasons. The negotiations were prolonged beyond the period which I had expected would have been necessary, because the Swiss showed a certain reluctance to come to the agreement I was seeking. I was assisted in attaining the desired results by the interests of certain Swiss circles in obtaining a resumption of payments. These circles helped me behind the scenes, because they were afraid that the German resources would be used to satisfy other claimants.

The results of the negotiations were laid down in correspondence between the Reichsbank and the Swiss National Bank, and were reported by me in letters to the Reich Economics Minister in his capacity as President of the Reichsbank. The practical result was to free the Reichsbank accounts for payments desired by us. Quotas were established for a three month period (ending at the end of April) for payments for interest payments on Standstill credits, "new credits", gold mortgages, and Dawes, Young and certain other bonds, payments for Swiss electric power exports to Germany, reinsurance payments, allowances for Swiss repatriates from Germany, and certain miscellaneous transfers.

These payments were in the mutual interest of Germany and Switzerland. The interest of the Swiss receivers is clear. German interests were as follows:

a. Standstill credits. If Germany had not paid the interest on standstill credits in free exchange, the Swiss banks would have had the right to denounce the Standstill Agreements, and we were afraid that they would have seized the assets of German debtors which were covered by these agreements. These Standstill credits were granted in free foreign exchange, and their maintenance was extremely important for the German economy.

b.

Statement by Emil Puhl about his April 1945 talks with Swiss government and Swiss National bank officials. (U.S. National Archives; Senator D'Amato's office) partment even confirmed that it knew the Germans were pillaging the property of residents of the occupied countries, "such as Jews." The Bergier Commission even determined that the central bank knew what had happened to the looted victims.[8]

Eizenstat says that at least some of the gold Switzerland purchased had been stolen from Holocaust victims, resmelted, and reached Bern. This finding, which created a storm in May 1997, was confirmed by the Bergier report one year later. The commission found that the $2.9 million in gold ($25.8 million in current values) that came from Germany was deposited first in a "Melmer Account" in the Reichsbank, an account in the name of SS Officer Bruno Melmer, and that the source was mostly Holocaust victims.[9] Nonetheless, it is important to state that Bern could not have known for certain the exact source of each gold bar. The Swiss knew that the gold they purchased originated somewhere in plundered Europe, but they had no way of knowing if it was stolen from Jews, Gypsies, or central banks.

How much gold was stolen from Holocaust victims and what happened to it? In research prepared for the World Jewish Congress, economist Sidney Zabludoff estimates $800 million in current terms as the value of all the gold stolen directly from citizens of occupied countries by various German forces. But, he cannot say how much of that sum was stolen from Europe's Jews.

A document in the British Public Record Office indicates that the majority of the gold remained in Germany. In May 1945, General Dwight Eisenhower, commander of the Allied forces, reported to the Joint Chiefs of Staff in Washington that gold was discovered in German territory conquered by the U.S. military. Although Eisenhower did not report the exact amount or value of the gold discovered at thirteen different sites, the Americans seized hundreds of crates, boxes, and bags containing hundreds of gold bars and thousands of gold coins.

Most of the gold was found in a salt mine in Merkers, in western Germany, in which hundreds of packages of stolen assets, including jewelry and gold, and hundreds of thousands of gold coins, were discovered. In another document, the British estimated the value at about $1 billion in current terms. Among other things, Passover dishes were found, which hints that other items had been stolen from Jews. In addition, gold was discovered by Soviet forces in Austria and East Germany. Although this has not been proven, Eisenhower mentioned rumors about hundreds of bags of gold brought to Berlin, before it was occupied by the Red Army, and it is a reasonable assumption that the treasures of stolen gold were not specifically concentrated in the western Reich.

U.S. military officers payed a great deal of attention to tracing German gold. Reichsbank documents were saved and the officers took statements from three key central bank officials, Vice President Emil Puhl, gold department head Albert Thomas, and Karl Gruefener, head of the gold division of the foreign currency department. The interrogations determined the location of almost all of the German gold, that which was held by Germany and that which was sold to other countries.

The gold stolen by the Wehrmacht, the SS, the Gestapo, and others, was distributed to three principal groups. The gold that came from the concentration camps was transferred to the Reichsbank in Berlin. The dental work was smelted by the government mint in Prussia. The smelted gold, worth $40–50 million in current values, was exchanged for Reichsmarks to finance SS activities. Another portion of the gold was included in the Reichsbank's monetary reserves, from which the SS could also withdraw gold or cash in exchange. More gold was discovered by the Allies in various parts of Europe, sometimes in concentration camps or nearby, when the retreating Germans had not had time to transfer it to Berlin.[10]

The primary Swiss motive for gold trading was the need to maintain the strength of the Swiss franc, which relied, as did most currencies then, on the gold standard. This meant that the Swiss central bank had to have sufficient gold reserves to buy any sum of francs offered to it. During the war, foreign currency movement in and out of Switzerland was volatile and affected the price of gold. The central bank was sometimes forced to regulate the currency by selling gold bars from its reserves. This required large amounts of gold, which Germany was willing to supply in generous quantities.[11]

Bern's claim that it acted in good faith in buying gold from Germany could no longer be used from January 1943 onward. That month, when Britain reached the conclusion that Switzerland was buying stolen gold, the Allies published a warning to all the neutral countries, invalidating gold or other stolen property originating in occupied countries. This meant that after the war the pillaged countries could demand the immediate return of their property from the neutral countries, which would be forced to return it and lose the money they paid, assuming Germany would be incapable of returning the money.[12]

In February 1944, the United States, Britain, and the Soviet Union made it clear, in no uncertain terms, that they would not purchase gold from any country that traded in gold with Germany. Switzerland was unimpressed. It continued to buy as much gold from Germany as the Third Reich was able to sell. Simple math proves that if Switzerland purchased a nominal total of $400 million, and the acquisitions had reached $200 million by January 1943, then after the first warning from the Allies, Switzerland continued to buy gold at the same volume.

The Allies had a hard time forcing Switzerland to stop buying gold from Germany. Their means of enforcement were limited to declarations, pressure, and warnings as the Allies themselves needed Switzerland as a center for intelligence activity, for the service it provided in handling prisoners of war, and as gold trading partners. According to Bergier Commission figures, Switzerland bought gold from the United States at a nominal $518 million, and from Britain, $154.5 million ($4.6 billion and $1.37 billion, respectively, in current values).[13]

In the meantime, the United States had decided on the Safehaven operation in May 1944, which has made the headlines often in recent years after the exposure of the German-Swiss relationship. The purpose of the operation was to prevent a safe haven for Nazi assets. U.S. military intelligence units in Europe were instructed to prevent the transfer of German assets to neutral countries—mainly Switzerland—to ensure that German property would be available after the war for rehabilitating Europe and paying reparations to the Allies; to allow stolen property to be returned to its rightful owners; to prevent the escape of senior Nazis; and, above all, to obstruct Germany's ability to renew the war.

In practice, the United States and Britain had a difficult time implementing Safehaven, first due to differences of opinion between two countries, and later due to difficulties in negotiating with the neutral countries, primarily Switzerland. Despite these problems, the United States preferred not to take any steps against Switzerland for the previously mentioned reasons. Swiss policy did not change until February 1945, when a U.S. delegation arrived in Bern, headed by presidential aide Lauchlin Currie, along with a British delegation headed by Dingle Foot, the parliamentary secretary of the Ministry of Economic Warfare. The Swiss side was represented by the number two person in the delegation, Walter Stucki. The purpose of the talks was to finally end trade between Switzerland and Germany and Swiss trading in stolen gold.

Only at that point, when Germany's collapse was only a matter of time, did Switzerland agree to freeze all German assets within its borders; the cabinet made the decision on February 16, 1945. The freeze meant that Germany could not withdraw any of its assets in Switzerland, and would certainly prevent the further transfer of property that would have been immediately frozen upon arrival. The United States was satisfied with the Swiss declaration, and it appeared that finally the United States had managed to close the biggest loophole in the embargo on Germany, although after most of the property had already escaped, but better late than never.[14]

In practice, Switzerland breached its agreement with the United States almost as soon as it was signed, in an agreement it made with the Reichsbank signed in April 1945, just three weeks before the end of the war, with the knowledge and blessing of Bern's Foreign Ministry. The German central bank was represented in the talks by its deputy governor, Emil Puhl, who was also responsible for gold looted by the SS from Holocaust victims and was tried for his crimes after the war. The Puhl Agreement was reached when it became clear that Germany was beaten and ruined, when everyone knew about Nazi atrocities, and Switzerland had already promised to abstain from economic ties with Germany. Therefore, the Puhl Agreement is the most important evidence concerning the nature of Swiss-German relations.

Puhl came to Switzerland on March 15, 1945, and stayed there until April 19, just three weeks before Germany surrendered. Puhl testified under oath to his American interrogators in November of that year and revealed—and this is the most important recent discovery concerning that period—that official representatives of the Swiss government took part in those talks for the first time along with representatives of the central bank. The senior Swiss government representative was Dr. Robert Kohli, the head of the legal department at the Foreign Ministry, who later became director general of the ministry and conducted negotiations with the Israeli government concerning Holocaust victims' property. He was joined at the talks by Dr. Jean Hotz, head of the trade department of the Ministry of the Economy.

When Puhl reached Bern, all German accounts in Switzerland were frozen. His goal was at least to thaw the accounts of the Reichsbank—the assets of the crumbling German government—if not all the accounts, including private German property. To his surprise, Puhl found an attentive ear among his Swiss colleagues, as he testified after the war:

My general impression was that the principal motive on the part of the Swiss in entering into this agreement was that they realized the importance of maintaining a friendly relationship between the Swiss National Bank and the Reichsbank, not merely at the time but for the future, regardless of what would happen to Germany at the end of the war. The Swiss saw the importance of maintaining good economic and financial relations with Germany after the war. This point was made to me repeatedly by Dr. Kohli, Dr. Weber [Ernst Weber, governor of the Swiss central bank] and all the other Swiss people concerned. We discussed openly and frankly the probability of Germany losing the war.

The Swiss people realized that the February 16 decree, blocking German assets, was written with a hot pen and involved Switzerland in a type of control which was not in the best interest of Switzerland.

At the end of the talks, Switzerland agreed to thaw Reichsbank deposits, and anchored its agreement in an exchange of letters that became known as the Puhl Agreement. A U.S. document from the end of May 1945, determined that in mid-May, the Reichsbank had 50 million francs in the Swiss central bank (220 million francs in current values). According to Puhl's testimony, some of the thawed moneys payed for the electricity Germany purchased from across the Alps, and some remained open for free use by the Reichsbank.

Puhl concluded that

CONFIDENTIAL

Rubin

GERMAN GOLD MOVEMENTS (ESTIMATE)
From April, 1938 to May, 1945 (In Millions of U. S. Dollars)

INCOME		OUTGO	
Germany started the war with estimated gold reserves of	100	Sold to Swiss National Bank . .	275 to 282
(Published gold reserves were only 29)		Possibly sold to Swiss Commercial Banks before 1942	20
Taken over from Austria	46	Washed through Swiss National Bank depot account and eventually re-exported to Portugal and Spain (larger part by far to Portugal) . . .	100
" " " Czechoslovakia .	16		
" " " Danzig	4	Rumania	32.5
" " " Poland	12	Sweden	18.5
" " " Holland	168		
" " " Belgium	223	Found in Germany (including 64 earmarked for Italy and 32 earmarked for Hungary)	293
" " " Yugoslavia	25		
" " " Luxembourg . . .	5	Sold to or used in Balkan countries and Middle East-- mainly Turkey	10
" " " France	53		
" " " Italy	64		**752**
" " " Hungary	32		
	748		

- -

SWISS GOLD MOVEMENTS (SWISS OFFICIAL STATEMENT)
From January 1, 1939 to June 30, 1945 (In Millions of U.S. Dollars)

Purchased from Germany	282.9	Sold to Germany	4.9
" " Portugal	12.7	" " Portugal	116.6
" " Sweden	17.0	" " Spain	42.6
		" " Turkey	3.5

Conclusions: (1) All gold that Germany sold after a certain date, probably from early 1943 on, was looted gold, since her own reserves, including hidden reserves with which she started the war, were exhausted by that time; (2) out of $278,000,000-worth of gold that Switzerland purchased from Germany, the larger part was looted gold; in addition, Switzerland has taken $100,000,000 looted gold in deposit, which later on was re-exported to Spain and Portugal for German account; (3) among the gold that the Swiss sold during the war to Portugal, Spain, and Turkey, there could have been looted German gold; (4) the gold that Switzerland bought from Sweden during the war could theoretically be German looted gold; monetary experts all over the world (Switzerland has monetary experts at her disposal) knew, or ought to have known, roughly the figures and movements as contained in the above estimate--certainly they knew the gold holdings and gold reserves of the German Reichsbank. Switzerland therefore was lacking good faith. In addition, she was warned that all Germany's own pre-war gold stocks had been used up by mid-1943 at the latest and therefore all the gold then in the possession of Germany must be presumed to be looted gold.

ES:CWFletcher:jd
2/5/46

German gold movements report, February 5, 1946. (U.S. National Archives; World Jewish Congress)

Although my original hope had been to obtain the complete freeing of the Reichs-bank accounts, I was perfectly satisfied with the agreement I obtained, because for all practical purposes it amounted to more or less the same thing. We were afraid of the institution of a complete financial blockade of Germany. By this agreement we maintained a limited opening in the wall of restrictions surrounding Germany.[15]

At the end of the war, the Swiss National Bank began to search for justifications for its policies, a trend that became more substantial after Germany's surrender. The Bergier Commission report notes four primary arguments used by the bank, and rejects all of them. The first was that the gold was purchased in good faith, without any way to know its origins. The bank pointed out Puhl's promises that the Reichsbank was not trans-ferring stolen gold to Bern. The Bergier Commission also noted that in Puhl's interrogation after the war, he stated that senior Swiss central bank officials knew precisely what the source of the gold was. The commission determined unequivocally that the bank knew very early on about the loot-ing of central banks and private citizens, and what happened to the victims.

The second argument was that neutrality meant Bern could trade with both Germany and the Allies. The Bergier Commission determined, how-ever, that in 1943, senior central bank officials said that neutrality did not require the bank to trade with both sides. The committee noted that Swe-den, also a neutral country, had refused to buy suspected stolen gold from Germany. It should also be added, although the Bergier report did not state this that there is no comparison between buying stolen gold from Germany and buying gold from the Allies, to which the Allies were legally entitled.

The third argument was fear that refusal to buy the gold would lead to German military action against Switzerland. The Bergier Commission says that this argument was not made in real time. Conversely, if this issue was discussed at all during the war years, it was that Germany had a vested interest in maintaining Swiss neutrality. The real justification for the gold trade, the committee states, was the central bank's desire to profit from the trade.

The fourth and last argument was that the central bank coordinated its policies with the government and therefore complaints should not be ad-dressed to them. The government, for its part, claimed that after the war it did not receive the necessary information about the gold trade from the central bank. The Bergier Commission's analysis concludes that the central bank's actions were mostly independent, although at the end of the war gold trade became a political issue in which the central bank became the ball in a game of "political ping pong."[16] The commission does not deal with Puhl's testimony that proves government involvement in the agree-ment with Germany in April 1945, and essentially does not discuss in depth the need for some government role in determining the gold policy and implementing it.

The question of the gold Switzerland purchased came up for discussion at the Washington Conference in March 1946. At the beginning of the talks, Swiss National Bank director general Alfred Hirs claimed that the gold trade stemmed from monetary policy considerations and the neutrality policy. Hirs even claimed that there was no reason to discuss the question of stolen gold, as the bank relied on Puhl's promise that no such gold was included in Reichsbank shipments. The Allies categorically rejected these claims, citing on the grounds of Puhl's own statements. It became clear to the Swiss government that the negotiations could not be left in Hirs's hands, and leadership was transferred to Walter Stucki. Stucki raised the argument that Germany as an occupying power had the right to appropriate the assets of the occupied countries, and opposed the Allied right to claim for themselves any German assets deposited in Switzerland.

The Allies had trouble with these legal arguments and raised moral issues, but the Swiss did not budge. Swiss stubbornness led the Allies to lower their estimates of the volume of gold purchased by Switzerland. Original nominal estimates had been $200–398 million (multiply by nine for current values). As mentioned earlier, Eizenstat now determines that the sum was much higher—$398–414 million. But at the start of talks, the United States and Britain set the amount at $250 million as a basis for the talks.

Later, the Allies reduced the sum to just $130 million, the volume of gold stolen from Belgium, for which they had hard evidence of its arrival in Switzerland. When the Allies demanded its receipt, Stucki stopped the talks. The Allies gave in and dropped down to $88 million, the amount Switzerland admitted to, although they claimed it had been a legal purchase. This was Switzerland's position throughout the talks, but since the United States had already decided not to use economic sanctions, the Allies were more or less subject to the extent of Swiss goodwill.

Their goodwill amounted to $58.1 million, which Stucki called Switzerland's final offer at the beginning of May. The Allies reached the conclusion that they would not receive a better offer, and agreed. Seymor Rubin, a senior member of the U.S. delegation, called the agreement "sufficient," as it ensured that respectable sums of money would be available for the rehabilitation of refugees. However, simple math indicates that the Swiss technique for wearing down the Allies resulted in the Allies having to do with just 15 percent of the stolen gold that Switzerland purchased. In addition, Switzerland promised to freeze German assets in its territory, so the Allies could use them to rehabilitate Europe and cover their war damages.

Anyone who thought that this was the end of the story apparently did not understand the Swiss very well. They evaded fulfilling their promises, despite the fact that the United States hastened to release Swiss assets frozen during the war. It should be noted that as long as German assets were held in Switzerland, primarily in the banks, the Swiss economy continued to benefit, as they provided the banks with a vast resource for their ongoing financial activities. Differences of opinion delayed the receipt of German assets and Swiss payment for refugee rehabilitation. But Switzerland immediately transferred payment for the gold to the Tripartite Gold Commission (consisting of the United States, United Kingdom, and France), established as part of the December 1945 Paris Agreement for the purpose of receiving and distributing the returned gold.

In the spring of 1951, the Allies and Switzerland finally agreed on changes to the Washington Accord (parallel with talks between West Germany and Switzerland). The results were the series of agreements made in August 1952. The basis was the August 26, Bonn Agreement between Switzerland and West Germany that settled the financial problems remaining between them stemming from the war. The agreement determined that Bonn would pay Bern 121.5 million francs (1952 worth, $28.3 million, $170 million in current values) against payment Switzerland would make to the Allies for German property without heirs.

The German owners of the property in Switzerland could donate one-third of its value to the German government or receive compensation from the Swiss government in marks. The West German government borrowed the 121.5 million francs from the Swiss banks. Meanwhile, the Swiss government again demanded that the West German government repay a war-era debt of 1.2 billion francs (then worth $275 million, now worth $1.65 billion). Bonn agreed to pay 650 million francs, holding East Germany (not a party to the agreement) responsible for the rest.

In the Bern Agreement between Switzerland and the Allies, signed on April 28, Switzerland agreed to pay the Allies 121.5 million francs against receipt of German assets, from which the 20 million francs Switzerland had contributed earlier to refugee rehabilitation was to be deducted. The Allies contributed 13 million francs to refugee rehabilitation of the total 101.5 million francs they received.

Let us now see how cheaply Switzerland got away in the complex maze of postwar agreements. First, the gold. We clearly saw that the Allies agreed to compensation of just 15 percent of the gold Switzerland purchased. Second, German property. The Allies estimated that this ranged from $250 to 750 million in property, and for the sake of simplicity, let us work with the average, $500 million. This sum was to be divided equally between Switzerland and the Allies. In practice, Switzerland transferred to the Allies just $28 million, and even that is a misleading figure. As we have just seen, Germany financed the Swiss payment using a loan from Swiss banks. Furthermore, Switzerland managed to deduct the sum it promised to pay for refugee rehabilitation from the German property instead of adding it on. How did Bern work this miracle? It had more patience than the Allies because it had the property. And Bern understood perfectly well that in the context of the Cold War, no one would push too hard on matters relating to the previous war.[17]

In response to the Eizenstat report, the Swiss government noted on May 22, 1997 its importance in revealing new details, but in the same breath also noted that most of the issues had been researched in the past. Bern stated that

At the conclusion of the Washington Accord in 1946 the parties to the signing realized all essential facts. Thanks to their intelligence sources, the Allies even had precise knowledge of the Swiss negotiating position. Regarding the agreement's implementation, the report confirms in writing that Switzerland had paid the settlement sum at the prevailing value of Sfr. 250 million agreed to in the gold negotiations.

This announcement was the first time that Bern dealt with the question of whether it had had to conduct gold trade with Germany to safeguard its existence: "Only hypotheses are possible to question whether Switzerland in 1943–44 would have been in a situation to break off business ties with the Axis Powers without provoking the risk of an invasion," is the Swiss government's answer to this key question. "The Federal Council [cabinet] regards the representation of Switzerland as the banker of the Nazis as a one-sided package judgment. However, it is justified to criticize financial transactions known [in real time] to be questionable." Bern explained its relations with Berlin after the Nazis rose to power in saying that today, too, its neighboring Germany is a valuable economic partner.

Concerning the claim that its actions prolonged the war, Switzerland says this claim is not proven by the report's findings:

Such a comment would be justified—if at all—if it were based on a comprehensive study of the German war economy, mutual dependencies [between Germany, Switzerland, and other countries], and [Switzerland's] economic relationships with the Allies. Such a study is not available. It is also not evident that the difficult situation faced by Switzerland had relaxed accordingly with the turn in the war by 1943.

Switzerland commented extensively on Eizenstat's criticism of its neutrality policies, and determined that

Neutrality led to a difficult tightrope walk between adaptation and resistance. Today we know that this also led to mistakes. The faint-hearted refugee policy concerning Jews was inexcusable. In the business and financial sector concessions were sometimes made to the Axis Powers which are very hard to comprehend today.

It must not be forgotten that Switzerland's neutral stance also served Allied interests. Switzerland took on numerous protective mandates in their behalf in order to serve their interests in enemy countries. Thanks to its neutrality, Switzerland could assume wide-ranging humanitarian tasks such as visiting prisoner-of-war camps in Germany and Japan and tending to civilians interned in Switzerland.[18]

The Swiss announcement does make a few valid points, along with others in which Bern embellished the truth. As stated at the beginning of the chapter, it is impossible to make an unequivocal determination, as Eizenstat did, that Switzerland prolonged the war. Bern correctly states that there is no proof of this in the report, and therefore it is a political and not a historical conclusion. Switzerland was also correct in describing the difficulties it faced, surrounded by Nazi Germany, annexed Austria, Fascist Italy, and occupied France.

It is also true that Swiss neutrality was of great assistance to the Allies, and Switzerland did fulfill important humanitarian roles. There is no justification for criticizing the neutrality policy in and of itself five decades after the fact, claiming it is impossible not to take a stance against Satan. Countries act according to self-interests and compulsions, and not according to moral considerations. The United States itself did not enter the war until it was attacked. Another correct claim is that the Allies knew in 1946 all the necessary details before signing the Washington Accord, and if they gave in to Switzerland, they can only blame themselves.

On the other hand, Switzerland continues to evade the toughest question: Why did economic cooperation with Germany continue until the last days of the war? Let us suppose that in 1943 and even in 1944 that there was still some fear of a German invasion. But did Switzerland really expect that anyone would believe fears of invasion after the Allied landing in France in June 1944? Was there even a hint of such fears in January 1945, after the desperate German attack on the Ardennes was repelled, and the Allied armies were closing in on Germany's borders? Why did Switzerland agree only in February 1945 to freeze German assets, and moreover, why did Switzerland violate the agreement in less than two months, just three weeks before Germany's surrender? Do Swiss actions at the end of the war teach a little about Switzerland's real motives—selfish and economic—at the beginning of the war, too?

In the opinion of the Bergier Commission, even if profit was not the only motive for the central bank's actions, there is no doubt it played a fundamental role. Gold trade contributed to 67 percent of the bank's profits in 1942, the peak year for trade with Germany, compared with just 39 percent in 1939. The bank made a total of $4.3 million ($38 million in current values) from its trade with Germany.[19]

Another principal question concerns Swiss refugee policy that cost the lives of 30–40,000 Jews when they were deported from Switzerland to their deaths. Bern calls it an "unforgivable policy" and does not even try to justify it. As we know that only Jewish refugees were deported, and that those responsible for the policy knew that this meant certain death, the question arises about whether this was simply lack of concern or whether the darkest sentiments were at work in Switzerland.

Jewish refugees amassed at the Swiss border from the moment the Nazis rose to power, but Switzerland was not interested in absorbing them. The Swiss solution was to demand that Germany stamp the passports of Jews with the letter J so that border police would immediately recognize and return them to the Nazis. When Germany hesitated to implement this measure, Switzerland threatened to demand entry visas from all German nationals seeking to pass through Swiss territory. The threat worked, and from October 1938, the Reich stamped a J in the passports of all its Jews. The idea came from Heinrich Rothmund, commander of the Swiss foreigners' police, which initiated and implemented the severe policy of deporting Jewish refugees back to Germany or occupied France, under the authority of the Minister of Justice and Police, Eduard von Steiger.

The limitations on the entry of refugees were imposed in October 1939, two months into the war, and they were stiffened after the occupation of Western Europe in 1940. It is now known that Rothmund and his superiors were aware as early as 1942 about the fate of the Jews of Eastern Europe, but their policy remained in effect. In the first years of the war, almost all the Jewish refugees who reached Switzerland were deported just for being Jewish.

When a Polish division that had been fighting alongside the defeated French army escaped to the Swiss border in June 1940, the Swiss singled out the Christian soldiers and allowed them to stay, while the Jewish soldiers were returned to France where they fell into the hands of the conquering Germans. Only in the last years of the war, due to the increasing pressure of local public opinion, particularly from the church leadership, did Bern agree to allow Jewish refugees to enter, and transported them to military camps. Conditions were reasonable in some places, while in others the refugees fell victim to maltreatment by the locals in charge, and some even lost their lives.

The Swiss Jewish community was asked to fund the maintenance of Jewish refugees in the camps, as opposed to funding provided by the government for other refugees. A total of 230,000 refugees found asylum in Switzerland, but only 22,000 of those were Jews. In light of these figures, it is clear that there is no validity to Swiss claims that economic reasons prevented the absorption of many more Jewish refugees. The claim concerning fears of angering Germany is also unacceptable, and certainly not in the later years of the war. After the war, Heini Borenstein, who was a Jewish refugee activist in Switzerland, met with Rothmund and asked him if he regretted his actions in light of what he now knew about the Holocaust. Rothmund's reply was, "No. The law is the law, and I had to defend my country's interests."[20]

The regret came fifty years later. On May 7, 1995, in a speech to Parliament marking the fiftieth anniversary of Germany's surrender, then Swiss president Kaspar Villiger asked forgiveness from the Jewish people for the refugee policy and for stamping their passports with the letter J. That year, Paul Grueninger's name was also cleared. He was a St. Galin police officer who helped 3,000 Jews enter Switzerland illegally. Grueninger was fired, dishonorably discharged from the police force, could not find employment, and died in poverty. The fact that Yad V'Shem declared him a Righteous Among Nations did not impress Switzerland, and it was only in 1995 that a St. Galin court determined that he was a noble man to whom a great injustice had been done.

Let us now return briefly to the gold affair. In mid-1997, then British Foreign Minister Michael Rifkind declared his country's intention to hold an international conference in London concerning the stolen gold. After the Labour Party's electoral victory, his successor, Robin Cook, announced his support for the conference, which was held in London on December 2–4, 1997. More than forty countries and organizations took part, although most of the delegations consisted of fairly low-ranking officials and experts. Nonetheless, the conference was a success in at least two areas. It returned the problem of the stolen gold to the public agenda, and it took practical steps to begin to help victims of Nazi persecution and those researching the matter.[21]

The international media dedicated a great deal of time and space to the three-day conference at Lancaster House. Dozens of television crews and reporters were located in a huge tent in the site's courtyard. The Israeli delegation and Jewish organizations, in a united and impressive performance, managed to quickly make over the conference from a general and rather dry academic discussion, to one that dealt with the distress of survivors.

In his opening speech, Cook announced the establishment of a fund to aid Holocaust survivors. He called on the attending nations to donate to the fund the gold worth $70 million that had remained undistributed since the end of the war. The United States announced a $25 million contribution on the spot. Since then, a total of fourteen countries have pledged approximately $40 million to the fund.

Another important issue taken up at the conference was the need for complete disclosure of all relevant documents. The United States led this appeal, even announcing plans to establish and manage an Internet site at which all the countries could post the information they had. But the response was divided. Britain, France, and the Tripartite Gold Commission (TGC) claimed they could not publish at that time all the documents, although they did not explain why. Apparently, they feared discovery that the Tripartite Gold Commission had not properly distributed the stolen gold that had been located and transferred to it, but apportioned it according to political considerations influenced by the Cold War. (However, in 1998 the TGC completed its work and announced that its documents were open for research.) The Vatican, which sent observers who never spoke a word at the conference, was also attacked for its policy of hiding documents.

The question of whether the postwar gold settlements should be reopened for discussion was raised only on the last day of the conference. In the closing speech made by the Israeli delegation, Ministry of Justice director general Nilli Arad said the delegation believed that "the time is right to re-open the discussions concerning the Accord that was established in Washington in order to ensure that Holocaust victims, survivors, legitimate heirs and the Jewish people as a whole are entitled to their rightful share of the looted gold." This was a sophisticated choice of words, as it was clear to Arad, an experienced lawyer, that there were no legal grounds for reopening those agreements.

The head of the Swiss delegation, Thomas Borer, immediately responded and said that this was a legally ratified international agreement and that there were no grounds to reopen it for discussion. Professor Yehuda Bauer, head of Yad V'Shem's research institute, answered quietly and elegantly, "From a legal perspective, I absolutely agree with Ambassador Borer. This is a binding international agreement. However, the question is not a legal one but a moral one. Is the Swiss government willing to take a moral stance?" Borer had no answer to that. The Israeli position was not supported by other delegations, but the fact that the London Conference was held at all proves that the gold issue was again in front of the public.

The gold issue attracted most of the media and public attention, but it was not the only point at issue in the web of German-Swiss relations. Those wide connections made Switzerland an essential economic base for Germany, in gold, banking, weapons, works of art, and raw materials. We will not go into the details of their cooperation here, but will mention a few outstanding instances that indicate the general rule.

The Swiss commercial banks served Germany and its senior officials very well, and at least in one case, it is clear that stolen Jewish property was deposited in a Swiss bank. A report sent by the U.S. embassy in Bern to the headquarters of the Safehaven operation in June 1945 dealt with German deposits in the Johan Wehrli Bank and listed findings later confirmed by the Price-Waterhouse accounting firm.

The Price-Waterhouse examiners found an account known as the Gustloff Stiftung (trust) named after the leader of the Swiss Nazi party, Wilhelm Gustloff who was murdered by David Frankfurter in 1935.

The U.S. embassy reported that "The examiner, who has a personal knowledge concerning the background of this trust as a result of his many years residence in Germany before the war, described the Gustloff Stiftung as a 'fund' in which were placed the assets and titles of property taken by the Nazis from Jewish businessmen in Germany and the occupied countries." The report also described another account found in this small bank that belonged to Joseph Angerer, described in the report as "Hermann Goering's agent for the acquisition of works of art."[22]

Goering, Adolf Hitler's heir apparent until the end of the war and commander of the Luftwaffe, was not the only senior Nazi to deposit property in Switzerland. According to unconfirmed reports, his colleague and rival, SS Commander Heinrich Himmler, found a safe haven beyond the Alps for treasures looted from the Jews of Europe. The London *Daily Telegraph* reported in 1995 that at the end of the war, Himmler transferred to Switzerland works of art, gold, diamonds, and cash valued at $750 million (apparently reported by the *Telegraph* in today's values), which he had stolen from European Jews. According to the *Daily Telegraph* report, which is not supported by any other source, the transfer was made on April 21, 1945, nine days before Hitler's suicide and eighteen days before the end of the war.[23]

Another unconfirmed report circulated that Max Amann, publisher of *Mein Kampf*, kept the book's royalties in UBS, although it is unclear whether this means Adolf Hitler's money or the publisher's revenues. UBS denies the claim, and it is almost certain the truth will never be known.[24] What is clear is that many Germans had a great deal of property in Switzerland; and it is very likely that a large portion of that came from the looting of Europe.

Switzerland also provided Germany an important outlet for artworks that were looted all across occupied Europe. Like gold, works of art were sold in order to turn them into hard currency or to convert them into art that better suited Nazi tastes. The Swiss market was flooded with stolen art, much of which had been stolen from Jews. Martin Weyl, who was director general of the Israel Museum for many years, says that some of the works of art were catalogued in the names of their original owners, and others were easily recognized by tags on the back of the paintings or on the bases of statues.

In one case, Paul Rosenberg, a well known French-Jewish art dealer, found in Switzerland paintings stolen from him during the Nazi occupation. Despite many appeals, diplomatic pressure, compromise offers, and the presentation of certification, the Swiss authorities refused to return his property after the war. Only a lawsuit in Lucerne in the late 1940s brought eight paintings back to Rosenberg; dozens of other paintings are still missing.

According to Weyl, there were other similar cases. The common thread among them all is the "closed eyes of the Swiss government in the years that trade in Jewish property was going on and easy to identify, and unwillingness to investigate and return art treasures after the war, even to those with complete certification who demanded their property. Moreover, Allied officers whose job was to aid in the return of the works of art, were methodically blocked."[25] If the Swiss refused to return works of art that were completely documented, it is fair to assume that they treated Holocaust victims' bank accounts in the same way, particularly if the heirs had the right documentation.

Finally, official Swiss government documents, published in mid-1997, revealed that Switzerland provided Germany with weapons and the means to manufacture weapons at current values of $1.5 billion. The shipments of arms and raw materials were stopped under Allied pressure only in September 1944, when it was already clear to everyone that Germany was about to lose the war. As we have seen, two-thirds of the German gold that reached Switzerland was used to pay for Berlin's procurements. It is therefore likely that Germany paid for the arms with stolen gold.[26]

As previously noted, most of the revelations described in this chapter are not new to Holocaust and World War II historians and researchers, but they are new to the general public, and came at the worst possible time from the Swiss perspective. Primarily, but not only the U.S. media described Switzerland in chilling tones, and created the erroneous image in the eyes of the public that the Swiss were Nazi allies. This apparently stemmed from the combination of sensational writing and the "good guy, bad guy" approach that is popular in the age of television.

Public opinion classified Switzerland as the "bad guy" along with the Nazis and Fascists. It is untrue and unfair, but Switzerland paid dearly for not understanding how public opinion works.

Many media reports relied on fragmented documentation, and made no comment about whether they were publishing official position papers or just bits of intelligence and personal thinking. Most of the articles did not contain a Swiss response, and if they did, it was buried so deep that it was almost invisible. A fair look must admit that in light of the media barrage of mixing truth and assumption, fact and fiction, it is easy to understand why many Swiss believe their country was the victim of an international conspiracy of some kind.

Even with all the failings of the media in their treatment of the Swiss, it was very effective in everything concerning the Jewish accounts. Although most Swiss deny it, there is no doubt that without these reports the deposits' problem would have continued to drag on in a grueling, bureaucratic process, and to fall victim to continued decades of intentional Swiss neglect. But, when the Swiss discovered that all of their country's deeds during World War II were under siege, even if in an exaggerated and not always accurate manner, they began to understand that they had to solve the problem that led to all these reports, the problem of Holocaust victims' deposits. Not surprisingly, as the wave of claims against Swiss actions during the war increased, particularly against its trade with Nazi Germany, Bern's willingness to reach an agreement with the Jewish organizations also increased.

10

"THE PARTIES WILL COOPERATE"
The Beginning of the Independent
Investigation into the Deposits Affair

THE APRIL 23, 1996, hearings in the Senate Banking Committee stunned the Swiss bankers. Hans Baer and Heinrich Schneider could almost physically sense the hostility toward them, along with the enormous American media interest in the affair. Baer, who had grown up and worked in the United States, certainly understood the significance of the transition to the public opinion arena. On this front, the banks had no chance of winning, even before the sensational headlines began.

On April 23, in between the hearings and Bronfman's meeting with President Clinton, Israel Singer met with Baer. In prior talks, Baer had asked to reach an immediate agreement on the establishment of the joint Jewish organizations and banks committee, clearly hoping to blunt the sting of the Senate Banking Committee. Differences of opinion remained on the two most central questions, Jewish representation and Swiss representation. The organizations insisted that they represented the Jewish side, while the banks were only willing to talk to Rolf Bloch the president of the Federation of Jewish Communities. The organizations demanded that at least one major bank be involved on the committee, while the Bankers Association insisted on being the sole representative.

The shock treatment in the Senate Banking Committee led Baer, certainly in coordination with Georg Krayer, to accept the Jewish demands on both matters that same day.

A few days before, Bronfman and Burg had announced they would convene the leadership of WJRO on May 2 in New York City. Baer now suggested using the opportunity to sign an agreement for the establishment of the joint committee. After the final hurdles were overcome, Singer and Barak agreed.

On May 2, the heads of the Swiss Bankers Association, Krayer and Baer, came to New York. They were accompanied by Josef Ackermann, then president of Credit Suisse.[1] When the representatives of the banks and the organizations met, there were still a few issues to work out. The key unresolved point was the question of Swiss government involvement in the entire process, a demand originally raised by Zvi Barak, who believed that the largest amounts of Jewish money were not in the dormant accounts but in the stolen property. Burg also took this position, and the banks eventually agreed to mention their government as a party to the investigation of looted property. The parties to the Memorandum of Understanding were the WJRO and the Bankers Association. The agreement, which led to the establishment of the Volcker Commission, read as follows.

(1) An Independent Committee of Eminent Persons will be appointed. Three persons will be appointed by the World Jewish Restitution Organization (WJRO) and three persons will be appointed by the Swiss Bankers Association (SBA). The Committee of six will jointly appoint an additional member as Chairperson. Furthermore, each side will nominate two alternates.

(2) The Chairperson will administer the budget of the Committee which will be funded by the SBA.

(3) The Committee of Eminent Persons will appoint an international auditing company; this company must be licensed by the Federal Banking Commission (FBC) to operate in Switzerland. The SBA will assure the auditors unfettered access to all relevant files in banking institutions regarding dormant accounts and other assets and financial instruments deposited before, during and immediately after the Second World War.

(4) The Committee of Eminent Persons will instruct the auditing company as to the scope of its duties. It [the accounting firm] will examine the methodology of the individual banks, the Swiss Bankers Association and the Office of the Ombudsman as regards the search for accounts and assets in question. The Independent Committee will publish progress reports from time to time.

(5) The parties of the agreement will cooperate to assure that the Swiss Government will deal with the question of looted assets in Swiss banks or other institutions which were not reported or returned under the relevant laws during the years before, during and immediately after the Second World War.

(6) All negotiations will be handled in an environment of absolute discretion with a view of reaching an amicable resolution of all issues.

(7) As soon as the contents of this Memorandum are agreed upon, there will be a summit meeting of the presidents and their delegations [of both sides] to affix their signatures and to announce the names of the members of the Committee and the scope of its task to the public.

From the Jewish side, the four groomsmen—Edgar Bronfman, Avraham Burg, Zvi Barak, and Israel Singer—signed the agreement. The Swiss bridesmaids who signed the agreement were Georg Krayer, Josef Ackermann, and Hans Baer. The Jewish representatives demanded Swiss government confirmation of the agreement, which was provided three days later, although no government representative signed the agreement.

In the discussion after the signing, Krayer asked if now it would be possible to ensure favorable public opinion of the banks. Burg replied, "The

MEMORANDUM OF UNDERSTANDING

BETWEEN

THE WORLD JEWISH RESTITUTION ORGANIZATION
and
THE WORLD JEWISH CONGRESS
representing also the
JEWISH AGENCY and Allied Organizations

and

THE SWISS BANKERS ASSOCIATION

(1) An Independent Committee of Eminent Persons will be appointed. Three persons will be appointed by the World Jewish Restitution Organization (WJRO) and three persons will be appointed by the Swiss Bankers Association (SBA). The Committee of six will jointly appoint an additional member as Chairperson. Furthermore, each side will nominate two alternates.

(2) The Chairperson will administer the budget of the Committee which will be funded by the SBA.

(3) The Committee of Eminent Persons will appoint an international auditing company; this company must be licensed by the Federal Banking Commission (FBC) to operate in Switzerland. The SBA will assure the auditors unfettered access to all relevant files in banking institutions regarding dormant accounts and other assets and financial instruments deposited before, during and immediately after the Second World War.

(4) The Committee of Eminent Persons will instruct the auditing company as to the scope of its duties. It will examine the methodology of the individual banks, the Swiss Bankers Association and the Office of the Ombudsman as regards the search for accounts and assets in question. The Independent Committee will also be authorized to retain the services of other experts, as necessary. The Independent Committee will publish progress reports from time to time.

(5) The parties of the agreement will cooperate to assure that the Swiss Government will deal with the question of looted assets in Swiss banks or other institutions which were not reported or returned under the relevant laws during the years before, during and immediately after the Second World War.

(6) All negotiations will be handled in an environment of absolute discretion with a view of reaching an amicable resolution of all issues.

(7) As soon as the contents of this Memorandum are agreed upon, there will be a summit meeting of the presidents and their delegations to affix their signatures and to announce the names of the members of the Committee and the scope of its task to the public.

Signed and agreed:
New York, New York, May 2, 1996

Edgar M. Bronfman

Dr. Georg F. Krayer

Avraham Burg

Dr. Josef Ackermann

Zvi Barak

Hans J. Baer

Israel Singer

The Memorandum of Understanding that established the Volcker Commission, May 2, 1996. (Author's files)

INDEPENDENT COMMITTEE OF EMINENT PERSONS

599 LEXINGTON AVENUE
40th FLOOR
NEW YORK, N.Y. 10022

PHONE: (212) 900-8188
FACSIMILE (212) 446-1305

PAUL A. VOLCKER
CHAIRMAN

To Members of the Committee

Mr. Bradfield will be sending you shortly a rather lengthy memorandum reviewing a number of key procedural issues that should be resolved at our scheduled meeting in Zurich on January 30 and 31. In view of the nature of this material and the decisions required, I suggest the meeting start earlier than proposed on the 30th, at three o'clock. With the possibility of running well into the evening, that should provide adequate time.

I understand we have not yet received confirmation of plans to attend the meeting from all members of the Committee or alternates. You should understand that, as Chairman, I believe the meeting both important and timely, and I intend to proceed with whatever members and alternates are at hand.

The most important question for us to consider will be placed first on the agenda: whether in the light of developments in recent days and weeks, there is any longer both the will and ability to proceed with the kind of cooperative, jointly-sponsored, fact-finding, truth-seeking investigation that has been contemplated.

My own view of this matter as an interested participant was clearly expressed in my recent testimony. I suggested there that a combination of our inquiry with the official Swiss Commission offered the best, and perhaps the only, practical way for achieving the agreed objective of finding the truth as nearly as that truth can be determined after 50 years. In agreeing to become Chairman, and in our earlier meetings, I had gathered that was the common view. But it has become obvious that our work cannot proceed effectively if an atmosphere of confrontation infects our membership and our work.

I realize much of the controversy arises from matters beyond the primary scope of our work. But I would underscore the comment made only yesterday by Ambassador Eisenstat in speaking to the B'nai B'rith Center for Public Policy that "it is important that we have a cooperative not a confrontational relationship with the government of Switzerland and the Swiss Banking Association, if progress is to be achieved." Cooperation is, of course, a two-way street. I feel strongly that without a renewed sense of cooperation and commitment within our Committee, the desired results cannot be achieved.

I believe it essential that those attending the meeting on January 30 and 31 be fully prepared to reach a renewed understanding on our cooperative approach, whether that approach needs to be changed, or indeed whether the work of the Committee should proceed at all.

Paul A. Volcker

Paul Volcker's letter to the members of the Independent Committee of Eminent Persons, January 14, 1997. (Author's files) key to favorable public opinion is appropriate public behavior, and if the banks act in such a manner, it will help their image." The banks' sensitivity to reports on the matter, made obvious by Krayer's question, is what led to the inclusion of the discretion clause in the agreement.[2]

The Jewish representatives also had a few questions, the most important of which was whether the Swiss government would support specific banks if it became clear that they could not return the sums uncovered. The Bankers' Association representatives could not answer that question, but Krayer mentioned offhandedly that the government had some very important documents relevant to the committee's work. Burg said, "It proved to be a very important remark, because it was the first time we knew where to look for the documents."[3]

There is no doubt that the agreement's importance was first and foremost in its very signing. For a year, the Bankers Association publicly denied the existence of a Holocaust victims' accounts problem, and was willing at the most to recheck itself. Now, the SBA explicitly admitted that there had been and still was such a problem, and that not only did past handling need to be reexamined, but the problem itself needed to be resolved once and for all. After a year of trying to ignore the involvement of international Jewish organizations in the affair, the SBA was forced to sign an agreement with them, and only with them, to investigate all aspects of the problem.

The details of the agreement were also very important. It determined that not only Jewish accounts would be investigated, but also stolen property. Not by the committee, but by the government, which had virtually been forced into the picture, but it would be investigated.

In contrast, the agreement contained no mechanism to locate the accounts, no solutions to the problems facing heirs, no means to locate accounts opened by trustees, and no mention of the level of documentation the banks still had or the fate of accounts allegedly closed by the banks. But, as we will soon see, most of these questions eventually made it to the table.

Although the agreement spoke of introducing the committee members to the public on the same day, time was needed to complete the composition of the group. The Swiss side came prepared. Its representatives were Dr. Curt Gasteyger, professor of international relations in Geneva, Professor Klaus Jacobi, a Jew and former secretary of state in the Swiss Ministry of Finance, and Dr. Peider Mengiardi, former CEO of the Swiss branch of the international accounting firm of Ernst & Young. They also appointed Hans Baer and Professor Alan Hirsch, an international banking expert, as alternates. Hirsch eventually withdrew for personal reasons and was replaced by Professor Reneé Rhinow, of the law faculty at the University of Basel.

The Jewish side needed a little more time to get organized, as happened more than once throughout the crisis when questions of honor and influence arose. After a few days of discussions, the Jewish side appointed Avraham Burg; Argentinean banker Ruben Beraja, who was also president of the World Jewish Congress in South America; and Ronald Lauder, CEO of the Estée Lauder cosmetics empire and treasurer of the World Jewish Congress. Israel Singer and Zvi Barak were appointed as alternates. Edgar Bronfman and Georg Krayer received supervisory status. All regular members, all alternates, and both supervisors took part in most committee meetings.

The question of committee chair remained unresolved. The Jewish organizations and the SBA each suggested six names, and each side vetoed the other party's suggestions one after the other. Finally, the last name on the Swiss list was left—Paul Volcker, Chairman of the Federal Reserve Board in the 1980s—the man who made that institution into one of the most important bodies in the global economy. He may have been recommended by the Swiss, but the Jewish side could also recognize his good points.

A year earlier, Barak and Singer had toyed with the idea of hiring Volcker to prepare research on the economic status of Europe's Jews prior to the war, after implications were made that Europe's Jews were too poor to have made significant deposits in Swiss banks. The idea faded when they considered the cost of financing the investigation, which they estimated would cost hundreds of thousands of dollars, so they never even talked to Volcker. But when his name was recommended as chair for the committee, Bronfman, who knows the New York business community inside out, said, "It's OK, he is James Wolfenson's partner." Wolfenson, a Jew, heads the World Bank. Volcker got the job.[4]

The first committee meeting was held in Volcker's Manhattan office on August 14, 1996. It was a tense and unceremonious meeting that exposed the significant gaps between the Jewish and Swiss sides concerning the committee's authority. "Ugh, what a revolting meeting," one of the Jewish representatives recalls. That some three months after its establishment the two sides still differed on what the committee was supposed to do, is indicative of the nature of their relationship.

The bankers were angry about the continuing and worsening anti-Swiss media reports that increasingly focused on the Banks' actions during World War II. Their anger was directed primarily against Burg and Singer, the former for his public anti-Swiss remarks, and the latter due to the assumption that he controlled Senator D'Amato's office and could determine what became public knowledge. After a dinner Bronfman held at Seagram's offices the same evening, tempers cooled, but only after four and a half hours of arguments.

The meeting opened with a lengthy discussion of the committee's fields of endeavor. Volcker expressed the opinion that the committee had to focus on the dormant accounts, which would require the accountants employed by the committee to use techniques that exceeded the usual auditing procedures. He was hinting at what is called forensic accounting, which not only examines reports and figures, but searches for signs of fraud and assets that have disappeared.

Volcker noted the need for cooperation with the Swiss government, which was about to investigate the stolen property, and that the government should bring any uncovered details to the attention of the government that could assist in that investigation. Nonetheless, Volcker emphasized that the committee could not and should not deal directly with the stolen property issue, for which Bern was responsible and for which the committee had no mandate.

The Jewish representatives rejected Volcker's stance, and claimed that the question of stolen property was as much a part of the committee's mandate as the dormant accounts. According to them, the committee had a moral and historical obligation to ensure that all Jewish property transported to Switzerland be returned to the Jewish people, including the stolen property deposited by Germans in Switzerland that had originally belonged to Holocaust victims.

The minutes of the meeting reveal that Burg and Singer also hinted at the Swiss alternative: "Working within the framework of the Committee these matters could be accomplished in a cooperative atmosphere, that handling these matters outside the Committee would result in bitterness." In other words, if the committee did not handle it, public discussion of the matter would continue, along with all the damage it would do to Switzerland and the banks.

The banks' representatives hastened to respond that although there was a need for cooperation with the government, the committee must limit itself to its mandated task—investigating the problem of the dormant accounts. In their opinion, only the Swiss government could deal with the stolen property, as only it could take steps as a result of its findings.

The stolen property was not the only stumbling block in the first meeting of the Volcker Commission. Even the meaning of the term dormant accounts was controversial. An unnamed attorney (apparently Michael Bradfield, who was officially appointed legal counsel in September 1996) expressed the opinion that the intention was any kind of financial assets, but not dormant stolen property. He claimed that it would be very difficult to recognize dormant stolen property using accounting techniques—the committee's primary tool. It is not clear if the Jewish representatives understood the significance of the remark, which certainly would have been a warning light to them. From the point of view of locating an account, there is no difference between a dormant account belonging to a victim and a dormant account belonging to a criminal. If the latter is difficult to locate using accounting procedures, then so is the former, in which case the committee's work would encounter a deadlock.

After further discussion of the committee's mandate, Burg suggested three principal guidelines, which were acceptable to all the members: (1) Jewish property left in Switzerland as the result of World War II would be returned to its owners; (2) the work would focus on dormant Jewish "belongings" in Swiss banks, defined as "all types of assets that might have been placed in the custody of Swiss banks, including deposits, financial instruments, and all other assets of all kinds"; and (3) if the Swiss Parliament did not pass a law on the matter of the stolen property, or if such a law handled the problem insufficiently, the committee would reopen discussions about its mandate in light of such developments.

The Jewish side saw this decision as ensuring that the problem of stolen property would be dealt with, as it mentioned all the dormant Jewish assets in banks, which could include gold dental work removed from Auschwitz victims, then smelted and sold to Switzerland. The banks saw this as a way to pass the ball to Parliament, as it specifically stated that the committee would deal with stolen property only if Switzerland did not do so itself. The stolen property issue was not raised during the next few meetings because other matters in question were discussed. Nonetheless, the accountants were later instructed to report to the committee any signs of stolen property, if found, while investigating the Jewish accounts.

The next subject on the agenda was the choice of an accounting firm to handle the investigation of the banks. Volcker recommended choosing a three-member subcommittee, consisting of himself and a representative from each side, to interview the candidates in Zurich in September 1996. Although it was not explicitly stated, it was clear to everyone present that only the six largest accounting firms in the world (which have since become five) could be considered for a task of this magnitude. Volcker also suggested beginning with a sample investigation of two to three banks in order to determine the accountants' working methods. Another important suggestion was to employ more than one firm to avoid conflicts of interest, as all the major Swiss banks employ one of the six large accounting firms. This would also create a professional level of competition for quality of service. All Volcker's suggestions were accepted unanimously.

Near the end of the meeting, the committee discussed its budget. Volcker suggested preparing one that took into account the cost of employing the accountants, which would be determined only after the accounting firms had been chosen. Additional sums would also have to be allocated for the committee's administrative costs, and the employment of other experts the committee might hire. Among other things, the budget had to cover the fee of attorney Michael Bradfield, a partner at Jones, Day, Reavis & Pogue, whom Volcker had chosen to serve as the committee's legal counsel and secretary, due to their long acquaintance. It was agreed that Volcker and Krayer would discuss the committee's budget, which was to be provided entirely by the banks.

At the beginning of the meeting, the banks suggested paying each committee member an annual honorarium of $50,000, in addition to covering all expenses. The Jewish representatives were opposed, and Burg stated that any sums he and his colleagues received would be transferred to the fund to memorialize Holocaust victims. It was thus written into the minutes that payment of honoraria were not agreed to, but at the next meeting, Hans Baer demanded a clarification: that the decision had been that each member could decide whether or not to accept honoraria. In practice, the Jewish side's money, $250,000 per year, was transferred to WJRO, while the Swiss representatives each apparently accepted the money.[5]

On September 12 and 13, 1996, Volcker and Bradfield received the proposals of the six accounting firms. After hearing them, Volcker held a series of meetings with senior Swiss officials: Minister of Finance Kaspar Villiger; Supervisor of Banks, Kurt Hauri and the director general of his office, Daniel Zuberbuehler; Mathias Kraft, then head of a Foreign Ministry team established to handle the deposits crisis; and Bankers Association ombudsman, Hanspeter Haeni.

Villiger emphasized the importance of the law establishing a committee of historians on the matter of Swiss policy during World War II, and promised that the Swiss government would provide all possible assistance. Volcker reiterated his position on the committee's mandate—to focus on the question of dormant accounts—and noted that the question of the stolen property had to be investigated by the Swiss government. Villiger agreed.

Volcker's most important meeting was with Hauri and Zuberbuehler. The two promised Volcker that his committee would have access to all information collected by the accountants, including the date the located account had been opened, the nationality of the account owner, and the sum located, everything except the owners' name. This was an important breakthrough in the committee's work, and was supported four months later in a special declaration by Hauri that required the banks to cooperate with the committee. Representatives of the Supervision of Banks also approved the employment of non-Swiss accountants by the chosen firms, another important element in ensuring impartiality.[6]

The Volcker Commission meeting on October 18, 1996, dealt primarily with the work of the accountants and the ongoing attacks on Switzerland. It was held in the Zurich airport convention center and lasted three and a half hours. First, the committee approved the instructions to be given to the accountants and agreed that the first stage, a sample examination of three banks, would be completed by June 1997. They decided that the complete report on the examination of all the banks would be completed by June 1998, however, in practice, the end date changed rather drastically.

It was now necessary to choose the accounting firms to conduct the investigation. Bradfield believed that Arthur Andersen, KPMG, and Price-Waterhouse had made the best presentations from the perspective of their Swiss branches' forensic accounting capabilities combined with the support of their New York and London branches. At the beginning of 1998, as the scope of the investigation became clear, Coopers & Lybrand was brought onto the team. (Later that year Price-Waterhouse and Coopers & Lybrand merged.)

Later in the meeting, Volcker reported on a number of developments, primarily the filing of a class-action suit against the banks, and the continuing media attacks on Switzerland for its ties to Nazi Germany. At this point, Baer launched a direct attack on the Jewish organizations: "The Jewish organizations are no longer living within the spirit of the Memorandum of Understanding. Attacking Switzerland as a country is unacceptable and creates bad will that undermines the work of the committee."

Baer's words came the very morning that then Swiss Foreign Minister Flavio Cotti demanded that Baer and Georg Krayer act to end the attacks. It is hard to avoid the thinking that Bern assumed that the international press was controlled by the Jews. The Jewish representatives' response, however, was conciliatory, as noted in this remark entered into the summary of the minutes of the meeting: "Both the Swiss banks and the Jewish organizations are better off in this process than outside it. The members unanimously agreed on the desirability of making the committee process work in harmony."[7]

The class-action suit that Volcker had mentioned was filed in New York on October 1, 1996. On October 18, the day the lawsuit was first mentioned in a commission meeting, another suit was filed, while on January 29, 1997, a third lawsuit was recorded. All three lawsuits sought to represent all the Holocaust survivors who registered with law offices, thus suing in the names of hundreds of thousands of Jews. For the banks, this meant lawsuits for tens of billions of dollars; lengthy and expensive legal proceedings; and the need to reveal documents and bring dozens of employees, including some of the most senior, to New York for interrogation, while a hostile American press peered into the entire process.

The first lawsuit was filed on behalf of Gizelle Weisshaus by attorney Ed Fagan against UBS and Swiss Bank Corp., and left open the possibility of adding more banks during the proceedings. The suit had a ceiling of $20 billion, half of which was claimed as compensation for Jewish deposits, and the other half as compensation for assets looted from Holocaust victims and deposited in Switzerland.

Fagan's expedient demands included an immediate accounting of all of the accounts and valuables deposited by class-action members in Swiss banks so they could be compensated for their losses. He also wanted an immediate calculation of the value of the stolen property deposited in Switzerland by Germany that had belonged to lawsuit petitioners or their relatives.[8] In the coming months, Fagan made the rounds of the media with Weisshaus and took the elderly woman as far as Bern to draw international press attention to her at Swiss government and bank events. He also disclosed that hundreds of applications to join the class action were received by his offices daily. He later filed a similar lawsuit against large European insurance companies who did not pay compensation to the relatives of the Holocaust victims they insured. In the public relations arena, Fagan had certainly proven his talent.

The most serious of the three lawsuits was the one filed on October 18, 1996 by attorney Melvyn Weiss, a well-known New York attorney, and Michael Husfeld, from Washington, D.C. It was not accompanied by a media ruckus and did not demand huge sums of money, but was based on a series of documents and testimony focusing on the stolen assets and Swiss ties with Germany. From the banks' perspective, this was the most dangerous lawsuit, as it was clearly based on vast knowledge.

The plaintiffs in this suit were divided into three groups: the owners and heirs of stolen property, forced laborers and their heirs, and depositors in Swiss banks and their heirs. The first plaintiff was Jacob Friedman, whose story was recounted in Chapter 6. Other familiar names among the plaintiffs included Elizabeth Trilling-Grusch and Charles Sonabend.[9] Another plaintiff was Lewis Slaton, who was eighty-five years old when the case was filed. Slaton's father, Bernard, was a well-known lawyer and stamp collector, whose hobby brought him to Switzerland, for which reason his son believed he had a bank account there. The fifth plaintiff was David Boruchowicz, who worked at forced labor for the German company Transvania from 1940 to 1943. Boruchowicz was later a slave laborer in the I.G. Farben factory at Auschwitz, and was finally transported to the concentration camps at Majdanek, Buchenwald, and Theresienstadt.

Weiss's case covered at length Swiss acts during World War II, and touched only briefly on the question of Jewish deposits. The case reviewed Swiss refugee policy; the banks' relations with Nazi Germany, the receipt of stolen gold and information concerning its origins, the use of the Red Cross and Swiss diplomatic representatives to transmit stolen property across the Alps; the Swiss breach of neutrality, the scope of the Nazi pillage, forced labor; the deposits' affair, the Washington Accord, the fate of property without heirs; the Bergier Commission, the Volcker Commission, and more.

The legal aspect of the lawsuit was particularly uncomfortable for the defendants, Credit Suisse, UBS and Swiss Bank Corp. Weiss based his case on a series of very serious accusations against the banks: the violation of international law in assisting the Nazi regime in crimes against humanity, breach of their obligation to their clients, breach of their legal obligations, breach of contract, money laundering, negligence, unlawful enrichment, conspiracy, and fraud. Weiss asked the court to find that the banks committed all the acts alleged in the lawsuit and committed all the alleged crimes, and to instruct them to locate and return all the victims' assets, as well as all assets of Nazi Germany and its representatives.[10]

The third lawsuit was filed on behalf of the World Council of Orthodox Communities by attorney Richard Appelby. Along with the organization, other participants to the suit were Irene Zarkowski, a Holocaust survivor; Joseph Wieder, who claimed his family had bank accounts and insurance policies in Switzerland; Erwin Hauer, the son of a wealthy family who remembers discussions in his childhood home about a Swiss bank account; and Lillie Ryba, another survivor.

The grounds for the Orthodox Communities' class-action suit were similar to those raised in Weiss's case, although in less detail. It did deal at length, however, with the stolen property, and most of the information on the deposits' affair was taken from the Hug-Perrenoud report. This case added a fourth group to the plaintiffs listed in Weiss's case: the heirs of the community property stolen by the Nazis. The grounds for the lawsuit and the requested recompense were similar to Weiss's suit.[11]

The banks filed a motion to dismiss all the class-action suits *in limine* with a series of supporting arguments. The key grounds for the motion were that the Swiss courts, not the New York courts, were the place to hear the lawsuits, and that under international law, the plaintiffs could not file these lawsuits. The plaintiffs argued that the New York courts could try the suits because the major Swiss banks had branches there, to which Holocaust victims' accounts and stolen property had been transferred.[12] These cases later proved to be a key factor in the achievement of a compromise agreement.

In November 1996, two important events took place. The Volcker Commission finally agreed on the instructions for the three accounting firms it initially hired, and the Bankers Association ombudsman published his initial findings. Hanspeter Haeni's report was presented at a crowded Zurich press conference on November 12: After examining 900 applications of the 1,055 received by September 30, eleven dormant accounts containing 1.6 million francs were located. In accounts opened before 1945, however, only 20,000 francs were discovered. The banks reported 11,000 francs belonging to three Holocaust victims, while the remainder was in two accounts from Romania and in one account of a couple killed in a car accident in the 1920s.

Haeni gave a comprehensive review of his findings to date. Most of the applications were from the United States (29 percent), Israel (16 percent), and Germany (10 percent). Seventy percent of the applications came from relatives of Nazi victims. Only fifty-five applications required the opening of bank files, and of those only eleven have been found. Of the eleven, two accounts containing less than 100 francs were found, there were two with between 100 and 1,000 francs, three contained 1,000 to 10,000 francs, one with up to 100,000 francs, one with up to 1 million francs, and one with more than 1 million francs.

Haeni said that the results were "in keeping with prior expectations," and that he had received the impression that the banks did their best to examine the applications. "I do not expect any unusual results," Haeni said of the rest of his work, and noted that he continued to receive about twenty applications a day. He explained that most Holocaust victims' property had already been located in the 1960s and in other cases had lost its value, as was the case, for instance, with Romanian bonds from the 1930s.[13]

As was expected, the Jewish organizations responded to Haeni's report with anger. "Miserable results," was how Kalman Sultanik, vice president of the World Jewish Congress, characterized the report, while also demanding that everything possible be done to ensure justice for the "thousands of other people who deserve money." Sultanik had already called Haeni's work a "cruel joke," and now it appeared to him that his estimation had been proved correct. "Haeni serves as the banks' photocopying machine," he said in outrage.[14]

One week later, on November 19, 1996, the Volcker Commission's memorandum of instruction sent to Arthur Andersen, KPMG, and Price-Waterhouse, granted the firms unprecedented authority, and practically removed banking confidentiality in the matters to be investigated. One of the most important items in the memorandum instructed the accountants to report to the committee on all findings concerning the deposit of stolen property in the banks, not just about Jewish property.

The accountants were instructed to use not only traditional auditing techniques, but forensic accounting. They were to burrow deep into the fabric of the banks, the SBA, and the ombudsman, to reexamine their working methodology about the dormant accounts, and conduct a detailed search for them. Aware of the increasing accusations about destruction of documents by the banks, the commission instructed the accountants to investigate whether this took place, and if so, was it accidentally or premeditated. They were also asked to determine if the banks upheld ethical principles and Swiss law concerning the preservation of documents pertaining to dormant accounts.

Three months were allocated for the first stage of the investigation, the collection of background data. The commission determined that at this stage the accountants would do little auditing of the banks, but primarily receive general information in addition to the information they already had as part of their regular work with the Swiss banks. This stage required the accountants to use the skills of historians, as they had to understand the background of those who smuggled property into Switzerland under pain of persecution by the Nazis. One source were the documents from the

Safehaven operation; another were the official reports of foreign capital movement to Switzerland from 1934 to 1946, in addition to all relevant laws and regulations concerning dormant accounts from 1934 to the present day. The accountants were also to report to the commission about the possibility of creating a database of all the accounts (without exception) opened in the banks from 1934 through 1946 and their fate.

After this stage, the first sample investigation would take place, with the express purpose of determining the methodology used at the more than fifty banks that had existed during the war. The commission decided to increase the number of banks in the sampling from four to five, and this stage was also expected to last three months. In light of the results of the sample investigation, the committee would decide on the final instructions and powers granted to the accountants for the overall investigation, scheduled to begin in June 1997, and estimated to take one year.[15]

What was Israel doing during all these months of significant developments? The subject was debated in the Knesset a number of times and a special committee for the restitution of Jewish property was established in 1997,[16] but the Israeli government, faithful to the course it had followed for years, preferred to leave the struggle to the Jewish organizations in order not to damage its ties with Switzerland. Prime Minister Benjamin Netanyahu, however, did make some changes: Israel would provide public support for the Jewish organizations, and would take an active role in practical negotiations with Switzerland, if such a time should come.

MK Avraham Hirschson was placed at the head of the Knesset committee, whose work centered on debates about the various aspects of the property problem. In addition, the committee collected information on 7,000 specific problems of property restitution, but no cases were reported in which the committee succeeded in helping to solve them. Even so, the very existence of the committee was important, as it helped to keep the subject in the Israeli public eye. Hirschson was himself appointed to the management of the fund Switzerland established in February 1997, to aid Holocaust victims.

When Gabriel Padon became Israel's ambassador to Switzerland in October 1995, he met with then Foreign Minister Shimon Peres, and asked to receive instructions about how the embassy should handle the matter. Peres replied, "The government of Israel has decided that, like in the matter of the restitution of property in Eastern Europe, it is not good for the State to be involved." The reason for this was fear of damaging relations between the two countries. Switzerland is an important client of the Israeli defense industry, and, as opposed to the European Union countries, was not then in the habit of attacking Israel for the political situation in the Middle East.

Peres advised Padon to work behind the scenes: "You are not a side in the negotiations of this matter, but I ask that you remain in contact with all the parties involved and report back to us." In practice, this meant maintaining contact with the Swiss Foreign Ministry, the Jewish community, the World Jewish Congress, and the Jewish Agency, primarily to collect information and occasionally to transmit proposals among the parties. The embassy advanced almost none of its own proposals. Nevertheless, there were a few exceptions. For example, Padon proposed that the World Jewish Congress and Rolf Bloch act together to publish the names of dormant account owners, and suggested that the Swiss appoint Israeli Professor Saul Friedlander as a member of the committee to research Swiss Second World War policy.[17]

The Swiss government favored the opposite approach. According to Foreign Ministry official Thomas Borer, he would have preferred to negotiate directly with Israeli representatives, one diplomat to another. "It is likely it would be easier that way," Borer said, "as diplomats have standing channels, accepted forms of behavior, accepted lingo, a regular working method, and the media is not involved. When the media is not activated, there is much less red tape, fewer disruptions, it is much easier and the results are much better."[18]

The Jewish side believes that although it might usually be preferable to place negotiations between countries in the hands of diplomats, in the case of the Swiss deposits there are also advantages to direct negotiations by the Jewish organizations. "Bronfman can allow himself to say things to the Swiss that an official Israeli representative could never say," says one source close to the negotiations. "The line where the WJRO is active is healthier from the perspective of the interests of the State of Israel." Yet, even this source says that Bronfman and Burg have made a few extraneous comments that a career diplomat would never have voiced.[19]

In the last two months of 1996, it appeared that it did not matter who was involved in the negotiations, since they were making progress, although slowly, and with conflicts at nearly every step. Undoubtedly, they did make significant progress in contrast to the beginning of 1996, when contact with the Swiss dragged along unproductively through unofficial channels. But then came January 1997, the stormiest of the entire crisis, in which scandals followed scandals at a dizzying pace. During these days of serious Swiss errors and belligerent Jewish responses, it seemed like the process was collapsing.

"OPPRESSION AND BLACKMAIL"
Serious Blunders Cause Switzerland a Series of Crises

FOR HUNDREDS OF years, the Alps protected Switzerland from invasion, and helped create its solidly neutral position in the worst wars Europe ever saw. But neutrality can breed isolation and Switzerland has come to understand that connection the hard way since mid-1995. Hundreds of years of voluntary detachment from world affairs caused Switzerland to make a series of errors in the 1990s, errors that cost Switzerland untold damage to its image.

Looking on, it is sometimes impossible to understand how a modern state at the end of the twentieth century could act as if nothing was wrong while the entire world was in an uproar over its performance. An outside observer has difficulty determining if Bern is serious when it says that ratifying a simple law in six months is "record time." It is problematic to explain why it took the Swiss government eighteen months of increasing attacks before it realized that it was in the throes of a tremendous crisis, and then to try to understand how the Swiss government could stand before the entire world and ask, "What have we done wrong? What more must we do? Why don't you believe us?"

Why were two years of crisis necessary to bring Switzerland to the beginning of an admission? Thomas Borer explains:

At first it appeared that this was not an important subject, and it was therefore not handled. In retrospect, the time we lost was critical, as we did not take the necessary steps, and there was no one who could work with the Jewish organizations and handle the press. This is not the first example, but possibly the most prominent, of our political system, specifically our cabinet, being inappropriate to handle modern challenges, particularly crises. That's the whole story.

The most influence was from the dormant accounts affair. On the refuge matter we could have claimed that we behaved better than other European countries. The subject of the Nazi gold came up only with the Eizenstat report, and we have explanations for that. But with the dormant accounts, the question is why didn't we handle that in a comprehensive and final manner? That is the central question.

I think the banks made many mistakes, but I wouldn't call it arrogance. It was insensitivity.[1]

An Israeli source following the affair gives an entirely different explanation of Swiss behavior:

The government approach was if we close our eyes maybe it will all go away. They didn't take the subject seriously. They thought this time was like in the past—every few years someone raised the subject and then it disappeared. The Swiss are complacent and nothing is urgent to them. Believe it or not, the Swiss government doesn't have a spokesperson. The famous Swiss efficiency exists in the business sector, but not in the government sector. Part of the price of the isolation is that they don't understand how the modern world works, and they really believe that ratifying a law in six months is express. The banks' arrogance also played an important role and they also thought: we'll duck our heads and this will pass right over us.[2]

Arrogance or not, there is no doubt that the banks made a series of mistakes, the most basic of which was made in the spring of 1995, when the heads of the banks thought they could continue to make the rules— who they would meet, what they would discuss, what would happen—in order to continue to claim that there was no such thing as "Holocaust victims' dormant accounts."

As we have seen, the heads of the Swiss Bankers Association (SBA) tried to bring about Jewish representation only from the Swiss Jewish community. When that did not work, the bankers tried to resolve the crisis by immediately offering to give the Jewish organizations the $32 million found in the dormant accounts. They also thought it would be enough for the Jewish organizations if they turned the handling of the problem over to the SBA's own ombudsman, who set rigid regulations for examining appeals. When that did not work, and the SBA was forced to enter negotiations, its representatives tried to buy time and thought they could eliminate the entire affair with the unilateral report of February 1996. When it became clear that the report only plunged them into a bigger pot of hot water, the association thought it would be possible to bury the matter by establishing a committee that would include just representatives of the Swiss Jewish community.[3]

This attitude began to change only after the first hearings in the Senate Banking Committee on April 23, 1996. Hans Baer and his colleagues were stunned by the fierce public attacks against them, the likes of which they had never seen. It is no coincidence that the talks that led to the establishment of the Volcker Commission began immediately after that hearing.

The banks also got mixed up in a series of apparently minor incidents that, taken together, created the impression of an uncaring attitude, as though the banks had learned nothing from their experience of the past fifty years. These episodes were primarily remarks that diminished the scope of the problem or disparaged the claims of the Jewish organizations. "I am sure that those who believe we are sitting on someone else's gold treasures will be disappointed," said one senior source at Credit Suisse in July 1995, when official contact between Jewish representatives and the SBA began. "It is gall to say we didn't accurately examine the figures of Holocaust victims' accounts; constantly repeating fictitious figures does not make them real," said UBS general manager Robert Studer in February 1996.[4] And of course, there was the document-shredding incident at UBS, covered later in this chapter, that seriously damaged the UBS's credibility.

These mistakes damaged the banks' reputations and cost them dearly on the public relations front. During the course of 1997, the signs were there in the wake of the deposits affair that other customers might demand the restitution of funds that had reached the banks from dubious sources. The first hints were seen in the first half of 1997.

The following anecdote indicates how seriously this threat was taken. On one trip, Avraham Burg came to Switzerland straight from Russia. That evening, he met with a group of public Swiss figures, including members of Parliament. Their conversation dealt with the Holocaust victims' accounts, and Burg decided to float a trial balloon. He told them that he had heard that Russia was following developments closely, and if and when the struggle ended successfully for the Jewish organizations, Moscow intended to demand that the banks return tens of billions of dollars it believed had been stolen by corrupt officials and deposited in Switzerland. The others in the room went pale and did not say a word.

"That story was 98% untrue," Burg admits. "In other words, I really was in Russia and I really did hear it, but from the mouths of such low level officials that it really couldn't be taken seriously." But the reaction around the table that night indicates just how real the fears were among Switzerland's decision makers.[5]

According to a senior Israeli banker who is active in Switzerland, the banks have become much more sensitive since 1995 about handling dormant accounts. "Outside concerns apparently now believe it is easier to pressure the banks," the banker adds. "This, along with objective factors, raises these specific problems."

Another senior Israeli banker, also working in Switzerland, sees it differently: "The banks have been committed for several years to very strict due diligence, regardless of the deposits affair, and the greatest failure for a Swiss banker today is to accept 'dirty money.' Nonetheless, since income tax offenses are not criminal in Switzerland, they can continue to accept undeclared money, so Switzerland continues to be the world's largest tax shelter. The banks are more vulnerable today on the public relations level, but not on the level of day-to-day activities."

And what did happen to the banks on a daily basis? Swiss Bank Corp. admitted in March 1997 that it had lost "a few clients due to the affair, although not the select private banking clients." Widespread opinion is that if a bank makes such a statement, it has lost more than a few clients, and apparently some of the loses are "heavy" customers. In their 1996 annual reports, the two major banks (UBS and Credit Suisse) noted the deposits affair as one of the central events of the year, and it was prominently positioned in the management review that accompanied the reports.[6]

Where was the Swiss government throughout the crisis? When the crisis intensified, Bern believed that it was none of the government's business. Then President and Minister of Finance Kaspar Villiger told Avraham Burg and Edgar Bronfman in September 1995, "I understand your moral argument and I support it, but this is between private banks and their clients."[7]

This attitude remained in effect until May 1996, when the Swiss government was essentially dragged into the affair by item 5 in the Memorandum of Understanding establishing the Volcker Commission, which stated: "The parties of the agreement will cooperate to assure that the Swiss Government will deal with the question of looted assets in Swiss banks or other institutions which were not reported or returned under the relevant laws during the years before, during and immediately after the Second World War."

On May 8, one week after the memorandum was signed, Bern publicly praised the establishment of the commission and began examining what was requested of the government.

The government still believed this was a legal problem, and handling of the subject was therefore assigned to Mathias Kraft, head of the Foreign Ministry's legal department. Kraft was placed at the head of an ad hoc committee of Foreign Ministry, Ministry of Finance, and Ministry of Justice officials. Their primary task was to be observers in the legislative process of a law establishing a committee of experts to examine Swiss policy during World War II. The committee was actually proposed by Verena Grendelmeier in February 1996, with encouragement from Israel Singer. Debate in Parliament was scheduled to begin in July. Kraft's team decided to support Grendelmeier's proposal and not submit a government bill, arguing that there was no need for two parallel bills.[8] Kraft says:

Minister Cotti [then Minister of Foreign Affairs Flavio Cotti] believed at that time, that the core was the legal issues surrounding the subject. We did not react in an efficient or timely manner to the political and emotional aspects, because the government had difficulty assessing their significance. Then a great deal of criticism of the Swiss government began to appear, primarily in the US and Britain, for lack of awareness of the moral and emotional aspects of the issue. We were unable to respond to the criticism and create a positive policy, and that was one of the most difficult periods of my life. We started receiving more and more calls from the ambassadors in Washington and London to be more active and create a media strategy.

The task had become too large for Kraft, and Cotti knew it. Kraft admits that he was wrong to believe that he could head the team and continue to fulfill his regular Foreign Ministry duties. He also admits to another mistake: "I waited too long to reach the conclusion that a special task force of lawyers, diplomats and politicians needed to be formed to deal full time with the subject. By October, there was already a general feeling at the ministry that such a task force was necessary. In retrospect, we should have done it four to six weeks earlier than that, immediately after the summer vacation." An Israeli source who followed the affair says simply, "Kraft failed, so he was replaced."[9]

Not ten days after Swiss officials returned from their summer vacation at the beginning of September 1996, a bombshell landed in the form of the British Foreign Ministry report on trade in stolen gold during World War II and the postwar negotiations for its return.[10] From the point of view of historical research, the British report is less important than the Eizenstat report, but it is a central event in the development of the deposits affair. Its principal conclusion is that the Swiss government ignored requests and warnings from the Allies concerning German deposits of stolen gold in Swiss banks. By early 1943, Bern should already have known that Germany was depositing stolen gold in Swiss banks, as the deposits at that time were already greater than the entire prewar Reichsbank gold reserves.

The British report led the Swiss Foreign Ministry to reexamine its entire handling of the affair. This was the first time an important government confronted Switzerland, as U.S. pressure until then had been inconspicuous and had not included explicit allegations against Bern. Cotti and his colleagues began to understand that they were facing an international diplomatic crisis and not a local bank-client problem.

On October 18, 1996, the Volcker Commission met in Zurich. Between meetings, the Jewish representatives noticed that Georg Krayer and Hans Baer disappeared for a few hours. When the pair reappeared, they looked rather troubled. Only later did it become clear that they had been urgently summoned to Bern to meet with Cotti, who reprimanded them for allowing the continued attacks on Switzerland. "You sit with Jewish representatives on the committee," Cotti ranted. "Make sure these attacks stop."

Krayer and Baer returned to Zurich and the angry and insulted Krayer tried a new tactic in the meeting with the Jewish representatives. Barak recounts that "He said to us 'We'll publish everything we know about the Jews and the Israelis.' " "I said, 'Who are you threatening? I don't have a single penny in Switzerland, Mr. Singer doesn't, Mr. Burg doesn't and Mr.

Bronfman doesn't, and about everyone else, you can publish whatever you want. You aren't threatening anyone.' Afterwards, Krayer commented that he hoped the Zionist Congress [the 100th anniversary of the first Zionist Congress in 1897] would be able to take place in Basel, the city where the Bankers Association headquarters are located, and said something about some poll. A whole story." The Jewish representatives answered with thunderous silence.[11]

When the committee reconvened, Baer tried to fulfill Cotti's demands, as the minutes of the meeting report: "The Jewish organizations are no longer living within the spirit of the Memorandum of Understanding. Attacking Switzerland as a country is unacceptable and creates bad will that undermines the work of the committee." At this point the debate started on Baer's claims. The Jewish representatives said that there were many voices in the organizations they represented, and they were not all of the same opinion.

Finally, a decision was made that probably did not satisfy either Baer or Krayer: "Both the Swiss banks and the Jewish organizations are better off in this process than outside it. The members unanimously agreed on the desirability of making the committee process work in harmony."[12] No one promised the banks that the attacks against Switzerland would stop, and many of them had originated in Senator D'Amato's office anyway, where no Volcker Commission member had any control.

One week later, Cotti decided that the time had come to completely change the Swiss government's attitude to the affair, and turn it over to a full-time staff. After a few discussions, Kraft recommended that Thomas Borer head the team. Borer speaks fluent English, had previously served his government in the United States, and is now married to a former Miss Texas. Attractive and photogenic, then-39-year-old Borer is a lawyer and a diplomat. Borer was then serving as the ministry's deputy comptroller in charge of ministry administration, a relatively low-ranking official. On October 23, Cotti summoned Borer and asked him to head the special task force on the Swiss role in World War II. Borer agreed.[13]

On his first day, the task force consisted of Borer and his secretary; at its peak, it employed 25 people. Its first job was to coordinate the activities of all the government ministries dealing with the crisis, but not to make decisions in cases of differences of opinion. That authority was left to the cabinet only. Another mission was the determination of Swiss policy concerning the items on the agenda, and the protection of Swiss interests.[14]

Borer created a plan that combined defense and counterattack. By the end of October 1996, then ambassador to Washington, Carlo Jagmati, was presenting the new Swiss approach. In a press conference, Jagmati called the $20 billion class-action suit against the banks "over exaggerated," and said that in his opinion "the real sum involved is much lower." Jagmati acknowledged that the banks had made "psychological mistakes" in handling the heirs, and said it was inconceivable to ask for a death certificate for Holocaust victims. He also stated, "On the other hand, if you were a bank customer, you would expect the bank to behave in a serious manner and not pay everyone who came along with unproven claims."[15]

One of the primary targets of the new Swiss strategy was Alphonse D'Amato, whom Bern justifiably considered a key threat. The harshest attacks came from Cotti in February 1997: "D'Amato is not Switzerland's judge and we cannot act in response to his attacks. I understand his interest in the question of Jewish property in the banks, but the manner in which he presents us and his unconcealed distrust of our good will, are unimaginable."[16]

Switzerland began to use Washington lobbyists who denounced D'Amato as a cynical politician and manipulator of the media who was acting out of selfish consideration for the upcoming 1998 Senate elections. According to one, D'Amato's interest is to raise issues as long as they serve his personal goals. "He has no other aspirations, and the Swiss affair is a textbook example of this. Jewish voters vote and contribute huge sums, as they are among the more well-off constituents. D'Amato is courting the Jewish vote, particularly the orthodox vote."[17] This is a rather correct, if biting, description of D'Amato's motives in the Swiss affair, but they are also the motives of nearly every politician on virtually every matter.

Running parallel to the new policy, the Swiss government began to involve itself in contacts concerning the beginning of a possible agreement between the Jewish organizations and the banks. The claim that this was a conflict between the banks and their customers disappeared; the crisis had become too serious to leave in the banks' hands. The first time the Swiss government was actually involved was when Greville Janner (today Lord Janner) went to Bern in November 1996. Janner is vice president of the World Jewish Congress and a leader of the British Jewish community. At that time, he was also a Labor Member of Parliament. At present, he sits in the House of Lords.

In agreement with Singer and Bronfman, but against the wishes of Burg and Barak, Janner spoke for the first time with Krayer and Baer about the need to establish an initial compensation fund to aid victims and their heirs until an overall solution was found. His argument was that survivors were becoming fewer in number with each passing day and could not wait for the results of the Volcker Commission's work. Krayer and Baer did not give a definitive answer, only promising to raise the matter with the major banks. The fact that they did not categorically reject the proposal, however, represented a significant change in attitude.

From there, Janner went to meet with Borer and Cotti, as he believed that "only government activity could force the banks to do something, along with the belief that revelation of the truth would affect their reputations and their business."

Janner told Cotti that to the best of his knowledge the banks would seek to raise some of the money from the government for the fund he had proposed. Cotti replied that he was hearing the idea for the first time and would consider it. "The banks are trying to buy time," Janner claimed to Cotti. "Some of them believe that if they delay handling the problem, the scandal will eventually dwindle. But there are too many people who will not let this scandal dwindle because the injustice is too great. The fact that thousands of Jewish refugees were deported from Switzerland and murdered and the gold extracted from their dental work came to Switzerland, cries out to the heavens." Janner says that he did not suggest an amount in his talks with Cotti, and that it was Borer who estimated that the banks would eventually contribute 200–300 million francs to the fund.[18]

In the first week of December 1996, Borer left for Washington to participate in the House Banking Committee hearings, headed by Jim Leach (R. Iowa). According to Barak, Leach's hearings were more important than D'Amatos because, for the first time, the question of the banks' license to operate in the United States might be called into question. This was also clear to the Swiss, and on December 10, one day before the hearings, Borer lunched with Bronfman and Singer at Seagram's Park Avenue offices.

The meeting began with both sides giving an overview of recent history and a look at the immediate future. What took place afterward, is the subject of serious conflict between both sides. "Borer offered 400 million francs," Singer says unhesitatingly. "Bronfman said 250–300 million would be a reasonable sum," Borer states with the same confidence. "He can say what he wants," Singer responds, "but he offered. There are two witnesses on our side and only one on his."

According to Singer, he showed Borer the draft of Bronfman's upcoming testimony in front of Leach's committee.

Borer wanted Edgar to change it, but that didn't happen. Borer said he thought that in a few months he would be able to get 400 million francs [$270 million] as a start, as an opening gesture. Those were his words. I am 100% sure of this. We said that that wasn't good enough, that in some months was too little too late. He said we needed to understand that Christmas was coming up soon, when everyone goes skiing, the whole country is closed and there is no one around but the tourists.[19]

Borer has an entirely different version of events.

We brought up all sorts of ideas, for instance the establishment of the Bergier Commission [formally named the Independent Commission of Experts: Switzerland–Second World War, described in this chapter], since Bronfman said all along that it wasn't about money but about justice. But he explained to me, that at the hearing he would request immediate aid for Holocaust victims, and ask the Swiss government to establish a fund to aid the victims. I asked what he thought should be the sum. He said he had no intention of naming a number, but clearly the $30 million in dormant accounts were not enough. Then I said I understood, but you agree that $1 billion was too much. Bronfman said yes, I know that's impossible, and it has to be a significant sum. I asked what "significant" meant. I said that a few weeks earlier a Swiss historian named Gorner had suggested 250–300 million. I asked if you agree that 250 million is a reasonable sum. He said 250–300 million is a reasonable sum. Then I said that we are of course talking in francs. He laughed and said, I think you are a very good diplomat. That's how it happened.[20]

According to Borer, he had had an earlier private meeting with Singer, "who said all sorts of things could happen in the US if there is no agreement, particularly all sorts of sanctions against the banks. From the way he presented it, it was clear that this was a reasonable possibility. I told him that sanctions never solve problems." After the meeting, Borer sent a report to Bern, the contents of which, as we will see later, are no less controversial than the contents of the meeting.

The following day, all the key players in the affair arrived at the House Banking Committee hearings; Bronfman, Krayer, Borer, Volcker, and Eizenstat. The most important testimony came from Bronfman, who raised, as planned, the possibility of establishing a fund to aid Holocaust survivors.[21] Bronfman described the banks' September 1995 commitment to keep not even one franc that belonged to a Holocaust victim, and added:

I must report to you today, however, that in the passage of that year not one franc has been transferred as restitution. I do not suggest that there have been no constructive developments. The presence of Mr. Volcker here is an instance of one such development. But to be candid, it is hard to deny that the positive developments have principally resulted from the moral force of international public pressure.

When the Swiss Banking Ombudsman, having received 2000 queries, reports that he has found only $8,000 in accounts, it is not merely pathetic but an indictment of his methods. Indeed, the fees he charged Holocaust survivors and the families of Holocaust victims to process their claims far exceeds the $8,000 he found.[22]

Bronfman reviewed for the committee a series of documents found in the National Archives in Washington, mostly "Safehaven" reports, which demonstrated Swiss economic cooperation with Nazi Germany, primarily on the matter of the gold. Most of his testimony was dedicated to this, for the clear purpose of embarrassing the Swiss. According to him, the documents only hint at the dimensions of the problem, and that the Jewish organizations were continuing to delve into hundreds of thousands of documents in the United States and abroad.

But while we work, Holocaust survivors now in their twilight years are dying. That is why the imperative to uncover historical truth must be weighed against the flesh and blood needs of the aging victims. While heirless assets, it has been agreed with [the] Government of Israel, should accrue to the World Jewish Restitution Organization, keeping in mind the urgent demand of the ever-shrinking population of Holocaust survivors must be met immediately.

We have repeatedly stated that . . . *moral and material restitution must be made*. The time has come for the competent authorities to make a good faith financial gesture—one that does not prejudice the outcome of any final settlement—so that those who have suffered so much may yet see in their lifetime some measure of justice done.[23]

At the same time as the hearings in the House of Representatives in Washington, the Parliament in Bern focused on steps leading to the establishment of the committee of experts on the matter of World War II. The law was unanimously approved by the Lower House on December 13, 1996, and by the Upper House a few days later. Ratification came six months after the process began, and the Swiss noted that this was "record speed," which they felt proved their seriousness and honesty.[24]

The law instructed the cabinet to appoint a committee of experts from various fields to research the fate of all the assets deposited in every possible place in Switzerland before and during World War II, including property stolen from Nazi victims and property deposited by German personages. The law also determined that all those involved must keep any documents that could be needed for the committee's work, and instructed them to permit committee access to those documents; in effect, annulling all the confidentiality laws for this purpose. The law also determined that anyone who destroyed documents would be arrested or fined 50,000 francs. It instructed the cabinet to publish the committee's findings and to provide it with all necessary funding.[25]

The cabinet published the makeup of the committee about a week later. It was headed by Professor Jean François Bergier, a professor of business administration and social history at the Zurich Polytechnic Institute. The members were Wladyslaw Bartoszweski, a historian and former Polish Foreign Minister; Saul Friedlander, a professor at the Hebrew University in Jerusalem and at Yad V'Shem's research institute, whose parents were deported from Switzerland during the war; Harold James, a history professor at Princeton University; Georg Kreis, a history professor at Basel University; Cybil Milton, a historian at Washington's Holocaust Museum; Jacques Picard, a Swiss Jewish historian and author of the book *Switzerland and the Jews* [1994]; Jacob Tanner, a history professor at Bielfeled (Germany) University; and Joseph Voyane, a lawyer and professor of law in Lussane University.[26]

What was the committee lacking? Economists and accountants, despite the fact that its primary mission was to locate property and determine its fate. Bergier said that he accepted the composition of the committee, but that he also planned to employ accountants and economists.[27] In practice, however, it was not done. Even the appointment of Bergier was puzzling. Rumor has it that he was a classmate of then Swiss president Jean Pascal Delamuraz, who got mixed up a shorttime later with somewhat anti-Semitic remarks. Borer does not deny the rumors about Bergier, and adds, "He was also in the army with Cotti, he knows many people." A source very familiar with Swiss alliances states, "It wouldn't surprise me at all if Bergier and Delamuraz are acquainted, because the Swiss elite is very small, because it includes relatively few academics, and everyone knows everyone."[28]

It appeared then, in mid-December 1996, that the crisis was marching slowly toward the beginning of a resolution: the Bergier Commission was established, talks on an initial fund to aid Holocaust survivors began, and Switzerland finally organized itself to handle the problem at a government level. In Washington, Senator D'Amato got ready for a Christmas vacation back home in New York, and in Bern, the ministers and senior officials were making final preparations for ski vacations in the Alps. In Jerusalem and New York, Avraham Burg, Edgar Bronfman, and Israel Singer each believed they could put the Swiss matter aside for a few days to handle their own business interests.

Then, on December 31, the biggest bombshell to hit since the beginning of the crisis landed. Delamuraz granted an interview to *Tribune de Genève* to mark the end of his term of office as Swiss president and made a few anti-Semitic remarks that angered the Jewish organizations and Israel, and brought the crisis to the verge of explosion.

What Delamuraz said is not in question, as his remarks appeared in print. Regarding the question of establishing a compensation fund, Delamuraz, then also minister of economics, said, "The sum named to Ambassador Borer, $250 million, is no less than oppression and blackmail. The fund will make it much harder to get to the truth. Such a fund will be considered an admission of guilt."

Delamuraz said that the attacks against Switzerland concerning World War II were directed at harming its status as an international financial center, and were inspired by behavior in certain Washington and London circles. He categorically rejected the establishment of a compensation fund, claiming that the end of the investigation should be awaited, and further emphasized, "When demands are made not in good faith, they must be rejected."[29]

What is in dispute is the question of why Delamuraz made the remarks in the first place. When the crisis was at its peak and the Swiss tried to understand what happened, Borer was accused of inciting the situation. According to this version of events, Borer reported to his government on the talks with Bronfman and Singer, and created the impression that the Jewish leaders were trying to blackmail Switzerland. Delamuraz read the report, became enraged, and then made his inflammatory remarks.[30]

Borer categorically denies this: "My report was sent to only four members of the task force and to Minister Cotti, and not to anyone in the cabinet."[31] A Swiss source who read Borer's report says it would be very difficult to reach the same conclusions that Delamuraz reached, and, in retrospect, it appears that this was only an excuse for what was apparently a crude mistake on the part of the outgoing president. The source also hinted at the possibility that Delamuraz had his own sources who misled him and caused him to make the remarks.

Burg first heard about Delamuraz's remarks in the late morning of December 31, when a foreign journalist asked him for a comment. He said that those were "serious remarks that should never have been made," but when alone, he did not feel that they were so bad. "Singer and I had argued a few weeks previously on Janner's proposal of $250 million," Burg recounts. "One of the claims I made directly to him was, Israel, that's extortion. Therefore, when Delamuraz said the same thing, my first thought was, I told you so."

Later in the day, Burg talked with some of his associates. "One of them said to me, 'Hey! That's a terrible remark.' And then suddenly the shoe dropped. Just because I think the Swiss will say something is blackmail, doesn't meant they really should say it." Burg called Singer who was just beginning his work day in New York and said, "We already have our job for the day."

The two planned their strategy during that conversation. Burg would be aggressive and extreme, while Singer would stand aside and let him "go wild" for a couple of days. "You always need a good cop and a bad cop," Singer says, "so I was the good cop." The idea was to use the strongest weapon the Jewish organizations had: the threat of a boycott by New York City and New York State institutions. As Singer was to arrive in Jerusalem in two days anyway for a regular meeting regarding Jewish property, the two also planned a joint press conference for January 5.[32]

When Singer got to Jerusalem, he talked about meetings already held with Governor George Pataki and Mayor Rudolph Giuliani in which the two had been asked to consider withdrawing state and city employee pension funds from Swiss banks. "We will not be quiet while they insult the Jewish people," Singer and Burg said.

Singer added, "The City of New York in which there are many Holocaust survivors, will discuss if it is appropriate to continue to support the Swiss banks. New York is just the first state, we will go on to Massachusetts, California, and all across the US." Burg threatened, "Now the battle will be much dirtier. Until now we have held back the international Jewish pressure."[33]

In Bern, on January 1, Thomas Borer realized that he had a problem. He didn't read the interview before it was published, and when he did read it, he was stunned. It was in direct contravention of the task force's established guidelines, issued just a few days earlier, concerning the manner of expression on all matters concerning the deposits problem.[34] It is true that the president does not have to listen to Foreign Ministry officials, but when a special staff is established to handle a specific problem, it should be expected that other branches of government will not undermine its work. At first, Delamuraz did not understand what the fuss was all about. It was only on January 4, when Burg began to talk about the boycott, did Delamuraz say that he was sorry if his comments hurt the feelings of Holocaust survivors. But, his spokesman emphasized, "Before clarification of the historical facts, no fund should be established in Switzerland to grant compensation."[35]

The leadership of the WJRO convened in Jerusalem on January 5, for an earlier planned meeting, but dealt with the Delamuraz crisis instead of its original agenda. They decided to wait one month for an official Swiss apology, and if that did not happen, they would propose that the Jewish organizations take a series of steps against Switzerland and the banks on February 11. These included a partial boycott of the banks, withdrawing investments, activities to cancel the banks' New York licenses, filing a class-action suit by the organizations against the banks, and increasing research about the deposits matter in order to increase public pressure on Switzerland. It was a weighty course of action, but devised to allow Bern enough time to find the right way to apologize before both sides went too far.

Singer was willing to threaten the Swiss from another direction:

So far we have covered only 5% of the documents pertaining to Swiss actions during World War II, and we have hundreds of thousands of documents that have not been examined in depth. Our intention was to share the information we have with the Volcker and Bergier Commissions. However, if Switzerland and the banks are not cooperating with us, we will be forced to expose the documents to global public opinion, in the same manner we read them—one per day.

Good public relations stem from good behavior. The last thing the banks need is negative publicity, and that is what the Swiss banks will get every day if they do not cooperate. We will deal with the banks one at a time, and we have documents on the banks, on Swiss personages, and on families whose money disappeared in the banks. We will do it until the banks say, "Enough. We want to reach a compromise." We don't want to do business to receive the compensation due the Jewish people—but committees are not money. We are not willing to put up with street gang behavior towards us, when we are acting fairly.[36]

That evening, January 5, 1997, the World Jewish Congress in New York published an American document from May 1946, in which it was claimed that Switzerland proposed to Germany that it forge a prewar date stamp on gold bars so Bern could claim it did not know it was purchasing stolen gold. Switzerland denied the allegation, which apparently really wasn't well-founded, but it was a clear hint of what lay in store if the crisis wasn't resolved quickly.[37]

Embarrassment in Bern increased. The share prices of Swiss Bank Corp., UBS, and Credit Suisse on the Zurich stock exchange dropped in response to the threatened boycott, and although the declines were moderate,[38] the trend was clear. Borer believed that "the Jewish organizations reaction, particularly Burg's, was exaggerated," but public opinion thought otherwise.[39] Delamuraz dug in his heels and refused to apologize, and his colleagues saw no possibility of changing his mind.

On January 7, the Swiss government announced its interest in immediate talks with the local banks and the Jewish organizations concerning the accounts, although it rejected the organizations' threats, saying they damaged efforts to locate Holocaust victim's property. A few hours later, the practical proposal was presented: the donation to a fund of the $32 million found in the dormant accounts to aid victims of Nazi persecution. Switzerland again proposed the same amount the banks had proposed in September 1995, as if sixteen months of talks, hearings, discussions, and crisis had not gone by. The only change was Borer's announcement that the money could be made available to the Jewish organizations by the end of January. Bern's declaration ignored the demand for an apology for Delamuraz's comments, which the government spokesman said, "were misunderstood and led to an exaggerated response."

The Jewish organizations had a long memory and rejected the offer on the spot. "It is amazing that the Swiss try to buy us with money that never belonged to them anyway," Burg said. "It is important to remember, that no one asked the Swiss to establish a compensation fund. We only want what belongs to us, and nothing more than that. We will have no contact with them until they apologize for Delamuraz's remarks, and the threats remain in effect until then."[40]

On January 11, Senator Alfonse D'Amato, the Jewish organizations' heaviest cannon, entered the fray. This was one day after Switzerland's new president, Arnold Koller, officially rejected the demand for an apology from Delamuraz, saying his predecessor had already expressed public regret for his words.[41] Koller's announcement, however, was inaccurate. Delamuraz expressed regret for the possibility that his comments hurt the Jewish people's feelings and claimed they were taken out of context, but he did not renege and certainly did not apologize. In contrast, then CEO of Swiss Bank Corp., Marcel Ospel, said that a boycott of the banks would have "serious consequences."

Ospel's comments played right into D'Amato's hands, who announced plans to hold hearings in the Senate Banking Committee on the question of renewing the licenses of Swiss banks in the United States. It was not a practical threat, as individual states grant licenses, but it was clear that these discussions would cause serious harm to the banks' image.[42]

After two weeks, the Swiss government finally understood that it had to resolve the problem. The behind-the-scenes activity once again took place in New York, at the same bar where Singer and Hans Baer habitually met. This time, along with Singer, was the Swiss general consul in New York, Alfred Defago, and Member of Parliament (MP) François Loeb (the owner of a chain of Swiss department stores bearing his name). The three drafted Delamuraz's letter of apology that would be sent to Edgar Bronfman, as well as Bronfman's reply.

Delamuraz's letter stated, "I am very sorry I hurt your feelings, as well as those of the entire Jewish community. I promise you that this was not my intention. The extent to which I based my comments concerning the compensation fund was inaccurate." Bronfman confirmed receipt of the letter and added, "I expect to return to constructive work together with Swiss authorities and banks, in order to resolve the pending issues, which will serve our purpose of reaching truth and justice." Bronfman and Burg officially announced that the threat of the boycott was removed.[43]

The letters were exchanged between Bronfman and Delamuraz on January 15, a few hours after an apparently marginal event in Zurich, which again raised tensions. It is likely that neither of them knew what had happen when they concluded the Delamuraz crisis. At that time exactly, the Zurich canton district attorney announced the launch of an investigation against UBS to look into the possibility that the bank was trying to destroy documents apparently pertaining to the Holocaust victims' deposits affair. In a matter of days, the process again was in danger of collapse.

Christopher Meili, the twenty-eight-year-old security guard who discovered the documents, became a media hero in the United States overnight. In fact, the Meili incident was nearly insignificant in and of itself, but it did rekindle in full view of the entire world, the key question in the entire affair. Where are the papers that document deposits made by Europe's Jews in Swiss banks? Is it possible they were destroyed en masse in order to hide a trail of looting the money by the banks?

Meili worked for a security company hired by UBS. On January 8, as Meili was patrolling the management wing of UBS's main building on Bahnhofstrasse in Zurich, which was undergoing renovations, he came to the shredding room. On the left side of the room, Meili saw bags of old papers, and began to search through them. He later said that he immediately suspected someone was trying to destroy documents concerning the deposits' affair. In one of the bags, Meili found books with green bindings written in 1926 and later. In skimming through them Meili found documentation of credit granted to German companies. He hid two books in his locker and took another one home. The next day it became clear to him that the rest of the documents had been shredded. After reading the books for the next two days, Meili and his wife reached the conclusion that "Holocaust survivors had to see this material."

On January 11, Meili called the Israeli embassy and offered to bring important documents to the legation. Security directives for Israeli representations abroad forbade them to respond to such offers, and Meili was asked to send the documents in the mail. He chose another route, however, and called the office of the Jewish community in Zurich and was immediately told, "Come to us with the documents." The head of the community, Werner Rom, read the documents and told Meili that he had to turn them over to the police. Meili called the police who transferred the matter to the district attorney. Daniel Kossandi announced that he was opening an investigation of UBS on January 15, on the grounds of violation of the December 1996, Parliament decision to establish the Bergier Commission that prohibited the destruction of documents necessary for the commission's work.

In the first days after the investigation was launched, uncertainty pertaining to the documents prevailed. Meili claimed that they dealt with the property of customers from Berlin deposited in the bank between 1930 and 1940. The bank responded by stating that it did not know the contents of the documents. UBS admitted that destruction of the documents was contrary to parliamentary instructions and claimed it was done because an anonymous clerk believed the documents were "unimportant." Only in July 1997, did the bank admit that the documents dealt with the forced sale of real estate by German Jews in the 1930s. This meant they were possibly relevant, at least indirectly, to the deposits investigation, and the bank violated the law in destroying them.[44]

The real question, as Werner Rom put it, was, what other documents were destroyed. The revelation also aroused the suspicions of the Jewish organizations, as the director general of the World Jewish Congress in Israel Avi Becker stated, "We have suspected for quite some time that Switzerland destroyed documents and this fact must be considered while investigating the affair." Paul Volcker appealed to the Swiss government and the SBA and expressed his fear that the Swiss had violated the agreement that required them to reveal to his committee all information concerning the Holocaust victims' deposits.[45]

Ironically, a parallel investigation was then launched against Meili, on suspicion of violating banking secrecy, and he was suspended from his job. Meili was later fired, but was granted asylum and citizenship in the United

States after appearing at hearings in both houses of Congress.[46] In October 1997, the Zurich district attorney announced the closure of both files in the case—against Meili and UBS chief archivist, Erwin Hagenmueller.

The argument for the closure of the second case was very edifying: destruction of the documents was not a criminal offense (which the bank itself admitted having committed, and if it had not been an offense why did it take nine months to investigate?), Hagenmueller did not receive instructions from superiors to destroy the documents (what does that matter?), and the relevant documents were shredded and unavailable for investigation (which was the offense in and of itself). UBS expressed regret for the unpleasantness caused Meili, but did not apologize to him. Only when an overall agreement on the deposits' affair was reached in August 1998, was it revealed that Meili received $1 million in compensation from the bank.[47]

The Delamuraz and Meili crises brought the Swiss government to seek a rapid resolution to the new situation. It was clear to Bern that there was only one solution and it was only temporary: the establishment of a compensation fund for Holocaust victims. The initiative that had been rejected by the banks when Greville Janner raised it in November 1996, began to take shape in just a few months time. The notion that had led Delamuraz to say what he did became the way out of the crisis created by his remarks.

The government and the banks conducted quiet but stubborn negotiations for months, with the government demanding some action (i.e., paying into a fund), and the banks opposing their demands. At the height of the January crises, Rolf Bloch said to Flavio Cotti, "You must do something before the Bergier Commission report, because that will take another five years." It was now agreed in talks between the government and the banks that one of the major banks would take the initiative, the other two major banks would join in, the government would praise them and then help implement the idea.[48] The task fell to Rainer Gut, the chair of Credit Suisse. Why him? In Bloch's opinion, "Credit Suisse had a more positive attitude the entire time."

Singer believes that the reason is far more cynical and goes back to February 6, 1996. On that day, the World Jewish Congress published the document about the bank account of Romanian war criminal Radu Lecca in Volksbank, which later became part of Credit Suisse. In Singer's opinion, that is the reason that the bank found itself in a moral position that eventually led to practical leadership. In addition, there was pressure on the heads of the banks from Richard Holbrooke, now U.S. ambassador to the United Nations, who was then in a senior position at First Boston, the investment bank that is owned by Credit Suisse.[49]

On January 21, 1997 the Swiss Parliament's Foreign Affairs Committee approved a proposal to transfer the property without heirs to the Jewish organizations, and a decisive step was taken the following day. Gut arranged for publication of an article he had written in the best known newspaper in Switzerland, *Neue Zuricher Zeitung*. In his article, Gut proposed to his colleagues the immediate establishment of a "very generous fund" to compensate Holocaust survivors, which would be a gesture of goodwill. Meanwhile, Gut said, the government must provide the banks guarantees against future claims by victims' heirs so that they did not pay both to the fund and to the heirs and the government must also take responsibility for all dormant accounts in the future. He did not specify the exact amount to be placed in the fund, but noted that one month earlier, 100 million francs (then $70 million) had seemed to be a reasonable sum. Now, after the Delamuraz storm, it would appear that a little more money was needed.[50]

Outwardly, it appeared that the Swiss government jumped quickly on the bandwagon, although in practice it had been riding the wagon since it began to roll. On January 24, the government decided to enter immediate negotiations with the Jewish organizations for the establishment of what it called a Memorial Fund to aid Holocaust survivors. Borer declared that Bern's goal was to reach an agreement with the Jewish organizations and the central bank within a matter of weeks concerning the financing of the fund and its objectives. Bern decided that the scope of the fund would be $70 million, which indicates that the government already had commitments from the major banks to contribute jointly to the minimum sum Gut had mentioned.[51]

The Jewish organizations at first praised the Bern decision, but noted that if this was the sum, the proposal would not be accepted. Their position was that the fund had to be much closer to the $250 million mentioned over and over again. A declaration the next day by the Bergier Commission, however, reawakened the suspicions of the Jewish organizations. It seemed that this might be another Swiss exercise in buying time.

Bergier said that his committee's task was "to form a basis for the decision to establish a fund." He estimated that the committee would need six months to publish a preliminary report on Swiss purchases of German gold, then Bern could progress toward establishing the fund.[52] Apparently, one more crisis was necessary in order to finally motivate the Swiss government to really act quickly, and that came on January 26, just two days after the decision to establish the fund.

It was Sunday, January 26, and Borer hoped for a little rest after the continuous crises of the preceding weeks. But, when he opened *Sonntag Zeitung*, he was shocked. The respected newspaper had acquired a confidential memo sent by Carlo Jagmati, Switzerland's ambassador to the United States, to Borer before Christmas, in which Jagmati commented on the struggle against the Jewish organizations: "This is a war . . . which Switzerland must win, both on the external front and on the internal front. Most of our enemies cannot be trusted," Jagmati added, hinting at D'Amato and the Jewish organizations. He even noted that Swiss agreement to establish the compensation fund stemmed from the need "to rapidly satisfy D'Amato and the Jewish circle," which was true in and of itself, but the whole thing looked very bad just three weeks after the Delamuraz interview.[53]

Singer was not too excited about the memo: "Basically, he was right: we were at war," but expressed sorrow at its contents.[54] Burg fumed, or at least pretended to fume. In retrospect, he admits that he exploited the opportunity to escalate the crisis and increase the pressure on Switzerland.

To the point of the matter, nothing that Jagmati said bothered me, except that he called us the "enemy." But I knew that global public opinion would not stomach two Swiss bad guys so I decided to hit full force. If this is war, as he said, then there are instances where you take no prisoners. My strategy the entire time was that we would make gains in the Volcker Commission if we pressured them from outside, and this was an opportunity to do so.[55]

Burg demanded that the Swiss government apologize for Jagmati's comments and fire the senior ambassador.[56]

Jagmati's remarks made big headlines in Israel and all over the world, particularly in the United States. D'Amato demanded that the Swiss government apologize for the comments, and the State Department spokesman also urged the Swiss to do so in his daily press briefing. The spokesman called Jagmati's comments "worrisome and erroneous," rather harsh terminology in the diplomatic lexicon. Within twenty-four hours, Bern realized that Jagmati would have to forfeit his job in order to prevent a repeat of the Delamuraz crisis. Jagmati, sixty-four, informed the Foreign Ministry that he did not believe he could continue until his planned retirement in July 1997, expressed regret at the injury to the sensibilities of the Jewish people, and resigned. Minister Cotti, who took care to immediately publish Jagmati's announcement, said that no pressure was applied for resignation. It stands to reason, however, that resignation was suggested and Jagmatic took the hint.

There is no doubt that the rapid Swiss response to the Jagmati crisis was influenced by actions against Swiss banking activities in New York that were gaining momentum at the time. On January 30, chairman of the New York City Council, Peter Vallone, proposed a municipal bill to forbid the city and its institutions from depositing moneys in Swiss banks before they established a compensation fund for Holocaust victims. Meanwhile, Sheldon Silver, the speaker of the New York House of Representatives, announced that hearings would begin on February 13, to deal with "whether the State of New York needs to reconsider its relations with Swiss banks, as a means of encouraging them to cooperate in locating the unclaimed assets and returning them." UBS spokesman immediately admitted that if American customers began withdrawing funds, it would be a "serious problem."[57]

January 1997, the stormiest month in the deposits crisis, drew to a close, but not before the Volcker Commission met in Zurich for a lengthy and difficult meeting. The meeting had been planned in advance for January 30–31, but the events of the month granted it special importance. By January 14, at the height of the Delamuraz crisis, Volcker was threatening to blow up the entire process. A source close to the committee says, "Volcker was very angry about Burg's harsh response to Delamuraz's remarks and the threat of a boycott, although he did not say so explicitly." "Delamuraz's remarks didn't interest him, because they had no direct connection, in his opinion, to the committee's work. The Jewish threats did affect it, and he was angry about that."[58]

The committee met on January 30 at 3:20 P.M. at the Savoy Hotel in Zurich. Burg arrived at the hotel accompanied by two police cars that had escorted him from the moment of disembarkation, due to threats on his life. The first question local reporters asked when they could approach him in the terminal was, "Why do you hate Switzerland?" Burg's reply was to roll up his sleeve and show off his wrist watch: "Could someone who has worn a Swatch all his life hate Switzerland?"[59]

The meeting continued until 11:50 P.M. that evening, with a break for a working dinner with Bergier, and resumed for a few more hours the following morning in the conference center at the Zurich airport. Volcker began with a report on his meeting with the New York State then supervisor of banks, Neil Levin, who had also begun to examine the affair, and hinted broadly at the possibility of taking action against the banks, especially in light of the steps planned against the banks by the state and city. Volcker and Levin agreed to cooperate, the key to which was the expansion of the Volcker Commission's accounts' investigation to include the banks' foreign branches.

The next item on the agenda was the Meili affair and the destruction of documents by UBS, which occupied the committee for several hours. Volcker summoned the bank's representatives, then CEO Mathis Cabiallaveta and legal counsel Urs Roth. In their presence, Volcker expressed his concern about the implementation of the Swiss parliament's decision concerning preservation of relevant documents. The Jewish representatives did not believe a word of the explanations they provided, and simply laughed outright when they heard them. "They tried to present the archivist [Erwin Hagenmueller] as if he were some low-level clerk although he is a member of the bank's management," one of them said. Burg sharply said to the UBS representatives, "The equation is very simple. The more you destroyed, the more you'll pay."[60]

Roth began to describe events that took place at the bank. According to him, the destroyed documents belonged to the German Eidgenossische Bank, which UBS acquired in 1945, and included only annual reports, board of directors' minutes from the bank's founding in 1863 until 1945, and a group of documents concerning the general financial situation of the bank. After UBS's July 1997, admission, according to which the documents did concern Jewish property (although held in Germany), there is no option but to conclude that the bank's representatives did not tell the Volcker Commission the whole truth.

Even more grave was the UBS report on the manner in which the bank handled the preservation of documents in general. According to Roth, on December 19, 1996, six days after the ratification of the law establishing the Bergier Commission, archivist Hagenmueller instructed that the Eidgenossische Bank's documents be examined and classified into two categories: those relevant to the deposits affair and those irrelevant to the deposits affair. Hagenmueller decided to destroy the documents that appeared irrelevant to him, and "there is no written documentation of the destroyed documents," a very important comment that verifies the suspicion that the banks do not habitually keep lists of destroyed documents. The significance for the investigation is clear.

Roth's comments about UBS had to raise concern. On December 10, when it was clear that the law ratifying the Bergier law was only a matter of days away the bank's chief of staff widely distributed a memo with instructions for the preservation of documents that could be subpoenaed by New York courts hearing the class-action suits against the banks. "However, the Archivist did not receive a copy of this memorandum, and the Archivist's knowledge concerning the Holocaust document preservation was solely derived from newspapers," Roth revealed. His comment is not an error: the person responsible for the bank's documents did not receive the instruction to preserve the documents. Roth even added that confirmation of the law did not lead to the issuance of a new memorandum, although, "now [at the end of January] efforts are being made to rewrite the December 10 memo."

Afterward, Curt Hauri, the supervisor of banks, appeared before the commission and officially summarized the details of the understanding he had reached with Volcker in October 1996. Hauri announced that he would use his authority for the first time in Swiss history to direct that the accountants hired by the Volcker Commission would be considered "special auditors" from the supervision of Banks. This meant complete access to all bank documents, including the names of clients, and the option to report their names to the Supervision of Banks. The client's names would not be reported to the Volcker Commission, but it could receive other information, including the nationality of the account owner, the date the account was opened, and how long it existed. This removed one of the chief stumbling blocks facing the commission: the fear that the banks would not cooperate with the accountants by claiming confidentiality. Hauri's declaration also enabled non-Swiss accountants to handle the investigation, just as the Jewish organizations had wanted.

The Volcker Commission moved on to discuss the accountants' work and heard reports from David Ashton of Arthur Andersen, Frank Plandioisi of Price-Waterhouse, and David Smith of KPMG. Ashton spoke about preliminary results of an investigation into bank responses to the 1962 law, which required them to report accounts whose owners may have been Holocaust victims. Ashton stated that only twenty-six banks bothered to report dormant accounts in 1962, a number that Jewish representatives later called "stunning." He noted that there were 500 banks in Switzerland in 1962, but "it didn't look like anyone bothered to investigate why so many banks did not report." The Jewish representatives jumped out of their seats as if they'd been bitten. Ashton's figure verified their suspicions about the partial reporting by the banks, and even more, faulty government supervision.[61]

After dinner with Bergier, at 8:45 P.M. the commision began to discuss the most charged subject on the agenda: its continued existence in light of the atmosphere created between the Jewish and Swiss sides. The minutes state that

In light of these developments and the real possibility that the Committee may not be able to live up to the expectations that some have for its work, the Chairman [Volcker] indicated his belief that the time had come for a frank discussion of whether the Committee should keep going. The Chairman recognized that given the charged political situation, it is unlikely that public attention on the issues being discussed by the Committee would diminish.

The Chairman expressed his view that it is the responsibility of the members of the Committee to refrain from participating in the public debate in such a way that the Committee itself would be the subject of their criticism. In particular, the Chairman stated the importance of keeping the Committee's discussions and confidential information on the work of the Committee within the Committee. He said that the need to protect the confidentiality of the Committee's discussions would become even more important as the work of the Auditors got underway and the Committee began to have concrete information regarding dormant accounts. Committee members agreed with Chairman's thoughts on this matter."

On another point, a tumultuous argument arose, expressed only partially in the minutes. According to the record, "Some members pointed out that there were many aspects of the public debate and public perceptions on the role of the Committee that were not totally within the control of the Committee Members. The Committee discussed the particular pressures individual members of the Committee faced in being both members of the Committee and also public figures with responsibilities to other organizations." This was an obvious reference to the representatives of the Jewish Agency and the World Jewish Congress. The banks' representatives, for their part, tried to exploit the opportunity to limit at least the committee's work, if not the public debate, to "the very narrow focus on the search for dormant accounts."

Not even hinted at in the minutes was the verbal confrontation, between Burg and Peider Mengiardi, who sharply criticized Burg's remarks condemning Delamuraz. "You are bringing a country to its knees, you are ruining its system," Mengiardi claimed. "You are letting the anti-Semitic genie out of the bottle. We have also had applications, and we can also respond to the pressure on us," he added in an unexplained threat.

When the attack was over, Burg answered him very quietly. He told of a meeting he had held the day before in London with a Holocaust survivor, and laid a yellowing document on the table. It was an authorization that a survivor received from a London doctor who had examined the man's mother—an Auschwitz survivor—for the purpose of receiving a disability stipend from Germany. Among other things, the document stated that while at Auschwitz "six healthy gold teeth [dental work] were removed from the woman's mouth for reuse."

Burg continued, "Gentlemen, I do not work for you. While your president calls me a 'blackmailer,' I represent only one thing here." He read the same line from the document, written in German, held out his hand to Mengiardi and said quietly, "I represent here six healthy gold teeth for reuse. Could you please return them to me? You don't have them? So this is the partner you have for the negotiations and I will not leave you alone until you return the last tooth." The room was absolutely silent. The stunned Mengiardi leaned back in his chair speechless. Burg leaned on the table a few seconds longer and then he leaned back also. That was the end of the Swiss attack.

We now return to the minutes, which state laconically that there was "wide-ranging discussion of the subject raised by the Chairman," and covers Volcker's summary.

Despite the difficulties facing the members of the Committee, there appeared to be a will within the Committee both to move forward and for the Committee Members to protect the Committee from becoming embroiled and possibly derailed by the wider public debate. It was agreed that within the Committee, Members must strive to preserve cooperation amongst themselves, despite these pressures, and that when directly engaged in activities in other arenas, Committee members should do their utmost to protect the Committee and its efforts from being adversely affected by such activities.

Concurrently with the Volcker Commission meeting, Israeli Prime Minister Benjamin Netanyahu, in Davos for the World Economic Forum met with then Swiss president Arnold Koller in an effort to reduce the tension between the two sides. Netanyahu announced in advance that he intended to raise the issue of the deposits at the meeting with Koller the first time the matter would be discussed at the highest rank. In an interview with a French newspaper a few days earlier, Netanyahu had said, "We must determine, in partnership with our Swiss colleagues, a mechanism that will enable us to correct this terrible historic injustice."[62]

In their meeting, Koller promised Netanyahu to act energetically to rapidly complete the investigation and determine the means to compensate the owners and their heirs. Netanyahu stated that Switzerland promised to cooperate with the Jewish organizations and the Knesset committee for the restitution of property, headed by Avraham Hirschson. At a press conference following their meeting, Koller publicly distanced himself from the expressions of anti-Semitism in his country due to the affair, and promised his government would not allow them to be overlooked.[63]

The bottom line is that the last few days of January were very different from the beginning days of the month. After a month of serious crises, the process was on a much faster track toward the beginning of resolution. Switzerland needed the fierce international attacks to understand that it could not keep acting in its usual slow and carefree manner. The combination of barely concealed anti-Semitism at the highest levels of Swiss government and the weird and embarrassing incident at Zurich's largest bank, changed the entire course of the deposits crisis.

12

"EASING THE SUFFERING"
Steps Toward Absolving the
Sins of the Past

IN THE ONE year that passed since the then president of Switzerland, Kaspar Villiger, said, "the deposits problem is a matter between the private banks and their customers," the problem appeared more and more frequently on the cabinet agenda. In the last months of 1996 and the first months of 1997, the matter was on the agenda of every single cabinet meeting. Naturally, this led to increasing media interest in developments, which led to a great deal of public attention to the events of the case.[1]

Swiss public opinion on the deposits' crisis, particularly reports surrounding the country's actions during World War II, is one of the main components of the affair. It is of fundamental moral and historical importance—what does Switzerland see when it looks at itself in the mirror. It also has an immediate practical importance in a country where a referendum can be held on any issue: public opinion does have a direct influence over government decisions and their implementation.

Then Foreign Minister Flavio Cotti, who was born just a few weeks after the outbreak of World War II, said in February 1997:

My generation has believed for a long time that its early years belong to history, as dramatic as it is. I am certain that 99% of Swiss citizens grew up with total confidence that the country's overall attitude during the war was completely correct, even if mistakes were made here and there. Now, we must consider that many mistakes were made, mostly in refugee policy.

For fifty years, only good things were said about Switzerland, and the positive aspects of World War II history in our country were described much more fully than the negative. It appears the time has come to emphasize the shadows, and in the future, the time will come for a more balanced view. There is never an absolute historic truth, and history is not black and white. I am sure, that if the Swiss are given the necessary time, it will be possible to create the proper balance of wartime events.[2]

Thomas Borer also commented at that time on the manner in which the citizens of his country saw the continuous attacks on Switzerland:

It must be understood that the accusations didn't stop even after Switzerland took steps that no other country has come close to taking. When the debate centered on money, many Swiss began to wonder whether this is about just money or about the truth? What is the real motive? Everything we do, they want more. There is a difference between the Swiss attitude and the American attitude. We are watch makers, want very accurate clocks, and it takes three years to make such an accurate watch. Americans want very fast solutions to every problem.[3]

Historian and MP Jean Ziegler stood up time after time in the Swiss Parliament to attack the banks. "The Swiss banks are robbers and money launderers for generations of the entire world's criminals. They will do anything to sabotage the committees trying to reveal the truth," Ziegler said. "Switzerland has no natural treasure except the moneys of foreign nationals. If the banks surrender even once and let someone from outside peek in their safes, the rumor will spread around the world and reach the ears of the drug barons and dictators of Africa. The banks must lie, they have no choice. Anyone who thinks otherwise, is naive."[4]

Ziegler's opinion, however, is far from the dominant one: Across from him stood the no less vocal Christoph Blocher—one of the wealthiest businessmen in Switzerland and MP representing the People's Party—whose representative is Adolf Ogi the minister of defense. Blocher led the attack against Swiss soul-searching, which has also led to pocket searching. Blocher presented a series of particulars, some true, some exaggerated, and some completely groundless, but since they concerned complex historical events, even the wise among his listeners had a hard time sorting out truth from equivocation in his remarks. Blocher was right when he noted that Switzerland remained a democracy and opposed Fascism. He was right in saying that Switzerland absorbed hundreds of thousands of refugees, and there was truth in the claim that if Switzerland had countered a German attack, Berlin would have had to bring many troops to the Alpine front.

In contrast, Blocher misled his listeners and readers when he claimed that Germany seriously intended to invade Switzerland, and that the danger of invasion increased near the end of the war. He described the deportation of Jewish refugees as a situation in which "Switzerland was unfortunately forced to restrain about 30,000 refugees outside its borders," and spoke not a word about their ethnic origins, the sole reason for their "restraint." The stamping of the letter J in the passports of Germany's Jews Blocher explained away as Swiss inability to withstand German pressure, while the opposite is true: Switzerland urged this action. In Blocher's opinion, this was at most, a "misunderstood step."

From here, Blocher went on to vehemently attack the Jewish organizations, calling their claims hypocritical and only desirious of money. In his opinion, those Swiss who present a pro-Jewish stance supported by moral arguments are essentially amoral and want to blame "economic and political decision makers" for the crisis. Had Switzerland behaved during the war as that moral group would have wanted, the country would have been lost. In his opinion, politicians who appeal to Switzerland to face its past are acting only in their own self-interest. He calls the Jewish organizations' demands "blackmail."

Blocher demanded no repentence for Switzerland's wartime trade policy, "which was not only legal but also essential for Switzerland. The country didn't have a chance for survival without this trade. If the economy, the banks, the State or anyone now decides to pay money for that policy or to apologize, this means unjustified criticism of our country at that time, which constitutes betraying our people!"[5]

While Blocher walked the fine line between evangelism and incitement, and nationalism and racism, there are a number of Swiss who have demonstrated unconcealed anti-Semitism since the affair gained momentum. The problem of anti-Semitism in Switzerland is not new, but was relatively dormant until the end of 1996. Until then, anti-Semitism was expressed primarily in the form of prejudice. Surveys showed that even the well educated believed that there were 200,000–300,000 Jews in Switzerland, while the real number was 18,000. The same surveys also indicated a high percentage of Swiss who believed that the Jews controlled the economy of the canton of Zurich, the largest and most important one in Switzerland.

The turning point for the worse, in the opinion of Jewish concerns, was the interview of then president Jean Pascal Delamuraz in December 1996, when Delamuraz accused the Jewish groups of "extortion and blackmail," he granted, even if unintentionally, legitimacy for Swiss anti-Semitism to come out of the closet.

After that interview, the Israeli embassy, the Jewish community, and the newspapers were flooded with hundreds of anti-Semitic letters, some of which were threatening. The embassy received anti-Semitic letters every day at that time, in contrast to the one per month it averaged before then.[6] Fortunately, so far the threats have remained on paper.

One of the letters was accompanied by a picture of a bearded Jew in a yarmulke pointing at a desecrated synagogue in Poland. The writer warned, "He is mourning his latrine. This could also happen in Switzerland due to the 'friendly' attacks of the gangsters Avraham Burg, Israel Singer and Alfonse D'Amato! Not one penny of Swiss citizens' taxes, no harm to the property of the Swiss people for a Holocaust fund!"

Burg, D'Amato, and Bronfman were the primary targets of the anti-Semitic profanity. On a photo of Burg, swastikas were drawn on his hands, and the sender added, "Scorn this anti-Swiss Jewish pig!" A Star of David was drawn on D'Amato's forehead with the caption, "Physically he could be a Jewish pig. If there is Jew-hatred in Switzerland today, it is to his credit!" A letter about Bronfman stated in broken English: "Wanted! Dead

Letters against Avraham Burg and Alfonse D'Amato sent to Jewish institutions in Bern. (Author's files)

or Alive. Edgar Bronfman ('Extortioner Eddy'). Reward: 0.50 US Cents. The Deputy Sheriff of Switzerland."[7]

The annual report of the Center for the Research of Anti-Semitism at Tel Aviv University, published in April 1997, indicated an unmistakable rise in anti-Semitism in Switzerland due to the deposits' affair. The report's authors noted that the struggle for the property brought a general rise in anti-Semitism in all the affected countries, particularly Switzerland, where there was latent anti-Semitism in the first place.[8]

It should be noted to the credit of the Swiss government that it immediately and decisively confronted the expressions of anti-Semitism. According to Rolf Bloch, the key problem is not the anti-Semitism itself, but that the "General attitude towards Jews has changed, and there is again a difference between Swiss Jews and Swiss Gentiles. There is a less-friendly feeling towards Jews. Beforehand, Jews were more or less one among the minorities living in Switzerland, now they are strangers again. I do not claim this is the general thinking, but it is the trend."

Bloch believes, as in June 1997, that the key problem is not the battle against anti-Semitism, but the need to handle its cause—external pressure on Switzerland and the ongoing attacks. "It is impossible to say that Switzerland bought Nazi gold, but that its central bank did, which is an independent body. This was not official government policy. From a legalistic standpoint, the Swiss said during the war: we need to be in contact with both sides. They could have said they didn't want to continue to be in contact with the devil, but we cannot judge their motives today."[9]

Bloch has a very ambivalent opinion of the activities of the World Jewish Congress and the Jewish Agency:

I believe that the involvement of the international Jewish organizations is entirely justified, as the Jewish community cannot speak for all the world's Jews. This is not only a Swiss issue, but also from the Jewish standpoint this is an international issue. I did not want to create the impression that this is a matter among Swiss citizens, but to receive the approval of all those affected. I therefore said to the Jewish organizations: we'll work together.

Today, the Swiss are naturally very hurt and they are responding. They believe that the Jewish organizations and the Americans are pressuring us and the response is anti-Semitism and anti-Americanism. We now find ourselves between a rock and a hard place—between the Swiss and the Jews, and between the Swiss and the Americans.

If the Jewish organizations act publicly, they must be more aware of the way things are done in Switzerland. They are not done the way they are done in Israel or in the US. The Swiss are not accustomed to pressure like this and they react as Swiss. If the organizations had consulted with us, not only occasionally [but on a regular basis], we may have been able to predict the results more clearly. We were not Holocaust victims, and we shouldn't have to be victims of the bank accounts.

However, I must be clear: without some external pressure, things would have moved very slowly, and may not have reached the same ends. It is only a question of the amount and kind of pressure. In practice, the amount of pressure didn't change [even when Switzerland took steps to resolve the crisis], and things were said that caused the Swiss to think that their good will and willingness were unrecognized. The organizations should have considered what was built here [Swiss willingness to investigate the affair and wartime history], instead of launching a new attack every day, justified or not."[10]

And what does Thomas Borer think, the man positioned on the front lines for the Swiss?

I do not see and never have seen the Jewish organizations as enemies. I see them as having a different set of interests. There is a lot of frank, honest motivation behind their interests. We didn't react well, and they used other means [the media]. The problem is that now they cannot control those means.

The people positioned at the forefront of the matter, have only the most honest motivation. I mean the World Jewish Congress and maybe also the Jewish Agency. I cannot express an opinion on Burg's motives as I have never met him. The second line are those hanging onto the matter hoping to profit from it, and not necessarily from honorable motives. Among them, there are a few who are not interested in Jewish history or the Holocaust, even including politicians.

When asked if he means D'Amato, Borer is evasive. "We have good working relations with D'Amato. I don't know him well enough to express an opinion. I have my own guesses concerning his motives, as anyone has the right to guess, but I'm keeping them to myself." About Bronfman, Borer says, "I was very impressed with him. I only met him two or three times, and we had open, frank talks [a diplomatic euphemism for differences of opinion]. I don't know him well enough to judge him." On Singer, he comments, "I have good working relations with him. I think he is a bright man and I respect him. I believe he respects me. He knows I'm a hard nut, and I know he's a hard nut. I think he is honest, and he is currently fulfilling a very important role."

Borer saves his most positive opinion for Rolf Bloch. "He fulfilled an extremely positive role, in an attempt to bridge the gap between the Jewish Congress's demands and the steps Switzerland took. He has a difficult job, as he is a member of the World Jewish Congress, but he is also Swiss. He tried to explain to the Jews how the Swiss think, and on the other hand, he tried to explain the Jewish organizations' demands to us. I think he is a good mediator, and very honest. He carried out his responsibilities excellently."[11]

Flavio Cotti provided a summary of the Swiss position at the beginning of 1997, after the January crises and prior to the establishment of the fund to aid Nazi victims, in a press release circulated after the February 12 cabinet meeting, which was dedicated entirely to the deposits' crisis. The cabinet reiterated its commitment to the rapid establishment of the aid fund, and decided to act in two stages.

Cotti said that a Special Fund would be established immediately, funded by contributions from the major banks and contributions from other sectors of the Swiss economy. Use of the funds would be determined in negotiations with the Jewish organizations and representatives of the Gypsies, the first time their inclusion was mentioned, in an attempt to prevent claims that the fund was meant only for Jews. Cotti emphasized that the Swiss government would not contribute to the fund from the State budget. It was later agreed that the Swiss National Bank would contribute an additional $70 million.

At the second stage, Cotti said, the Swiss government would plan a separate foundation whose scope and objectives would be determined by the interim report submitted by the Bergier Commission concerning gold trade and refugee policy. Cotti reiterated that the government's contribution would be based only on established facts, which is why the Bergier Commission was asked to submit those two reports first.[12] The Jewish organizations praised the Swiss cabinet's decision, although they made it clear that they did not see the establishment of a foundation as the end of the matter or as an alternative to the restitution of all the Jewish property to its owners.[13]

The practical negotiation's for establishing the fund were conducted in Bern during the last week of February 1997. February 25–26 were forty-eight hours of intensive talks that nearly collapsed completely at least twice. Heading the Jewish side were Israel Singer, Zvi Barak, and Bobby Brown, then Prime Minister Benjamin Netanyahu's advisor for Diaspora matters. The Swiss side was headed by Flavio Cotti, Ruth Dreifuss (the Jewish minister of the interior who was filling in for the minister of justice), Thomas Borer, and Alfred Defago (ambassador designate to the United States).

When both sides sat down to open the talks in the Parliament building, the Swiss pulled out a printed document, and said, "It's all set up." Brown and Barak looked at the document and were incensed. It stated that the foundation's management would have three members, one of whom would be Rolf Bloch, and none of whom would be representatives of the Jewish organizations or Holocaust survivors. When the Swiss saw the shock on the faces of the Jewish representatives, they said, "we already arranged everything with Maram Stern" (the World Jewish Congress representative in Brussels, who also participated in the talks).

"When we read that thing, Bobby and I nearly fainted," Barak said. "I said to Singer in Hebrew, Look, someone set us up. I don't care if it was the Swiss or you or one of your people. We are taking a break, clearing up between us what happened, and coming back.' Singer got angry and said that Bobby and I were acting like bulls in china shops. We finally all stepped outside and Stern said that the Swiss cheated him and that he hadn't seen the document in advance. In contrast, Bloch did see it. I am sure of that, because he was not surprised when the document was submitted. He came out with us and I sort of yelled at him that they couldn't run this, because it wasn't an issue for Swiss Jewry, it was an issue for the entire Jewry, and they just couldn't do that sort of thing."

The Jewish representatives returned to the conference room and announced that the proposed composition of the foundation's management was not acceptable to them. The meeting went on for several hours. In the evening, the professional delegations met, without Cotti and Dreifuss, and with legal advisors from the Foreign Ministry, and reached an agreement. The management would be composed of seven members, four of whom would be appointed by the Swiss government, and three appointed by the WJRO. According to the draft agreement from that evening, the chair of the fund would be one of the WJRO representatives.

The next morning when Cotti joined the talks he announced, surprisingly, that the agreement was not acceptable to him. It again appeared that the talks would collapse, but then the Jewish representatives agreed that Bloch could be the fund's chair, whereupon Cotti agreed to the four-three composition. Afterward, the question of the fund's steering committee came up for discussion and Cotti proposed that the committee, which would supervise the management, have ten members.

Barak was quick to agree, "Fine. Nine of ours and one of yours." Cotti was astonished, "Why nine of yours?" Barak explained, "We have nine organizations in the WJRO, and I cannot go back to Jerusalem without giving each organization a representative on the steering committee. I don't care what you do. From my point of view, you can appoint 600 people to the steering committee—we will have nine." So Cotti said, "Fine. There will be eighteen members—nine from each side."

Another important point was the agreement that not all the money would be directed toward Jewish victims; the exact division was left up to the steering committee. In September 1997, it was decided that 15 percent of the fund's moneys would be granted to non-Jewish victims. The reason for this was that the Swiss did not want to create the appearance that this was a special fund only for Jewish survivors, for fear that this would lead to criticism from local public opinion. The Jewish organizations did not mind, as they also preferred it to look as if they were dealing with a principal, and not a private financial matter. It was agreed in general that most of the remainder of the fund would be granted to the Gypsies, at least 200,000 of whom were murdered by the Nazis. Support for others who were persecuted, such as homosexuals and political opponents of the Nazis, was also discussed, but a decision was not made about that issue.[14]

The establishment of the fund was approved by a Swiss cabinet decision on February 26, 1997, wherein it was stated that the fund was designated to compensate Holocaust victims and their heirs who were in financial distress. There were to be seven members of the foundation's management—four Swiss including the chair, and three WJRO representatives (one from Israel, one from the Diaspora, and one Holocaust survivor). There were to be eighteen members of the steering committee, nine from each side. The fund would employ an accountant to audit its reports, and would be subject to Swiss government supervision.[15]

In the next month, the fund's management and budget slowly came together. The 100 million francs donated in advance by the three major banks were transferred on March 1 to a special account in the Swiss National Bank in Bern. Due to exchange-rate fluctuation, the original $70 million at the time of the announcement was now $67.5 million. That month, the Swiss Employers Association announced the contribution of 65 million francs ($44 million) and the board of directors of Swiss National Bank decided in September 1997 to contribute 100 million francs.[16]

President of the Bankers Association, Georg Krayer, called on all its members to contribute to the fund, but no banks other than the three major ones responded. As part of its effort to convince the banks to contribute, the SBA sent a circular to all domestic and foreign banks in Switzerland, including the foreign banks, which included Israeli banks. The Israeli banks reacted with astonishment, mixed with mockery and anger. It seems that this apparently marginal incident indicates a great deal concerning the character of Swiss actions, set in predetermined casts with insufficient flexibility of thought.[17]

More complex was the composition of the fund's management, and this time it was the Jewish organizations that caused the delay. The Swiss government quickly chose its representatives at the beginning of March. They appointed Rolf Bloch; René Bacher, a former prosecutor; Josi Meier, former president of the Swiss Senate; and Bernard Ziegler, former minister of finance for the canton of Geneva.

The Jewish organizations, affected by internal power and prestige struggles, raised and defeated a series of names. On May 1, the Swiss cabinet approved the three representatives from the WJRO: Elie Wiesel, Nobel laureate in literature and a Holocaust survivor; Dr. Joseph Burg, chair of the Yad V'Shem Holocaust Memorial Museum, father of then Jewish Agency chair Avraham Burg, and former minister in the Israeli government;

and Avraham Hirschson, chair of the Knesset committee on the restitution of Jewish property.[18]

But the story does not end here. Two weeks later, Wiesel, in a surprise announcement, withdrew his candidacy for membership of the fund's management. The official statement was that he felt incapable of determining compensation based on who had suffered more. The real reason, however, was the fact that the Swiss asked to name Wiesel as the "international chair of the fund," an honorary title empty of authority. Wiesel was insulted and left. Edgar Bronfman was temporarily appointed to replace him, in order to allow the fund to begin functioning. He was later replaced by Benjamin Meed, chair of the survivors' organizations in the United States. By March 1999, the fund approved applications for a total of $149 million, and actually paid $56 million. Most of the money ($30 million) was given to Holocaust survivors in the United States and in Eastern Europe ($20 million). $57 million were approved for survivors in Israel.[19]

Just one week after the decision to establish the fund, then Swiss president Arnold Koller spoke to the Parliament on March 5. The title of his speech was "Switzerland and Its Modern History," and it hinted that Koller would speak about the deposits' crisis and the Swiss role in World War II. Koller did just that, in a speech that wove apology with self-respect, and repentance with patriotism.

The MPs listened to their president patiently, although as the speech progressed, there were certainly some who began glancing at their watches and even yawning. When Koller began to summarize the need for a balanced view of Swiss history, it was clear that he was reaching the end of his speech. "If we succeed in this, we will succeed in mastering our present and future," Koller said, in what seemed to be his concluding statement; but it was his additional remarks that caused his sleepiest colleagues to sit up straight in astonishment:

Distress, poverty, injustice, genocide and the disrespect of human rights are not only historic incidents, they also belong to today's conspicuous and disturbing realities. Therefore, there are many reasons to create a work of solidarity on a broader scale.

If we really want to set a sign to reinforce Switzerland's humanitarian tradition and to prove our gratefulness for having been spared during two world wars, if we want to do some good to those who endured unspeakable sufferings fifty years ago, if in Switzerland and abroad we want to give new meaning to the sense of solidarity and to public spirit, virtues today at risk, then we must effect, with inner conviction and as an act of will of a self-conscious nation, something capable of easing today's and tomorrow's sufferings.

It is in this spirit that the Federal Council, in agreement with National Bank and with regard to the national celebration of 1998, has developed the idea of the "Swiss Foundation for Solidarity." The object of the Foundation would be the easing of pressing human needs in Switzerland and abroad. The Foundation would be funded by the returns from the management of those parts of the gold stock of the National Bank made available for other public purposes following the necessary reform of the money and currency constitution.

The total assets of the Foundation would probably amount to about seven billion Swiss francs. The Foundation would manage the respective gold stock according to open market rules. With careful management the average return per year would result in the long run to several hundreds of millions of Swiss francs, which would have to be used half in Switzerland and half abroad. Such money is then to be destined to victims of poverty and catastrophies, of genocide and other severe breaches of human rights, such as of course victims of the Holocaust and of Shoa.[20]

The idea of the foundation was raised by the Swiss National Bank because it was interested in decreasing its gold reserves, which are the highest in the world (in per capita dollar terms). For more than twenty years, Swiss gold reserves totaled a standing amount of 83 million ounces, with a March 1997 value of about $30 million. Only the United States has greater gold reserves, with a population about forty times larger. The price of gold has not changed in real terms in the fifty years that have passed since the end of World War II, so this was not a successful investment in the long term. Another problem is that Swiss law required the central bank to list the gold at historical cost prices of just $3,100 per kilo, while the market price in March 1997, was $12,500 per kilo.

One week before Koller's speech, the governor of the central bank, Hans Mayer, met with Koller and Minister of Finance Kaspar Villiger. Mayer proposed a linkage between the deposits crisis, Switzerland's image problem, and the need to take action concerning the gold reserves. The idea was to change the law so that gold would be listed on the books at 60 percent of its real value, instead of at 25 percent of its real value. Then some of the gold would be sold over the course of ten years, the money invested, and the interest on the investment would serve humanitarian purposes. Villiger and Koller were quick to adopt the idea as preventive medicine for the expected blow from the Eizenstat report on gold trade between Switzerland and Germany.

The Swiss government published more details concerning the foundation in the next days, despite the fact that a clear and complete plan did not yet exist. Bern made it clear, that in contrast to the fund to aid Nazi victims, the Solidarity Foundation would be managed only by Swiss hands, and "would be almost invincible to demands from outside Switzerland." The cabinet estimated that it would take six to eight years from the establishment of the foundation until the interest on the sale of gold reached the targeted annual sum of 300–400 million francs ($200–260 million).

The foundation's aims, Bern reported in the spring of 1997, would be to aid poor and needy people both inside and outside Switzerland, victims of genocide, torture, and other violations of human rights (including Holocaust survivors or their needy relatives); and victims of military conflicts or natural disasters. It was also possible that some of the money would be transferred to organizations dealing with disaster victims, such as the International Red Cross.[21]

When the Swiss Ministry of Finance proposed the bill for the establishment of the foundation in June 1998, it became clear that it would not grant any practical aid to Holocaust survivors. According to the proposal, the foundation's goals included the struggle against poverty and discrimination, the creation of opportunities for youth, the promotion of mutual understanding and peaceful coexistence, the reconstruction of communities, the prevention of murder, and aid to the victims of crimes against humanity. Holocaust victims could be included only in the last category. The proffered bill only mentioned Holocaust victims indirectly, and noted the possibility of aiding them to overcome the traumas of their past. It was clear to everyone that the foundation would only reach its targeted sum by the middle of the first decade of the next century, when almost no Holocaust survivors would remain alive.[22]

After the dramatic events of February and March, the handling of the deposits' crisis continued along previously opened channels. On April 16, 1997, the Volcker Commission met for the fourth time. The meeting was dedicated primarily to the accountants' work.[23] At the previous meeting, committee members had heard about the trifling bank response to the 1962 law, and this time David Smith of KPMG reported that lawyers, insurance companies, and other brokers for the most part also avoided reporting to the Claims Registry. As well, Smith reported that the supervision of reporting was faulty, and that very few follow-up examinations were made.

It was agreed at the meeting that the sample inspection would include ten banks. Five of the banks would undergo a comprehensive investigation through a long questionnaire covering internal procedures for opening accounts, documenting accounts, and handling dormant accounts, while the other five would be inspected only for relevant documentation. The choice of the banks was left to Volcker, in consultation with Singer and Baer.

Prior to the April 16, meeting, the three accounting firms submitted detailed reports on their work to date and projections for its continuation. The SBA in Basel certainly paled when they read the reports, as the accountants had only just begun to collect data, but had already charged ten of thousands of francs in fees. At that time, payment to each firm amounted to 600,000 francs a month including reimbursements, meaning the SBA was spending 2 million francs per month only on the work of the accountants. "They were already completely worn down by the expenses," Burg said with a small smile. "We didn't care. The investigation would cost what it did, but it would be carried out thoroughly." In December 1998, it was estimated that the accountants had already been paid over $300 million.[24]

Anyone who thought that the Volcker Commission had reached calm waters was proven wrong at the next meeting. On June 2, when the group met in Jerusalem, a conflict developed very quickly between the Jewish representatives and the commission's legal counsel, Michael Bradfield. The issue was apparently marginal, a request from Arthur Andersen for a 150,000 franc budget to locate relevant data at Yad V'Shem. The SBA was opposed, and Bradfield supported them.

Barak led the charge against Bradfield at the meeting. "Do you think you interest me, Bradfield? If the accountants can't take material from Yad V'Shem, then do I give a hoot about all your work?" Bradfield insisted, "There will be no special budget for the collection of data from Yad V'Shem." Barak got angry and said to Singer in the middle of the meeting, "I demand that Bradfield be fired. Someone else must be appointed." Now Bronfman was mad too, unaccustomed to wasting time on peripheral matters. He rose in real anger, directed primarily at Bradfield, and said, "All these stories don't interest me, and I don't want to hear any more." Bronfman left the room, slamming the door behind him.

After a few seconds of shock, Bradfield understood that he had gone too far, and he withdrew his objection to financing the investigation at Yad V'Shem. Bronfman did not return to the meeting, only to the commission's dinner. The commission, particularly the Swiss members, did not forget Bronfman's actions, and the talks moved faster after that.[25] Among other things, the accountants reported that it appeared the banks had at least 20,000 dormant accounts under Swiss ownership, and Burg immediately determined that the majority certainly belonged to trustees who opened them for Jews. He demanded that the names be published, and the SBA announced its agreement a few days later.[26]

A number of important decisions were made during the talks in Jerusalem, the foremost of which was an unprecedented mechanism for handling ownership claims on dormant accounts. This was after the Swiss government and the banks agreed to publish the names of the owners of dormant accounts uncovered by the banks in their 1995 investigation, the first such publication in the history of Swiss banking. As the Jewish organizations had already stated openly that they had no faith in the SBA ombudsman, they asked for another way to handle applications concerning those accounts.

It was agreed that the mechanism would consist of three members— judges or banking experts—one Swiss, one Jewish, and one American who would also serve as chair. (Later, the number of members was increased to sixteen.) Anyone who thought he had the right to inherit from someone whose name was published, could apply to the banks through Ernst & Young, the firm hired by the Volcker Commission as its own accountants.

If the application was rejected, the potential heir could request a final ruling by an international panel. The commission emphasized that the banks and the panel would adopt "liberal standards of proof," which would take into account the time passed since the opening of the account, and the special circumstances of the Holocaust.[27]

The commission also decided to identify the banks whose procedures would be inspected in the sample investigation: Swiss Bank Corp., Credit Suisse, Spur und Laikhasse, Banque Cantonale Vaudoise, and Picket & Cie. The banks in which document preservation would be examined were UBS (a successful choice in light of the Meili affair), Bauman & Cie., Banque Cantonale de Genève, Julius Baer Bank, and St. Gallische Kantonalbank. "We are finally reaching the stage of going into the banks," Volcker stated with justifiable satisfaction. The principals of the preliminary reports on the investigations at the banks were reported to the commission in September 1997 (see Chapter 1).[28]

Meanwhile, launching the aid fund was progressing slowly. The fund began its practical work only five months after its February introduction, when it decided to distribute $11.6 million to Holocaust survivors living in difficult conditions, particularly in Eastern Europe and the former Soviet Union. In the coming months, differences of opinion would arise between Rolf Bloch and the heads of the Jewish organizations concerning who determined the criteria for entitlement and the list of those entitled. Bloch asked to establish his own mechanism. The organizations claimed that the lists should be based on those of the Joint and the Israeli National Insurance Institute (similar to the American Social Security System).

In the end, a compromise was reached. The WJRO gave the Swiss government a list of 40,000 names of Holocaust survivors potentially entitled to the aid, and a list of recipients was compiled based on that data. The first check, for $400, was presented in November 1997 to Rebecca Shaeffer from Riga, Lithuania, after which tens of millions of dollars were distributed to survivors worldwide, including Gypsies.[29]

In the United States, the first, if limited, sanctions were imposed at that time on the banks—a significant forewarning of things to come. In the last week of May 1997, the city of Los Angeles decided to withdraw $400 million deposited by its pension funds in UBS "overnight" accounts. This followed a remark by a senior UBS bank official that "It's a good thing our banks don't have Jewish management."

In October 1997, New York City comptroller Alan Hevesi ordered UBS disqualified from a consortium the city was about to enlist for raising $1.3 billion in municipal bonds. Hevesi stated explicitly that he was taking this step due to the bank's actions concerning the deposits, primarily the Meili affair and the insulting remarks made by a senior bank official. Although the bank lost a mere $500,000, in commission for raising funds, the symbolic significance of the step was enormous. Within days, California and

Massachusetts also announced steps against the banks in general and UBS specifically, while Illinois reported reexamination of its overall relations with the Swiss banks.[30]

There was no summer vacation for the deposits crisis in 1997, and the month of July was rich in events. On July 8, the SBA announced that the banks had located the heirs of Holocaust victims who had a total of $6.8 million in dormant accounts. In addition, the association reported that it had located the owners of other dormant accounts valued at $4.5 million.[31]

On July 23, the first list of dormant accounts was published at a press conference held at the conference center in the Zurich airport. Those waiting for the list of 1,000 names representing 775 accounts located by the banks at the end of 1995, were surprised. It now included 1,872 names of 1,765 account holders. Those expecting 40 million francs in the accounts were also surprised. Their value now amounted to 60 million francs. The explanation was a list of 1,000 accounts at Swiss Bank Corp. which the bank claimed had not been located earlier due to "their incorrect recording in computers in the 1970's." The truth is that the list of 1,000 accounts was discovered by the World Jewish Congress at the American National Archives, College Park, Maryland. It included accounts transferred to the bank's U.S. branches in 1941, and returned to Zurich in 1946. When Singer threatened to publish the list himself, Swiss Bank hurried to append it to the SBA list of dormant accounts.

According to SBA figures, about 90 percent of the money was in 10 percent of the accounts. Two-thirds of the accounts contained 5,000 francs or less, an unsurprising figure in light of the fact that the banks had charged over fifty years' worth of fees on the accounts and paid interest on only some of them, fees are always higher than interest. Singer did not intend to waive serious accounting of the value of the accounts, and a subcommittee was established at his request to investigate this point. The subcommittee was headed by Henry Kaufman—former chief economist for Credit Suisse First Boston—and included a Jewish and Swiss representative. They decided in September 1998—as they reported to the Volcker Commission— that current accounts should be multiplied by 6.81, and that no fees should be charged. Bonds should be multiplied by 10.17, and management accounts should be multiplied by 18.89. Shares, according to the subcommittee, should be multiplied by 70.45. (all terms for investment held from 1939 to 1998).

Upon publication of the list, supervisor of banks Kurt Hauri made one of the most important announcements of the entire affair. In the future, names uncovered by Volcker Commission accountants would be published in a similar manner. "Banking confidentiality does not exist concerning the accounts of Holocaust victims," Singer determined. Hauri hurried to claim that that was not true, but it appears that Singer was right. When custom-

Surname	Given name(s)	City	Country
Leutelt Dr.	**Helmut**	**Shenyang**	**China**
Runge	*Hans*		
Levi	**Jeanne and Berthold and Renaud and André and Jean-Claude and Pierre and Marianne**	**Paris**	**France**
Levy	**Klara**	**Dantzig / Gdansk**	
Rosenthal	*Ella*		
Lewin	**Max**	**Zurich**	**Switzerland**
Lewy	**Isak**	**London**	**United Kingdom**
Lewy	*Heinz Albert*		
Lichtenstern	**Max**	**Zagreb**	**Croatia**
Lienbacher	**Johann**	**Graz**	**Austria**
Lindauer	**J.**	**Paris**	**France**
Lindenberg	**Luise**	**Cologne / Munich**	**Germany**
Linsin	**Karl**	**Rheinfelden**	**Germany**
Lintner	**Josef**	**St. Maddalena**	**Italy**
Lintner	*Anna*		
Lintner	*Maria*		
Lintner	*Terese*		
Lipmann	**Ernst**		**Cuba**
Lippe Zur	**Seine Durchlaucht Prinz Hermann**	**Budapest**	**Hungary**
Blumgrund	*Leo*		
Liquornik	**Albert**	**Bucharest**	**Romania**
Llorente	**Maria**		**Italy**
Loeri	**Heinrich**	**Vienna**	**Austria**
Loiseau	**Anne Marguerite**	**Evry**	**France**
Lomsky	**Karel**	**Prague-Hodkovicky**	**Czech Republic**
Lomska	*Rosa*		
Lorenz	**Odette**	**Aleppo**	**Syrian**
Lorenz	*Hermann*		
Lotter	**Alice**	**Stuttgart**	**Germany**
Lovas	**Stefan**	**Budapest**	**Hungary**
Lovizio-Fornino	**Angelo**		**Italy**
Luchsinger	**Enrico**	**Bergamo**	**Italy**
Lückemann Prof.		**Wroclaw**	**Germany**
Huber & Lutz			
Luib	**Coloman and Irene Marie**	**Budapest**	**Hungary**
Lundgren	**Guilhermo Alberto**		**Brazil**
Lupas	**Nicolae**	**Bucharest**	**Romania**
Lupu	**Basile**	**Jasi**	**Romania**
Lupu	*Elena*		
Lussenhop	**Martha**		
Lutt	**Enrico**	**Ludesch**	**Austria**
Lux	**Adolf and Frieda**	**Constance**	**Germany**
Maatschappij Voor Industriele En Finance		**Amsterdam**	**Netherlands**
Macé	**Etienne and Odette**	**La Haye-Fossard**	**France**
Macherette	**Carlos**	**Diepoldsau**	**Switzerland**
Macius	**Silvio**		**Switzerland**
Mackiewicz	**Zygmund**	**Post Janova**	**Lithunia**
Madero	**Hector**	**Rome**	**Italy**
Madrenas	**Jaime**	**Saarbrücken**	**Germany**
Madurga Val	**Mariano**	**Zaragoza**	**Spain**
Magazin Universal		**Chisinau**	**Moldania**
Kuna	*Josif*		
Kuna	*Schlioma*		
Novak	*Jtco*		
Magnan	**Amedee and Gabrielle**	**Marseille**	**France**
Magnan	**Raphäel**	**Marseille**	**France**
Magnan	*Denis*		
Magyar	**Irene**	**Covassna**	**Romania**

List of dormant accounts, published by the Swiss Bankers Association, July 23, 1997. (Author's files)

Swiss Monitor

AN UPDATE ON SWITZERLAND'S PROGRESS IN MAKING RESTITUTION TO HOLOCAUST SURVIVORS

Comptroller: Ask if Swiss firms have contributed to fund

Stating that it would both protect pension assets and accelerate the funding of the Special Fund for Needy Victims of the Holocaust/Shoah, New York City Comptroller Alan G. Hevesi is urging public pension funds to write to Swiss companies in which they are shareholders to determine if the companies have made contributions. The Comptroller wrote such a letter to 27 Swiss companies last month (*see page 3 for the full text of the letter*).

> An important humanitarian gesture that will aid poor and elderly Holocaust survivors who are most in need.

Intended to support financially needy Holocaust survivors and their descendants, the Special Fund was established with an initial donation of Sfr. 100 million from Credit Suisse, Swiss Bank Corporation and Union Bank of Switzerland. Other members of the country's business community contributed another Sfr. 70 million.

Hevesi said that there have been "some small successes in bringing justice to those who have waited more than fifty years," most notably the donations. On July 7th, the Special Fund's Executive Board announced the initial distribution of Sfr. 17 million to those most in need (*see page 2 for details*).

Hevesi stressed the potential value of corporate participation in the Special Fund. By contributing, companies could avert long-term damage to their public image, in addition to minimizing the possibility of international sanctions and boycotts.

The five New York City retirement systems had 780,720 shares, worth more than $462 million, in publicly traded Swiss corporations as of December 1996. ∎

Swiss publish list of bank accounts dormant since 1945

The first list of World War II-era dormant accounts in Swiss banks was published on July 23rd this year by the Swiss banking community. Publicizing the list is part of a response to international efforts to ensure that assets held in bank accounts of Holocaust victims are returned to their rightful owners.

This major breakthrough is the first time Swiss banks have stopped using the famous Swiss banking secrecy rules as a shield against returning money to Holocaust survivors and victims' heirs. They are now encouraged to come forward and settle the accounts.

The Swiss Bankers Association paid for space to print the names and hometowns of dormant account holders in newspapers in the U.S., Europe, Switzerland and Israel. The list was placed in the New York Times, London Times, Washington Post, Jerusalem Post, Frankfurter Allgemeine Zeitung, Le Monde, the Star (Johannesburg), and Pravda.

In addition, the information is available on the Internet at http://www.dormantaccounts.ch or by telephone at 1-800-662-7708.

"We hope this will be yet another chapter in bringing the matter to a close, with dignity and honor," said an Association spokesman.

The Swiss bankers agreed to list the accounts after the Swiss Federal Banking Commission (SFBC) distributed a circular letter—a form of banking directive—to all Swiss banks, requiring them to report the accounts of residents and non-residents of Switzerland that have been dormant since 1945.

In addition to the first list of foreign dormant accounts (those of foreign residents or nationals) published on July 23, an information booklet and claim forms have been made available at contact offices in Switzerland, Israel and other countries.

In a joint press release, the SFBC, Paul Volcker, Chairman of the Independent Committee of Eminent Persons (ICEP), and the Swiss Bankers Association

continued on page 2

Produced by the Office of New York City Comptroller Alan G. Hevesi   August 1997

1 Centre Street, New York, New York 10007   212/669-4766   www.financenet.gov/financenet/state/nycnet/nycnet.htm

Swiss Monitor, produced by the office of New York City comptroller, Alan Hevesi, August 1997. (Author's files)

ers' names are published, even without identifying a specific bank, confidentiality is nullified. After publishing names for the first time, it is much easier to demand that it be done a second and third time.

The list enabled the banks and the Jewish organizations to each maintain that it reinforced their original claims. Among the names, only 20% appeared Jewish, and, as stated, the money did not come to a huge amount. The Jewish organizations said that they had claimed for two years that the banks had appropriated Jewish money for themselves and destroyed relevant documents. The banks for their part could claim, "we told you so."

There were many well-known names on the list, but not of Jewish ones. It identified princes Hermann zur Lippe and Erwin zu Lukowicz; Ramona Serrano Suner (minister of finance during Franco's regime in Spain) who reported that he had opened the account for his children who attended Swiss schools; and Paul Esterhazy, one of the wealthiest men in Hungary before the war. Nevertheless, in the first days after the list's publication, a number of Jews reported recognizing the names of their relatives. Among others, U.S. ambassador to Switzerland Madeleine Kunin, who is Jewish, identified her father.

A number of other names made headlines when the Wiesenthal Center in Los Angeles claimed that some of the accounts were left in the banks by Nazis. One was Vili Baur, the alias of Anton Berger, one of Adolf Eichmann's assistants and the deputy commander of the Theresienstadt ghetto. Another, Heinrich Hoffman, was Adolf Hitler's personal photographer. Other names hint at a relationship with Nazi Germany. The list includes Elise Eder, the wife of Gestapo commander Ernst Kaltenbrunner; Herman Esser, vice president of the Reichstag; Herman Schmitz, one of the heads of I.G. Farben (the manufacturer of Zyclon-B) that used tens of thousands of forced Jewish laborers at Auschwitz; Karl Jaeger, one of the commanders of the Final Solution in Lithuania; and Hans Wendland, one of those responsible for looting artwork from occupied countries. The banks hastened to announce that the names would be investigated and that in any case, Nazi criminals were not entitled to withdraw moneys deposited in Switzerland.[32]

On October 29, the SBA published a list of Swiss nationals whose accounts were dormant. At first, the association had reported the existence of 20,000 names to the Volcker Commission, but further investigation revealed a much higher number, close to 64,000. Of those that the banks reported, 54,000 accounts included less than 100 francs to date; therefore, the names of the owners were not published and the moneys donated to charity. A total of 14,000 names were published including foreigners who had savings accounts (the accepted assumption is that Holocaust victims mostly had current accounts so that the moneys would be available as soon as they were needed), that contained $12 million in nominal values. It is worth remembering that in February 1996, the banks claimed they had 775 dormant accounts of all types.

Unofficially, the banks said that a significant portion of the Swiss accounts apparently belonged to the needy and orphans, who had received gifts of small savings accounts from the banks decades earlier. The banks also admitted, however, that a significant number of accounts belonged to trustees who acted primarily for Jewish individuals. The big problem would be identifying the trustees who acted for Jews, and it does not appear that there is much chance of doing that.[33]

Another event that contributed to the increasing international pressure placed on Switzerland was the London Gold Conference held in December 2–4, 1997 (see Chapter 9). Despite the fact that the conference was entitled "Nazi Gold," almost all eyes, and the accompanying criticism, were on Switzerland. It was again clear that international public opinion did not believe Bern's explanations.[34]

One week before the London conference, Bronfman revealed the Jewish side's financial demands: "I want $3 billion or northward in order to end it all, the class action suits, the Volcker process and the rest." The timing of the demand was not coincidental, as Singer and the banks' representatives were negotiating an overall settlement at that time. In the background hung Alan Hevesi's threat to impose sanctions on the banks beginning December 8, if no agreement was reached. Hevesi now represented not just New York City, but a growing number of comptrollers and financial managers from more than 800 states and cities. At the London conference itself, Bronfman said that he expected the sum of the overall settlement to be "9–10 digits." Borer rejected his demands categorically, saying that since the Jewish organizations had insisted until now on claiming that this was a moral issue and not a financial one, he had trouble understanding Bronfman's stance.

Nonetheless, the talks went on behind the scenes, and when Hevesi and his steering committee met at the end of December 1997, Bronfman asked them to postpone the imposition of sanctions for three months, in order to exhaust all possibilities. Hevesi naturally agreed. Stuart Eizenstat also entered the negotiations at that time. Eizenstat hoped to create a compromise that would both avoid imposition of sanctions, likely to be detrimental to Swiss-U.S. relations, and ensure fair compensation to Holocaust survivors and their heirs. At the beginning of 1998, it appeared that an agreement was close, and Bronfman even stated in public that he expected within a month to reach an agreement on "less than $10 billion and more than $1 billion."[35]

The next weeks were replete with turnarounds. First, Borer announced that the Swiss government was opposed to an overall settlement. In response, the Jewish organizations discussed the renewal of the sanction option. California State comptroller Matt Fong called on his colleagues to give the banks an ultimatum: agree in principle to an overall agreement by March 31, and conclude the agreement by May 31, 1998. The comptrollers' steering committee met in New York on March 26, where the atmosphere prior to the meeting was pessimistic. "Sanctions are inevitable," senior officials in the Jewish organizations said.

In talks held until the last moment, the banks offered $500 million, but their proposal was rejected. Meanwhile, Singer and Burg reached an agreement with attorneys Melvyn Weiss and Michael Hausfeld, who filed one of the class-action suits, that they would accept any agreement the Jewish organizations reached. This agreement removed a central obstacle to an overall agreement, as the bankers kept asking, justifiably: suppose we make an agreement with you, what happens to the class-action suits?[36]

On March 23, the heads of Credit Suisse, UBS, and Swiss Bank sent a letter to Eizenstat in which they promised for the first time to enter negotiations for an overall settlement. Eizenstat met with Singer and Burg the next day and showed them the letter. The two immediately rejected it. Negotiations would be conducted only with the Jewish organizations and not with the U.S. government, they declared. The crisis atmosphere worsened. D'Amato announced additional hearings, and Governor George Pataki of New York announced his administration's opposition to approval of the huge UBS–Swiss Bank merger. The U.S. and Swiss governments applied counterpressure, and on March 26 made a joint announcement of their opposition to sanctions.

When the comptrollers' steering committee meeting began, Eizenstat pulled out the same letter from the banks and showed it to Singer and Burg—but this time it was addressed to Israel Singer. This paved the way for an agreement to negotiate an overall settlement, in order to achieve what the banks called in the letter an "honorable and moral solution, through an overall settlement of Holocaust-era issues directly related to us." This sentence led to almost instantaneous differences of opinion. What had been agreed to? The Jewish organizations claimed that looted gold and works of art also had to be discussed, since at least some of the gold and artworks had reached the banks. The claimed that the gold and art were relevant to the central bank and the government, and that they were directly related only to the deposits. In any case, the comptrollers allocated three months for completion of the negotiations, and suspended the decision to impose sanctions until the end of June.[37]

The additional three months did not bring about an agreement. In mid-June, when the WJRO leadership felt that there had been no progress, they made an official ultimatum: an agreement by June 30, or the organization would file its own class-action suit against the banks in every state where

MEDIA RELEASE

CREDIT SUISSE | GROUP    UBS

DEUTSCH   FRANCAIS

US class actions: banks reach a settlement

New York/Zurich, 12/13 August 1998 ½. On Thursday, shortly after 12 midnight Swiss local time, at a status conference in New York, Credit Suisse Group and UBS AG, as well as the World Jewish Congress and the lawyers representing the US class action plaintiffs, reached agreement on a settlement initiated by Judge Edward Korman. The settlement amount of USD 1.25 billion will be paid in four instalments over a period of three years.

This settlement, which has been endorsed by the US government, will satisfy conclusively all claims on Swiss banks in connection with dormant accounts and the banks' activities during the Second World War. At the same time, the plaintiffs have committed themselves to renouncing all claims against the Swiss state, including the Swiss National Bank, and against Swiss companies. Only claims against Swiss insurance companies, which together with other European insurance companies are the subject of a separate class action lawsuit, are excluded from the settlement.

The agreed settlement amount of a total of USD 1.25 billion is a lump-sum consisting of the offer of UOD 500 million made by the banks on 10 June 1000 and all dormant assets identified as part of the Volcker audits.

Furthermore, the banks have said that they are ready to pay an additional amount in order to meet the demands of the plaintiffs for a global settlement and in order to ensure that a settlement can be reached at all.

The aim of the additional payment by Credit Suisse Group and UBS is to avert the threat of sanctions as well as long and costly court proceedings. The banks assume that other Swiss companies and institutions will contribute to the financing of this sum.

Credit Suisse Group and UBS are convinced that the agreed settlement can now be implemented without delay and that it represents a fair solution for all parties. Above all, however, they hope that the money can be made available quickly to the victims of the Holocaust. At the same time, the banks express their continued and unreserved support for the work of the Volcker and Bergier Committees.

Enquiries:

CREDIT SUISSE GROUP   Tel. +41-1-333 6700 or +41-1-333 8844

UBS AG   Tel. +41-61-288 6595

Media release by Credit Suisse and UBS concerning the global settlement, August 13, 1998. (Author's files)

they operated. The warlike tone was Burg's, even though Singer preferred to continue quiet negotiations. At this point, there were real and significant differences of opinion between the two men.

The Jewish organizations proposed a formula for the agreement, which would have led the banks to pay $990 million. The aim was to come as close as possible to the $1 billion line, which the banks had resolutely refused to cross. The banks refused and announced they would pay no more than $600 million. On June 23, the negotiations collapsed. In a meeting between the organizations and the banks in which Eizenstat participated, no agreement was reached and no new date for talks was set.

On July 1, Hevesi's steering committee reconvened, and decided to impose sanctions on the banks. The group decided that each state and city would independently determine the type of sanction, its scope, and the starting date. Fong announced that California would immediately stop new business with the banks. Alan Hevesi and Carl McCall announced a graduated package of sanctions by New York City and the State beginning September 1, 1998, that would lead to complete severance of ties with the banks within nine months. The Swiss government and the banks called the sanctions "illegal" and announced that they would not surrender. The U.S. government condemned the move, while Flavio Cotti appealed to U.S. president Bill Clinton asking him to act to prevent the sanctions.

In July, talks began on a merger between Credit Suisse and the J.P. Morgan investment bank. Credit Suisse CEO Rainer Gut, who opposed an overall settlement of significant proportion, called Singer and asked if he would create a stumbling block against the merger. Singer replied, "The fact that we allowed the UBS–Swiss Bank merger means we are stupid. If we agree to another merger, we will be something far worse." The two did not reach an agreement.

On August 9, the banks' representatives came to Hevesi's New York office. He relates, "They threatened me. At first they said that 12,000 New York residents would lose their jobs if I liquidated their branches in the city. I said that I was willing to promise that whoever took their business would take their employees as well. Then they said they would file a personal law suit against me. I replied: Just be sure to spell my name right.

"Afterwards, they asked if the $990 million formula had been OK in June, why wasn't it OK now? I answered: I'm not negotiating, but one good reason comes to mind—because then you rejected the proposal. In the end, they asked me what number seemed reasonable to me now. I reiterated that I wasn't negotiating. They pressured me, and then I said: I'll give you a number if you'll promise first to pay it—and they naturally didn't agree to that."

On August 10, Brooklyn Judge Edward Korman, scheduled to hear the class-action suits, convened the representatives of all the parties, the heads of UBS and Credit Suisse in the United States, Israel Singer, and the lawyers. Each group was cloistered in the jury room in the eighth district courthouse in Brooklyn. The conditions were the same as for jurors: meals ordered in, no talking on the telephone, and they could only go home at night.

In separate meetings, Korman began to threaten the parties. He told the Jewish organizations and the lawyers that he might throw the case out of court. He told the banks that he might require them to pay billions of dollars. Korman moved among the rooms, bringing proposals and responses, and sometimes summoned the parties to a joint meeting. He basically ran a pseudo-trial in which he brought the sides to reveal their evidence and arguments to him. The first day ended at 2:00 A.M. After a few hours rest, the parties returned to the courthouse, far from the prying eyes of the media. The following day, the talks were much shorter, until 10:00 P.M. and the day after that, agreement was reached at 7:00 P.M.

The banks reiterated the $990 million proposal plus the money in the dormant accounts, net the $70 million already transferred to the aid fund. Under pressure, the banks increased the sum and agreed to cross the $1 billion line. Much of the debate surrounded the question about whether the agreement would also cover Swiss insurance companies. Credit Suisse was particularly interested in that question, in light of its ownership of one of the largest insurance companies in the country, Wienterthur. Singer insisted that the insurance companies should be not included, and the banks gave in.

The agreed sum was $1.25 billion. It was also agreed that the Volcker Commission would continue to try and locate additional accounts, identify the owners, and pursue historical research on the deposits' affair. Accounts whose owners were identified would be returned. If additional accounts were uncovered, they would be added to the agreed sum. The payments would be spread out over three years, and 4–5 percent annual interest rate would be added on for a total rate of $150–200 million.

It was decided that the first payment of $250 million would be made within ninety days of Korman's official approval of the agreement. The remainder would be paid out in three payments of $333 million each year on a date approved by Judge Korman. In addition, the $20 billion class-action suits against the banks would be dropped. Each of the 31,500 plaintiffs would receive a few hundred dollars. The lawyers' fees would be determined by Korman. Some of them have already announced their intention to seek only reimbursement of costs. All the threatened sanctions would be withdrawn.

The use of the funds left after paying the plaintiffs and their lawyers would be determined by Korman according to a plan submitted by the Jewish organizations and the lawyers, without any involvement from the banks. The funds would be primarily designated to aid needy Holocaust survivors (55 percent) and organizations that aid survivors (25 percent) as well as for documentation, memorialization, and education (20 percent).

The Swiss government and its central bank were not partners to the agreement, although the Jewish organizations announced they would drop their suit against the central bank for its trade in stolen gold. Korman made it clear to Singer that in his opinion only the U.S. Supreme Court was qualified to hear that case, as it was essentially a case against a sovereign country. Korman noted that five long years could pass before the nine-judge panel decided whether to hear the case. Nevertheless, the commercial banks expected that the central bank would help finance the settlement. Another possibility was that the Swiss government would pay compensation later, after the publication of the Bergier Commission report on the wartime deportation of Jewish refugees from Switzerland.[38]

Swiss public opinion was mixed on the agreement. There were those who praised the end of the affair, and others who claimed the banks brought shame to their country. The banks immediately announced that they hoped other sectors of the Swiss economy would help them finance the agreement. The chances of this were very slim, since the level of response to the request for donations to the aid fund was very low. The Jewish side was generally satisfied, although there were some fears that ugly internal struggles would erupt over the use of the funds.[39]

For Switzerland, the deposits' affair was not only a problem of money and credibility, but also a deep soul-searching about its actions during World War II. But how did the world see this soul-searching? An unusual answer came on February 17, 1997, from Lance Morrow, a senior commentator at *Time* magazine. After a month of crises and prior to the establishment of the fund to aid victims of Nazi persecution, he told the bankers, "There are many forms of bankruptcy. The moral one is worst of all." Afterward, Morrow quoted Elie Wiesel: "If all the money in the Swiss banks were turned over, it would not bring back the life of one Jewish child. But the money is a symbol. It is part of the story. If you suppress any part of the story, it comes back later, with force and violence."[40]

And yes, the money is a symbol, but in a wider sense than Wiesel saw it. In the context of the Holocaust victims' deposits in Swiss banks, the money is a symbol of a liberal, democratic, European country and its attitude toward those who carried the physical and emotional scars of the worst crime in history. The demand to provide death certificates for Holocaust victims was not just bureaucratic stupidity, it was emotional and moral density. It is certainly permissible to leave pending the possibility that these demands would never have been raised about other victims, and not a single witness has come forward to testify that the heirs of other victims of the war—also not always documented and brought to proper burial—had to meet the same demands requested of the heirs of Holocaust victims.

This is not anti-Semitism, at least not in its most familiar form. This attitude, "the Jews are dead, the hell with them," as Edgar Bronfman calls it,[41] says that the Holocaust was just another event, unfortunate though it may be, and there is no reason to believe that the Holocaust deserves special attention of any kind. From this point it is a short trip to seeing the Holocaust as just another crime on a list of Nazi crimes, and maybe not even the worst of them.

Therefore, the money is a symbol, due to the manner in which the Gentiles related to it, and not the Jews. This obtuse stance began in the 1940s, worsened in the 1950s, reached its peak in the 1960s, and continued until the 1990s. But in the middle of the last decade of the twentieth century, fifty years after the survivors of the extermination camps came out from behind the barbed wire and the hiding places, Switzerland was forced, by external pressure and not by its own initiative, to admit its sins toward the survivors and their heirs, and change its attitude entirely.

The real soul-searching of all of Western Europe concerns not only the war era, which is already researched and documented, but the treatment of Jews after the Holocaust. After Switzerland, many other European countries began investigations into the fate of Jewish property. The same phenomenon is apparent in each country: theft during the Holocaust, disdain and apathy afterward. But even if theft can be excused as a fear of invasion or greed, there are no explanations or excuses and certainly no justification for what happened after the war. Treating a Holocaust survivor begging to receive what little is left of his property as a bother to be disposed of, is unforgivable. Now, European countries, including Switzerland, face the possibility of choosing between repeating the sin—the continued theft of Jewish property and its retention by those who are not entitled to it—and real penitence: restitution of the looted property while asking forgiveness from the Jewish people. This is the greatest moral test facing Europe at the end of the twentieth century. This will be the real test of the Continent's treatment of the Jewish people.

NOTES

CHAPTER 1

1. Helen Junz's report to the Volcker Commission, February 11, 1997.
2. Gitta Sereny, *Into That Darkness* (Andre Deutch, 1974), 101.
3. Journalists' meeting with Hanspeter Haeni, February 26, 1997 (hereafter, Interview with Haeni); interviews with Israel Singer, May 30, 1997, July 2, 1997, July 14, 1997, September 7, 1997 (hereafter, Interview with Singer); *Globes*, June 4, 1997, October 29, 1997.
4. Israel State Archives, Foreign Ministry (hereafter ISA), file fo 3347/45.
5. ISA, files fo 3347/12; fo 3347/46.
6. Ibid., file fo 3347/47.
7. Letter from Senator Alfonse D'Amato to attorney Mark Cohen, February 27, 1996; *Ha'aretz*, April 9, 1996; *Ma'ariv*, April 2, 1996.
8. *Yedi'ot Aharonot*, January 30, 1997.
9. *Ma'ariv*, March 6, 1997.
10. *Globes*, July 24, 1997; *Yedi'ot Aharonot*, July 27, 1997.
11. *Globes*, February 11, 1997.
12. Ibid., March 13, 1997. The published names appear on a website managed by the Simon Wiesenthal Center at http://204.254.71.206/Swissquery.cfm
13. Peter Hug and Marc Perrenoud, *Assets in Switzerland of Victims of Nazism and the Compensation Agreements with East Bloc Countries* (Bern: Federal Department of Foreign Affairs, English edition, 1997) (hereafter, *Hug-Perrenoud report*), 62.
14. ISA, file fo 2544/12.
15. Ibid., file fo 3347/12.
16. Ibid.
17. *Ma'ariv*, April 1983.
18. Journalists' meeting with high-ranking Swiss banker, February 26, 1997 (hereafter, High-Ranking banker).
19. Interview with Silvia Matile-Steiner, October 26, 1994.
20. Interview with Martin Wirz, October 25, 1994.
21. Meeting with Julius Baer Bank official, October 17, 1994; meeting with UBS official, October 19, 1994; Arthur Andersen's report to the Volcker Commission on Julius Baer Bank, August 1997.
22. *Globes*, June 5, 1997; KPMG's report to the Volcker Commission on UBS, August, 1997.

23. *Globes*, December 17, 1997. On Lecca see *The Holocaust Encyclopedia*, (Tel Aviv and Jerusalem: Yad V'Shem and Sifri'yat Poalim, 1990 [Hebrew]) (hereafter, *The Holocaust Encyclopedia)*, vol. 3, 653.

24. Arthur Andersen's report to the Volcker Commission on Credit Suisse, August 1997.

25. *Hug-Perrenoud report*, 44–46.

26. *Der Spiegel*, March 17, 1997.

27. KPMG report on Vaduz Cantonal Bank report; KPMG report on Picket Bank; Price-Waterhouse report on Spar und Leikhasse; Price-Waterhouse report on Swiss Bank Corp.; Arthur Andersen report on St. Gallen Cantonal Bank; Price-Waterhouse report on Baumann Bank. All reports submitted to Volcker Commission, August 1997.

28. *Globes*, September 10, 1997.

29. Ibid., January 29, 1999; February 4, 1999.

CHAPTER 2

1. State Department, *U.S. and Allied Efforts to Recover and Restore Gold and Other Assets Stolen or Hidden by Germany During World War II* (Washington, D.C./U.S. 1997) (hereafter, *Eizenstat report*), 49–50.

2. Ibid., 59–61.

3. Ibid., 76–77.

4. Ibid., 83–84.

5. Ron Zweig, "The Restitution of Holocaust Victims' Assets and the Refugee Problem" [Hebrew] in *Ha'apala*, ed. Anita Shapira (Tel Aviv: Tel Aviv University and Am Oved, 1990), 245–61.

6. *Eizenstat report*, 91–95; Central Zionist Archives (hereafter CZA), file S35-2126; file S35-3.

7. *Eizenstat report*, 101–103.

8. Ibid., 104–105.

9. *Hug-Perrenoud report*, 22–23.

10. *Eizenstat report*, 101–103.

11. CZA, file S57–242.

12. *Eizenstat report*, 121–22; *Hug-Perrenoud report*, 15.

13. Public Record Office (hereafter, PRO) file fo 192/205.

14. KPMG's report to the Volcker Commission on the banks' procedures in handling dormant accounts, August 1997; Interview with Singer.

CHAPTER 3

1. *Globes*, October 18, 1996.

2. Ibid., October 24, 1996, December 25, 1996.

3. *Hug-Perrenoud report*, 27, 31–32.

4. Ibid., 28–29.

5. Ibid., 94.

6. Ibid.

7. Ibid., 95–96.

8. Ibid., 96–97, 104.
9. Ibid., 98, 110.
10. Ibid., 99.
11. CZA, file S43–243.
12. *Hug-Perrenoud report*, 100.
13. Ibid., 100–101.
14. Ibid., 101–2.
15. Ibid., 103–4.
16. Ibid., 105.
17. Ibid., 105–6.
18. Ibid.
19. Ibid., 107–8.
20. Ibid., 110.
21. Ibid., pp. 100–111, 114–15, 122, 128.
22. Ibid., 111–12.
23. Ibid., 114.
24. Ibid., 117, 119–20.
25. Ibid., 117–18.
26. Ibid., 118–19.
27. Ibid., 119.
28. Ibid., 121–23.
29. Ibid., 124–29.
30. Ibid., 129–33.
31. Ibid., 135–38.
32. Ibid., 138–41.
33. Swiss Federal Department of Foreign Affairs press release, February 26, 1997.

CHAPTER 4

1. *Hug-Perrenoud report*, 26–27.
2. Interview with Thomas Borer, June 18, 1997 (hereafter, Interview with Borer).
3. *Hug-Perrenoud report*, 49.
4. Ibid., 57–64.
5. Ibid., 63–64.
6. On Swiss refugee policy see Heini Borenstein, *The Isle of Switzerland* (in Hebrew) (Tel Aviv: Moreshet, 1996) (hereafter, Borenstein); see also Chapter 9, n 20.
7. *Hug-Perrenoud report*, 63–66.
8. Ibid., 62.
9. Tom Bower, *Nazi Gold* (New York: HarperCollins, 1997) (hereafter, Bower). On pages 1–8 Bower describes a meeting on the same subject with the same participants, which he says took place in November 1952. There is no evidence in the Israeli document of a similar meeting on that date, so it appears Bower seriously mistook the date. His book is based primarily on Swiss and British documents, and no use was made of Israeli or Jewish sources, which seriously discredits the quality of the research.

The book is also shamelessly unilateral and sensationalist, which is obvious from the subtitle of the American edition (which I used), *The Full Story of the 50-Year Swiss-Nazi Conspiracy to Steal Billions from Europe's Jews and Holocaust Survivors*. I have made use of Bower's book, sharply criticized by several central players in the story, only in cases where its credibility is trustworthy—where he bases his writing on reliable sources or whose accuracy is evident in their content and context.

10. *Note about the Problem of Banking Accounts and Heirless Assets in Switzerland*. Memorandum presented by the Jewish Agency to the Senate Banking Committee (Jerusalem, 1996) (hereafter, Jewish Agency Memorandum), appendixes 11, 13, 14, 15; ISA, file fo 2544/12.

11. Eli Nathan, later a Jerusalem District Court Justice, continues to be involved in the issue of restitution of Jewish property. At the time of this writing, he is the legal counsel for WJRO, and composed the memo in note 10.

12. ISA, file fo 2418/5.

13. Ibid., file fo 2544/12.

14. Ibid., file fo 3347/46.

15. Ibid. At least one of the bankers with whom Horowitz met saw the meeting in a positive light. Credit Suisse general manager Mr. Rheinhardt sent him a friendly letter in August 1961 thanking him for his letter and visit, and expressing regret that they could not talk more at length. Rheinhardt expressed his support for the need to find a means to return assets left to their family members by Jews who fell victim to an unjust government. He even passed Horowitz's letter to the SBA.

16. All applications taken by the Jewish National Fund are preserved in the KKL 15 division of the Central Zionist Archives. For the protection of privacy, they are not available for public perusal, but the archive's management granted me access to a few forms in order to receive general information on the process. All identifying details are deleted.

17. *Hug-Perrenoud report*, 41–42.

18. Bower, 17–28; interview with Charles Sonabend in Nazi Gold, BBC documentary, broadcast in Britain in June 1997.

19. BBC interview with Elisabeth Trilling-Grusch, undated.

20. BBC interview with Estelle Sapir, undated. See also, *Die Zeit*, September 13, 1996; *Time*, November 4, 1996.

21. *Globes*, February 12, 1997.

22. Ibid., May 13, 1998.

23. Adam LeBor, *Hitler's Secret Bankers* (London: Pocket Books, 1997), 2–9, 10–13, 18–29 (hereafter, LeBor). LeBor's book is based exclusively on American and British sources, mingling the deposits affair and the gold affair. *Newsweek*, June 24, 1996; *Die Zeit*, September 13, 1996; *London Times Magazine*, November 6, 1998; *Time*. February 24, 1997.

24. Swiss Bankers Association's press conference in Zurich, February 26, 1997.

25. Interview with Borer.

CHAPTER 5

1. *Hug-Perrenoud report*, 66–69.
2. The text of the 1962 Swiss law and legal analysis can be found in ISA, file fo 3347.
3. Ibid. file fo 3347/46.
4. When added, the sum remaining for distribution by the fund established according to the law and the sum of property identified does not equal the sum reported by the ministry. The reason for this is that the ministry's funds were interest bearing and included income from nonmonetary property such as diamonds and securities, in case the Ministry of Finance decided to sell them. The KPMG accounting firm, investigating for the Volcker Commission the implementation of the 1962 law (report submitted August 1997), found that the Swiss National Bank and the government's Accountant General destroyed some of the relevant documents. These included the Accountant General's annual reports of financial transactions in the fund and the Swiss National Bank's annual reports on physical objects deposited by the Accountant General (art, jewelry, etc) before these were transferred to the Claims Registry. Both bodies explained that they regularly destroy documents after 10 years [in contrast to the usual documentation policy in government archives around the world] KPMG further note that the Claims Registry didn't make its own assessment concerning the value of the property transferred and trusted exclusively the valuations provided by the banks [also relevant to bank accounts, due to many years of charging fees without paying interest]. Updated valuations conducted only when the registry sold physical assets in order to include the yield in the fund.
5. *Hug-Perrenoud report*, 69–70, 72.
6. The similarity to the faulty way the Swiss handled the deposits crisis in 1995–96 is very obvious. See Chapter 11.
7. *Hug-Perrenoud report*, 76–78; KPMG report on implementation of 1962 law submitted to Volcker Commission August 1997 (hereafter, 1962 Report). The accountants suggest that some of the surplus documents served the banks to prepare copies of the reports submitted to the Claims Registry. This is unlikely as the number of forms requested was 14 times higher than the number of assets reported. As noted above, a senior UBS official said in real time that the number of forms was nearly identical to the number of assets the bank might report; he did not mention preparation of duplicates.
8. *Hug-Perrenoud report*, 78–79.
9. *1962 Report*.
10. *Hug-Perrenoud report*, 79–80.
11. There is a significant 370,000 franc difference between this report and the figures included in the Hug-Perrenoud report, 72. It seems the difference stems from similar reasons to those noted in note 4.
12. In the 1950s, an Israeli citizen tried to locate a relative's account in Switzerland, and he was then charged with violating Israeli law. However, an entirely different approach was taken in Israel, so this single case apparently stems from the lack of consideration of a specific official.
13. *Hug-Perrenoud report*, 81–82; 1962 report.
14. *1962 report*.
15. *Hug-Perrenoud report*, 76–77.

16. Interview for BBC with Herta Arbets and Zvi Weigel, December 29, 1996.

17. CZA, KKL 15, Switzerland files, box 193, file 202. My thanks to then Archive director general Yoram Majorek for allowing me access to the Hass, Farkash, and Katz files.

18. Ibid., box 192, file 200.

19. Ibid., box 193, file 213.

20. *Ma'ariv*, September 15, 1996.

21. *Hug-Perrenoud report*, 83–88.

22. Ibid., 88; 1962 report.

23. *Hug-Perrenoud report*, 88.

24. CZA, file L34-1051.

25. Interview with Singer.

CHAPTER 6

1. *Globes*, May 1, 1995. The instructions set down here were written in 1994, but the banks never claimed that they received different instructions from SBA in the 1970s and 1980s.

2. The Ministry of Justice's response to applicants concerning property without heirs, 1994. Here too, there is no claim that the response was different during an earlier period.

3. *Newsweek*, June 24, 1996.

4. *Vanity Fair*, March 1997.

5. *Globes*, June 5, 1997.

6. Interview with Amram Blum, August 10, 1994.

7. Interview with Avraham Burg, June 5, 1997, July 24, 1997 (hereafter, Interview with Burg); Interview with Zvi Barak, July 14, 1997 (hereafter, Interview with Barak); Interview with Singer; Interviews with Akiva Lewinsky, September 28, 1994, June 30, 1997.

8. Interviews with sources who asked to remain unnamed, June–July 1997.

9. The CZA contains dozens of files dealing with property restitution, beginning with documentation of the looting as part of reports on the Holocaust, and continuing in talks that began as early as during the war on compensation. Therefore, for instance, in October 1944, the Jewish Agency drafted a proposal for the establishment of a Jewish organization to centralize the handling of the matter (CZA, file S25–5188); in April 1945 the Jewish Agency drafted a 20-page memo on the "special character of Jewish people's claims for compensation" (CZA, file S35-2).

10. Interview with Singer.

11. *Sonntag Zeitung*, September 11, 1994.

12. Interview with Otto Piller, July 13, 1997.

13. Text of Otto Piller's motion, submitted to the Swiss Parliament on December 6, 1994.

14. The Swiss Federal Council's answer to Piller's motion, undated.

15. Interview with Singer.

16. Interview with Rolf Bloch, June 18, 1997, hereafter, Interview with Bloch.

17. Avraham Hirshson's letter to Shevah Weiss, April 27, 1995.

18. Interview with Burg.

19. Kaspar Villiger's speech in the Federal Assembly, May 7, 1995; *Globes*, May 12, 1995.

20. Interview with Burg; Interview with Singer.

21. Actually, the Israeli government did not receive a single franc of the property without heirs (see Chapter 5), and it appears this was an error on Shochat's part.

22. Shochat's remarks appeared in the Knesset's session minutes of May 17, 1995.

CHAPTER 7

1. Interview with Barak.
2. Ibid.; Interview with Singer.
3. Interview with Singer.
4. Ibid.; Interview with Barak.
5. Interview with Burg; Interview with Singer.
6. *Dormant Accounts at Swiss Banks* (Basel: Swiss Bankers Association, 1997).
7. *Globes*, September 14, 1995.
8. Swiss Bankers Association's press release, September 12, 1995; *Globes*, September 13, 1995.
9. Interview with Burg; Interview with Singer.
10. The appointment is described based on interviews with Singer, Burg, and Barak. Some details are based on Bower, 296–98, and *Globes*, September 15, 1995.
11. Interview with Burg.
12. Ibid.
13. Interview with Haeni.
14. Interview with Singer.
15. Arthur Andersen report to the Volcker Commission on ombudsman Haeni's work, August 1997.
16. Interview with Barak.
17. Interview with Singer.

CHAPTER 8

1. Interview with Singer; Interview with Barak.
2. Most of the events in the United States are described according to the interviews with Singer. Some details were provided by sources who asked to remain unnamed, June–July 1997.
3. Hans Baer's written testimony presented to the Senate Banking Committee, April 23, 1996.
4. My own attempts in June 1997, to get the SBA version of events and details of the affair were unsuccessful, as the SBA did not respond to my request for a meeting with a senior official. The SBA claimed that this was because the request was submitted without sufficient prior notice and that none of its senior officials were available on such short notice. It should be noted that Thomas Borer of the Swiss Foreign Ministry was kind enough to make himself available for a long interview and that there were at least five SBA officials intimately involved in handling the dormant accounts crisis.

5. The wider context of the affair gives the Lecca document great importance because it testifies that in the 1960s Volksbank claimed it did not keep documents longer than ten years.

6. See *Vanity Fair* (March 1997). After a number of months, a document was uncovered in the National Archives in Washington, D.C., that contained a list of Swiss lawyers the CIA suspected of assisting German financial activities in Switzerland. Among them was Elois Grendelmeier, Verna's father. She related that at first she was stunned by the discovery, particularly since her father was known as a virulent anti-Nazi. Later, after looking at the list, she discovered quite a few Jewish names, which she felt indicated a level of inaccuracy in the list of names. It is possible she is right, and the document is a clear example of raw intelligence reports, which should not be given too much weight.

7. Interview with Burg.

8. Bloomberg, February 21, 1998.

9. KPMG's report to the Volcker Commission on the Swiss Bankers Association 1995 survey, August 1997.

10. *Globes*, February 27, 1996. Studer said at the press conference that UBS located 10 million francs in dormant accounts. In 1994, the bank claimed that it did not have any accounts that might have belonged to Holocaust victims.

11. Senator D'Amato's office press release, March 27, 1996.

12. *Jewish Agency's memorandum*, 1–5.

13. *Globes*, April 18, 1996; Bloomberg, April 17, 1996.

14. Letter from Shimon Peres to Avraham Burg, April 21, 1996.

15. Interview with Singer.

16. Quotes from the Senate Banking Committee meeting are taken from a transcript prepared by the company Federal News. The quotes from written testimony are from the copies distributed by the various witnesses. Avraham Burg, although invited, did not participate in the hearing, as it fell on Memorial Day for Israel Defense Force Soldiers, and he preferred to be in Israel.

17. See *Globes*, April 26, 1996; *New York Times*, February 17, 1997; *Time*, February 24, 1997.

CHAPTER 9

1. *Eizenstat report*, v. Although this discusses neutral countries in general, the Swiss admit it refers to them (Interview with Borer).

2. Arthur Smith, *Hitler's Gold* (Oxford: Berg, 1996) (hereafter Smith). It should be noted that Smith's excellent book doesn't mention the Swiss government's role in the Puhl Agreement (to be discussed later in the chapter) uncovered in American documents discovered in 1996. Smith's book covers Switzerland's role in gold trade with Germany only on pages 48–92.

3. In the margins of the Swiss reports, details were also published of aid Berlin provided the Bank for International Settlements, an international bank founded to coordinate German reparation payments. (See, for instance, *Newsweek*, October 27, 1996). The only Swiss "sin" in this context was that the bank's offices were in Basel; it's governor throughout the war was an American and there are no signs of undue Swiss influence of any kind. The inclusion of Switzerland in the Bank for

International Settlements was a clear example of the lack of seriousness and unfairness of these reports. For considered coverage of the bank's role see *Eizenstat report*, 189–195; Smith, 52–60.

4. *Switzerland and Gold Transactions in the Second World War: Interim Report* (Bern: Independent Commission of Experts, Switzerland—Second World War, 1998) (hereafter, *Bergier report*), 18.

5. *Bergier report*, 32, 49. See also *Nazi Gold: Information from the British Archives* (London: Foreign and Commonwealth Office, 1996) (hereafter *Gold Report*).

6. *Eizenstat report*. A detailed analysis of trade conducted by Spain, Portugal, Turkey, Sweden, and Argentina with Germany as the headstone of the Swiss role in funding that trade through gold it received from Germany appears in the second part of the *Eizenstat report*, June 1998.

7. *Der Spiegel*, issue 12, March 1997.

8. *Bergier report*, 5, 86, 88, 120–21.

9. Ibid., 31–33. Re the Melmer account, see Jean Ziegler, *The Swiss, the Gold and the Dead* (New York: Harcourt Brace, 1997), 116–117.

10. *Globes*, January 30, 1997; PRO, file fo 1046/267; file fo 1046/33.

11. *Bergier report*, 60–63.

12. Ibid., 87; *Eizenstat report*, 6–7.

13. *Eizenstat report*, 9–10; *Bergier report*, 44.

14. *Eizenstat report*, 28–33. See also, Smith, 68–92; *Bergier report*, 108–110.

15. *Globes*, August 2, 1996. The American document quoted here was published by World Jewish Congress, July 1, 1996. See also, Smith, 52, 72–75.

16. *Bergier report*, 115–130.

17. *Eizenstat report*, 63–91, 97–123; *Bergier report*, 183–186.

18. Swiss Federal Council's press release, May 22, 1997.

19. *Bergier report*, 131–132, 190.

20. *The Holocaust Encyclopedia*, vol. 5, pp. 1197–1200; Borenstein, 65–95; LeBor, 173–208; Interview for BBC with Eliyahu Elon, December 29, 1996; Interview for BBC with Heini Borenstein, December 29, 1996; Interview for BBC with Yitzhak Kramer, December 29, 1996. For the first report on the subject see Carl Ludwig, *Die Fluchtlingspolitik der Schweiz Seit 1933 Bis Zur Gegenwart* (Bern: 1957). For additional important research see: Alfred Hasler, *Das Boot isf Voll* (Zurich: Pendo, 1992).

21. The London Gold Conference is described according to my notes, as I acted as an advisor to the Israeli Delegation. See also *Nazi Gold—The London Conference* (London: The Stationary Office, 1998).

22. The document was published by the World Jewish Congress.

23 *Yedi'ot Aharonot*, August 19, 1995.

24. *Ha'aretz*, August 15, 1996.

25. *Ha'aretz*, March 4, 1997. See Lynn Nicholas, *The Rape of Europa* (New York: Vintage Books, 1994), 82, 108–9, 162, 165, 168–69, 270, 291, 415–21, 426–27.

26. *Globes*, May 30, 1997.

CHAPTER 10

1. Interview with Barak; Interview with Singer.
2. The Swiss banks' hope to improve their international image with the establishment of the joint committee collapsed within two days. The British weekly, *The Economist*, criticized them harshly in a May 4, 1996, editorial, determining the affair was a "public relations disaster for the banks" and saying the banks exploited banking confidentiality to prevent victims' heirs access to their property. The magazine also held against Switzerland its Jewish refugee policy, its neutrality in two world wars, and the Cold War, and its lack of membership in the United Nations.
3. *Globes*, May 6, 1996; Interview with Singer; Interview with Barak; Interview with Burg.
4. Interview with a source who asked to remain unnamed, July 1997.
5. The meeting is described according to the minutes of the Volcker Commission meeting of August 14, 1996 and to interviews with sources who asked to remain unnamed, July 1997.
6. Memorandum by Michael Bradfield to Volcker Commission members, September 12, 1996.
7. Minutes of the Volcker Commission meeting, October 18, 1996; interview with a source who asked to remain unnamed, July 1998.
8. The class-action lawsuit on behalf of Gizelle Weisshaus was filed in New York Eastern District Court, file cv 96 4849 on October 1, 1996.
9. In October 1997, Sonabend filed a 100,000 franc lawsuit in Switzerland against the local government, as compensation for his parents deportation, resulting in their deaths at Auschwitz. See *Globes*, October 13, 1997.
10. New York Eastern District Court, file cv 96 5161.
11. Ibid., file cv 97 0461
12. Interview with Advocate Joe Oper in Melvyn Weiss' office, July 15, 1997. About the banks' arguments at the beginning of the trial, see *Globes*, August 4, 1997.
13. Written statement presented at the press conference of Hanspeter Haeni and Leon Schlompeff, November 12, 1996.
14. Reuters, November 12, 1996.
15. Memorandum from the Volcker Commission to the audit firms, November 19, 1996.
16. Press releases by Avraham Hirschson, December 23, 1996, January 5, 1997.
17. Interview with a source who asked to remain unnamed, June 1997.
18. Interview with Borer.
19. Interview with a source who asked to remain unnamed, June 1997.

CHAPTER 11

1. Interview with Borer.
2. Interview with a source who asked to remain unnamed, June 1996.
3. Interview with Burg.
4. *Globes*, February 27, 1996.
5. Interview with Burg.

6. *Globes*, April 19, 1997. See also Swiss Bank Corp. 1996 annual report, March 1997; Credit Suisse 1996 annual report, April 1997.

7. Interview with Burg.

8. Interview with Mathias Kraft, June 18, 1997 (hereafter, Interview with Kraft).

9. Interview with Kraft; interview with source who asked to remain unnamed, June 1997. An example from my own experience clarifies how the Swiss government handled the crises at the end of 1996 and the beginning of 1997. In September 1996, I asked the Swiss Embassy in Israel to set up interviews on my behalf with senior government and banking officials in my capacity as a journalist for *Globes*. In October, when it was too late to add a trip to Switzerland to my European travel agenda, I was told it would only be possible to submit questions in writing to Foreign Minister Flavio Cotti, which I did. On December 30, I was told answers would be sent after the New Year vacation. In the end, the answers to only some of the questions, and not in Cotti's name, were handed to me personally when I visited Switzerland at the government's invitation during the last week of February.

10. *Gold report*; see also, *Globes*, September 25, 1996.

11. Interview with Barak.

12. Volcker Commission minutes, October 18, 1996.

13. Interview with Borer.

14. Ibid. The Task Force was abolished in Febuary 1999, and Borer was nominated as Swiss ambassador to Germany.

15. *Globes*, November 1, 1996.

16. *Ma'ariv*, February 17, 1997.

17. LeBor, 307.

18. Interview with Greville Janner, November 28, 1996; Interview with Singer.

19. Interview with Singer.

20. Interview with Borer.

21. For the first reports on the fund idea, see *Globes*, December 2, 1996; December 6, 1997.

22. Edgar Bronfman's written testimony to the House Banking Committee, December 11, 1996.

23. Bronfman's testimony to House Banking Committee, December 11, 1996.

24. Journalists' meeting with Flavio Cotti on February 24, 1997 (hereafter, Cotti meeting); Interview with Borer. Borer admitted that in the eyes of the world this was hardly record time. "From our point of view, this is a time for the Guinness Book of Records," he said. I commented, "In its Swiss edition," and Borer smiled and nodded, "In its Swiss edition."

25. Decision by Swiss Federal Assembly, December 13, 1996.

26. Swiss Federal Department of Foreign Affairs press release, December 19, 1996. The Commission's Web site: www.euk/ch.

27. Interview with Jean Françqis Bergier, February 26, 1997.

28. Interview with Borer; interviews with sources who asked to remain unnamed.

29. LeBor, 316; *Globes*, January 2, 1997.

30. *New York Times*, January 26, 1997.

31. Interview with Borer.

32. Interview with Burg; interview with Singer.

33. *Yedi'ot Aharonot,* January 5, 1997.
34. Interview with Borer.
35. *Yedi'ot Aharonot,* January 5, 1997.
36. *Globes,* January 7, 1997.
37. *Globes,* January 8, 1997.
38. Swiss Bank shares dropped 0.6 percent, UBS shares dropped 1.8 percent, and Credit Suisse shares dropped 2 percent. Local analysts told wire service reporters in Zurich that the Jewish organizations' threats were the only apparent reason for the drop. *Globes,* January 8, 1997.
39. Interview with Borer.
40. *Globes,* January 10, 1997.
41. Ibid., January 13, 1997.
42. Ibid., January 15, 1997.
43. *Ma'ariv,* Febuary 28, 1997; *Globes,* January 10, 1997; *Ha'aretz,* March 7, 1997; *Yedi'ot Aharonot,* July 2, 1997; *Wall Street Journal,* July 29, 1997; *Yedi'ot Aharonot,* September 17, 1997; *Ma'ariv,* January 20, 1997.
44. *Globes,* January 16, 1997; January 20, 1997.
45. *Ma'ariv,* February 28, 1997.
46. Reuters, October 2, 1997.
47. Interview with Bloch; Israel Radio August 14, 1998.
48. Borer told me he didn't know in advance about Gut's article and was happy to read it. However, all indications are of prior coordination between the government and the major banks, at least on the principle of the action if not the details.
49. Interview with Bloch; Interview with Singer.
50. *Financial Times,* January 23, 1997; *Globes,* January 23, 1997.
51. *Globes,* January 27, 1997.
52. Ibid.
53. Interview with Borer.
54. Interview with Burg.
55. *Globes,* January 28, 1997.
56. *Yedi'ot Aharonot,* January 30, 1997; *Globes,* January 31, 1997.
57. Interview with a source who asked to remain unnamed, July 1997.
58. Interview with a source who asked to remain unnamed, July 1997.
59. Interview with Burg. The meeting is described according to Volcker Commission's meeting minutes, January 30–31, 1997; and to interviews with sources who asked to remain unnamed, June 1997.
60. I raised suspicions that the Swiss banks destroyed documents in my first investigative report on the subject, published in *Globes,* April 1995. They were rejected disdainfully by both the Swiss Ministry of Justice and the SBA.
61. Interview with source who asked to remain unnamed, July 1997. In a more comprehensive report submitted to the Volcker Commission in 1997, KPMG reported that forty-six banks reported assets according to the 1962 law, which is still less than 10 percent of all the banks active in Switzerland at the time.
62. *Globes,* January 29, 1997.
63. *Yedi'ot Aharonot,* February 2, 1997; *Globes,* February 3, 1997.

CHAPTER 12

1. Interview with a source who asked to remain unnamed, February 1997.
2. Cotti meeting.
3. Journalists' meeting with Thomas Borer, February 2, 1997.
4. *Ma'ariv*, February 2, 1997.
5. Blocher's remarks appeared on his website: http://www.blocher.ch
6. Interview with a source who asked to remain unnamed, July 1997; Interview with Bloch.
7. The author wishes to thank an unnamed source who placed the letters at his disposal.
8. Center for the Research of Anti-Semitism, *Anti-Semitism Worldwide*, 1996/97 (Tel Aviv University, 1997). See the chapter about Switzerland, 135–141.
9. Interview with Bloch.
10. Ibid.
11. Interview with Borer.
12. Declaration by Flavio Cotti, February 12, 1997.
13. *Globes*, February 14, 1997.
14. Interview with Barak.
15. Swiss cabinet decision, February 26, 1997.
16. *Globes*, March 7, 1997, March 12, 1997, March 28, 1997.
17. Ibid., April 8, 1997.
18. Swiss cabinet decision, May 1, 1997. See also, *Globes*, March 31, 1997, April 2, 1997, April 8, 1997, April 17, 1997, April 18, 1997, May 5, 1997.
19. *Globes*, May 14, 1997, May 23, 1997; Interview with Barak; Reuters, March 10, 1999.
20. Arnold Koller's speech, March 5, 1997.
21. Interview with Borer; Interview with Bloch; *Globes*, June 3, 1997, March 7, 1997.
22. *Globes*, June 29, 1998.
23. The meeting is described according to Volcker Commission minutes, April 16, 1997.
24. Interview with Burg; speech by Eizenstat in the Washington Conference on Holocaust-Era Assets, December 2, 1998 (author's notes).
25. Interviews with sources who asked to remain unnamed, July 1997.
26. *Globes*, June 4, 1997, June 13, 1997, June 16, 1997.
27. Volcker Commission press release, June 2, 1997; *Globes*, July 24, 1997.
28. Reuters, June 5, 1997.
29. *Globes*, July 9, 1997, September 17, 1997, September 19, 1997, October 13, 1997, November 19, 1997.
30. *Globes*, October 31, 1997.
31. *Globes*, September 7, 1997.
32. For complete information regarding the dormant accounts problem, see the website: http://www.dormantaccounts.ch. See *Globes*, July 24, 1997, July 25, 1997; *Yedi'ot Aharonot*, July 25, 1997 (including the formal ad by the Swiss Bankers Association), July 27, 1997; Reuters, July 26, 1997; *Ha'aretz*, July 29, 1997;

Ma'ariv, August 19, 1997; Conversation with Israel Singer, September 24, 1997; *Globes*, September 16, 1998.

33. *Globes*, October 30, 1997.

34. *Gold Transactions in the Second World War: Statistical Review with Commentary* (Independent Commission of Experts: Switzerland—Second World War, December 1997).

35. *Globes*, November 27, 1997, November 28, 1997, December 8, 1997, December 10, 1997, March 5, 1998.

36. *Globes*, March 13, 1998, March 16, 1998, March 23, 1998, March 27, 1998.

37. *Globes*, March 30, 1998.

38. *Globes*, May 18, 1998, June 26, 1998, July 3, 1998, July 6, 1998, August 3, 1998; August 14, 1998; November 17, 1998.

39. Reuters, August 13, 1998; *Wall Street Journal*, August 14, 1998; *Financial Times*, August 14, 1998; *Yedi'ot Aharonot*, August 14, 1998; *Globes*, August 17, 1998.

40. *Time*, February 17, 1998.

41. *Newsweek*, October 27, 1996.

BIBLIOGRAPHY

PRIMARY SOURCES

Israel State Archives, Jerusalem: files fo 2418/5, fo 2544/12, fo 3347/12, fo 3347/45, fo 3347/46.

Central Zionist Archives, Jerusalem: files L34-1052, S25-5188, S35-2, S35-3, S35-2126, S43-243, S57-242. Division KKL 15, Swiss files, box 192, file 200; box 193, files 202, 213.

Public Record Office, London: files fo 192/205, fo 1046/33, fo 1046/267.

Volcker Commission, New York: Commission's meetings minutes, reports by accounting firms, pilot report by Helen Junz, agreements, letters.

The Swiss Government, Bern: press releases, decisions, announcements to Parliament, presidential and ministerial speeches in Parliament, announcements by Foreign Ministry Task Force.

Office of Senator Alfonse D'Amato, National Archives, Washington, D.C. and College Park, MD: documents, press releases, letters, speeches.

World Jewish Congress, New York: National Archives documents, press releases, letters, speeches.

Swiss Bankers Association, Basel: reports, press releases.

Jewish Agency, Jerusalem: letters, press releases, memorandums.

The Knesset, Jerusalem: minutes, press releases, letters.

District Court of the Eastern District, New York: files CV 96 4849, CV 96 5161, CV 97 0461.

Swiss Bank Corp. 1996 Annual Report, March 1997.

Credit Suisse 1996 Annual Report, April 1997.

Interviews

Amram Blum, August 10, 1994.

Akiva Lewinsky, September 28, 1994, June 30, 1997.

Martin Wirz, October 25, 1994.

Silvia Matile-Steiner, October 26, 1994.

Greville Janner, November 28, 1996.

Herta Arbetz and Zvi Weigel, December 29, 1996.

Eliyahu Elon, December 29, 1996.

Heini Borenstein, December 30, 1996.

Yitzhak Kramer, December 31, 1996.
Flavio Cotti, February 24, 1997.
Thomas Borer, February 24, 1997, June 18, 1997.
Jean Pierre Roth, February 24, 1997.
High-Ranking Banker, February 26, 1997
Hanspeter Haeni, February 26, 1997.
Jean François Bergier, February 26, 1997.
Israel Singer, May 30, 1997, July 2, 1997, July 14, 1997, September 7, 1997.
Avraham Burg, June 5, 1997, July 24, 1997.
Rolf Bloch, June 18, 1997.
Mattias Kraft, June 18, 1997.
Otto Piller, July 13, 1997.
Zvi Barak, July 14, 1997.
Joe Oper, July 15, 1997.
Elizabeth Trilling-Grusch, undated (interview by BBC)
Estelle Sapir, undated (interview by BBC)

SECONDARY SOURCES

Books

Anti-Semitism Worldwide, 1996–97. Tel Aviv: Tel Aviv University, 1997.
Borenstein, Heini. *The Island Switzerland.* Tel Aviv: Moreshet, 1996. (Hebrew).
Bower, Tom. *Nazi Gold.* New York: HarperCollins, 1997.
Hasler, Alfred. *Das Boot ist Voll.* Zurich: Pendo, 1992.
The Holocaust Encyclopedia. 6 vols. Tel Aviv and Jerusalem: Yad V'Shem & Sifri'yat Poalim, 1990. (Hebrew).
LeBor, Adam. *Hitler's Secret Bankers.* London: Pocket Books, 1997.
Ludwig, Carl. *Die Fluchtlingspolitik der Schweiz Seit 1933 Bis Zur Gegenwart.* Bern: 1957.
Nazi Gold: The London Conference. London: The Stationary Office, 1998.
Nicholas, Lynn. *The Rape of Europa.* New York: Vintage Books, 1994.
Sereny, Gitta. *Into That Darkness.* Andre Deutch, 1974.
Smith, Arthur. *Hitler's Gold.* Oxford: Berg, 1996.
Zabludoff, Sidney. *Movements of Nazi Gold.* Jerusalem: Institute of the World Jewish Congress, 1997.
Ziegler, Jean. *The Swiss, the Gold and the Dead.* New York: Harcourt Brace, 1997.
Zweig, Ron. "The Restitution of Holocaust Victims' Property and the Refugee Problem." In *Ha'apala,* edited by Anita Shapira. Tel Aviv: Tel Aviv University and Am Oved, 1990, 245–61. (Hebrew).

Research and Reports

Hug, Peter, and Marc Perrenoud. *Assets in Switzerland of Victims of Nazism and the Compensation Agreements with East Bloc Countries.* Bern: Federal Government, 1997. In text references, Hug-Perrenoud reports.
Nazi Gold: Information from the British Achives. London: Foreign and Commonwealth Office, 1996.

State Department. *U.S. and Allied Efforts to Recover and Restore Gold and Other Assets Stolen or Hidden by Germany During World War II.* Washington D.C.: GPO, 1997. In text references, Eizenstat report.

Switzerland and Gold Transactions in the Second World War: Interim Report. Bern: Independent Commission of Experts, Switzerland—Second World War, 1998. In text references, Bergier report.

Press

Globes (Hebrew)
Yedi'ot Aharonot (Hebrew)
Ma'ariv (Hebrew)
Ha'aretz (Hebrew)
Financial Times
Newsweek
Economist
Jerusalem Report
New York Times
The Times (London)
The Wall Street Journal
Time
Vanity Fair
Le-Matin (French)
Der Spiegel (German)
Die Zeit (German)
Sonntag Zeitung (German)

Electronic Media

Nazi Gold, BBC Documentary, 1997.
Reuters.
Bloomberg.

Websites

Simon Wiesenthal Center site at http://204.254.71.206/swissquery.cfm.
http://www.blocher.ch.
http://www.dormantaccounts.ch.

INDEX

Defago, Alfred, 206
Delamuraz, Jean Pascal, 186–90, 192, 194, 198, 202
Denes, Adolf, 84
Denes, Elizabeth, 84
Deutsch, Elizabeth, 10
Diegi, Ruth, 4
Dinitz, Simha, 96, 105
Dreifuss, Ruth, 206–7

Eder, Elise, 217
Eggenschwiler, Walter, 52
Ehrenstein, Egun, 10
Eichmann, Adolf, 64, 67, 217
Eidgenossische Bank, 196
Eisenhower, Dwight, 144
Eizenstat Report, 140–41, 144, 150–51, 180, 210
Eizenstat, Stuart, 17, 133, 136, 140, 144, 150, 152–53, 184, 218–19, 221
Englaender, Erna, 10
England, 4
Epstein, Ernst, 7
Ernst & Young, 165, 212
Esser, Herman, 217
Estee Lauder, 166
Esterhazy, Paul, 217

Fagan, Ed, 170–71
Farkash, Egun, 82, 84–85, 89
Feigenbaum, Stanislav, 7
Feldman, Markus, 11, 52–57
Feldstein, Isaac, 5
Fischer, Julie, 10
Fischer, Milka, 10
Fong, Matt, 219, 221
Foot, Dingle, 146
France, 5, 7, 19, 21–22, 24, 37, 61, 63, 112; Swiss gold trade, 141, 151, 153–55, 155
Frankfurter, David, 156
Friedberg, Michael, 7
Friedlander, Emil, 5
Friedlander, Saul, 185
Friedman, Jacob, 90, 171
Friedman, Margarita, 90
Friedman, Martin, 90

Gasser, Hans, 74
Gasteyger, Curt, 165
Germany, 1, 19–24, 28–29, 32–33, 50, 57, 86, 95–96, 103, 112, 130, 151, 154, 196; gold trade, 140–42, 144–47, 149, 152–53, 180, 189; trade with Switzerland, 156–58
Gestapo, 85, 90, 145, 217
Giladi, Yehiel Michel, 88
Ginzburg, Eli, 22
Giuliani, Rudolph, 187
Glicksman, Moshe, 7
Goebbels, Joseph, 141
Goering, Hermann, 157
Goldmann, Nachum, 11, 58
Goldstein, Stanislav, 7
Gorner (historian), 184
Gottleib, Friedrich, 7, 10
Graber, Lina, 10
Graber, Louis, 10
Greece, 5
Greenberg, Hannah, 89–90
Grendelmeier, Alois, 230
Grendelmeier, Verena, 127, 129, 230
Grossman, B., 82, 84, 86
Gruefener, Karl, 145
Grueninger, Paul, 155
Gugenheim (family), 7
Gugenheim, Paul, 37, 54–55
Gustloff Stiftung, 156–57
Gustloff, Wilhelm, 156
Gut, Rainer, 192–93, 221

Haeberlin, Heinz, 79–80
Haeni, Hanspeter, 2, 115–19, 169
Hagenmueller, Erwin, 192, 195–96
Halasz, Eugen, 45
Halpern, Baruch, 5
Hasan, Nissim, 5
Hass-Axelrad, Zilla, 82, 84–85, 90
Hauer, Erwin, 172
Hauri, Kurt, 105–6, 169, 172–73, 196–97, 214
Hausfeld, Michael, 171, 219
Herascovici, Leib, 5
Herschkovitz, Simon, 5
Hevesi, Alan, 124–25, 127, 213, 218, 221

Thomas, Albert, 145
Tolkowsky, Shmuel, 54–57
Tomarkin, David, 4
Traschel, Otto, 16
Treblinka, 2 , 65
Trilling-Grusch, Elizabeth, 62, 171
Tripartite Gold Commission, 151, 155–56
Troendle, Max, 34, 43
Truman, Harry, 19
Turkey, 7, 19, 22

UBS, 4, 15, 45, 90–91, 104, 123, 157, 171, 178, 189, 195, 213; dormant accounts, 75–76, 78, 99–100, 128, 212, 228; Meili affair, 178, 190–92, 195–96, 212; negotiations with Jewish organizations, 105; settlement with Jewish organizations, 219, 222
Ullman, René, 10
Union Bank of Switzerland. *See* UBS
Union of Swiss Jewish Communities, 10–11
United Bank, 17
United Jewish Appeal, 22
United States, 19–26, 38, 67, 80, 93–94, 137, 153, 155, 190, 209, 219; dormant accounts in Swiss banks, 74, 112, 123; Holocaust victims' assets, 179–80, 183–84, 194; negotiations with Switzerland on German property, 145–46, 151
U.S. Comptrollers Association, 125

Vallone, Peter, 194
Vatican, 156
Villiger, Kaspar, 103, 106–7, 112, 121, 155, 167, 179, 200, 210
Volcker Commission, 1, 17–18, 171, 177, 182, 188, 194, 212, 214, 217, 222; accountants, 16–17, 31, 76, 78–80, 119, 128, 172–74, 228; establishment of, 161–66, 179; meetings, 166–70, 180–81, 195–9, 211–13
Volcker, Paul, 17, 166–70, 191, 195, 197–98, 211, 213
Volksbank, 15, 127
Voyane, Joseph, 185

Wahlen, Friedrich Taugott, 53–54, 57
Waldheim, Kurt, 93
Warburg Bank, 99
Warburg, Edward, 23
Washington Accord, 21–22, 24–26, 28, 37–38, 47–48, 51, 67, 106, 120, 152–53, 171
Weber, Ernst, 142
Weber, Hans, 75–76, 82, 84
Weigl, Zvi, 81–82
Weinberg, Berthold, 7, 10
Weiss, Melvyn, 171–72, 219
Weiss, Shevah, 102
Weizman, Isaac, 7
Wendland, Hans, 217
Wermas-Rosenberg, Bella, 7
Weyl, Martin, 157
Wieder, Joseph, 172
Wielich, Gotthard, 10
Wienterthur, 222
Wiesel, Elie, 208–9, 223
Wiesenthal Center, 217
Wintenberg, Rudolph, 45
Witz, Martin, 14
WIZO, 92
WJC. *See* World Jewish Congress
WJRO. *See* World Jewish Restitution Organization
Wohl-Landau Bank, 90
Wolfenson, James, 166
World Bank, 166
World Council of Orthodox Communities, 172
World Jewish Congress, 2, 15, 18, 31, 88, 93, 95–96, 104–5, 119, 121, 126, 130, 141, 144, 166, 173, 182, 191, 207; negotiations with Swiss banks, 11, 125, 132, 137, 139, 175, 189, 192, 198, 204–5, 217; negotiations with Swiss government, 26–27, 58
World Jewish Restitution Organization, 22, 94, 96, 104–5, 125, 131, 160–61, 169, 175, 185, 188, 207–8, 219

Yugoslavia, 7, 10, 22, 46, 86, 130

About the Author and Translator

ITAMAR LEVIN is Deputy Editor in Chief, *Globes—Israel's Business Newspaper*. Levin has led the world's media in reporting and uncovering the fate of looted Jewish property in Europe. A frequent lecturer on the subject, Levin also is an advisor to various public institutions, including the Israeli government.

NATASHA DORNBERG is Managing Editor of *Israel's Business Arena*, *Globes'* internet site.